CICERO

AND HIS FRIENDS

CICERO

AND HIS FRIENDS

A STUDY OF ROMAN SOCIETY IN THE TIME OF CAESAR

BY

GASTON BOISSIER

OF THE FRENCH ACADEMY

TRANSLATED, WITH AN INDEX AND TABLE OF CONTENTS, BY
ADNAH DAVID JONES

NEW YORK: G. P. PUTNAM'S SONS
LONDON: A. D. INNES & CO.
1897

CONTENTS

CICERO AND HIS FRIENDS

INTRODUCTION

CICERO'S LETTERS

No history is more readily studied now-a-days than that of the last years of the Roman Republic. Learned works have recently been published upon this subject in France, England, and Germany,[1] and the public has read them with avidity. The importance of the subjects which were then debated, the dramatic character of the events, and the grandeur of the characters warrant this interest; but the attraction we feel for this singular epoch is better explained by the fact that it is narrated for us in Cicero's letters.

A contemporary said that he who read these letters would not be tempted to seek the history of that time[2] elsewhere, and in fact we find it much more living and true in them than in regular works composed expressly to teach it to us. What more would Asinius Pollio, Livy, or

[1] The course of this work will show that I have made great use of works published in Germany, especially the fine Roman History of M. Mommsen, so learned and at the same time so living. I do not always share his opinions, but the influence of his ideas will be perceived even in passages where I do not agree with him. He is the master of all who study Rome and her history now.

[2] Corn. Nepos, *Att.* 16.

Cremutius Cordus teach us if we had them preserved? They would give us their personal opinion; but this opinion is for the most part open to suspicion because it comes from persons who could not tell the whole truth, from men like Livy, who wrote at the court of the emperors, or who hoped, like Pollio, to get their treason pardoned, by blackening the character of those whom they had betrayed. Instead of receiving a ready-made opinion it is better to make one for ourselves, and the perusal of Cicero's letters enables us to do this. It throws us into the midst of the events, and lets us follow them day by day. We seem to see them pass before our eyes, notwithstanding the eighteen centuries that intervene, and we find ourselves in the unique position of being sufficiently near the facts to see their real character, and sufficiently distant to judge them dispassionately.

The importance of these letters is easily explained. The politicians of those times had more need of correspondence with each other than those of the present day. The pro-consul starting from Rome to govern some distant province felt that he was withdrawing altogether from political life. To pass several years in those out-of-the-way countries which the public rumour of Rome did not reach, was very irksome to men accustomed to the stir of business, the agitations of parties, or, as they said, the broad daylight of the Forum. They did indeed receive a sort of official gazette, the *Acta diurna*, the venerable ancestor of our *Moniteur*. But it appears as though every official journal is condemned by its nature to be somewhat insignificant. The Roman journal contained a rather tame official report of public meetings, a short summary of important cases tried in the Forum, besides an account of public ceremonies and accurate notice of atmospheric phenomena or prodigies occurring in Rome or its neighbourhood. This is not precisely the sort of news that a praetor or pro-consul wished to know, and therefore, in order to fill up the gaps in the official journal, he had recourse to paid correspondents, who made "news-letters" for the use of inquisitive provincials, as was the fashion among ourselves in the last century; but while, in the eighteenth century, literary men of reputation, intimate with the nobles and well received by ministers, undertook this duty, the Roman correspondents were only obscure compilers, workmen as Caelius calls them, usually chosen among those hungry Greeks whom want made ready for anything. They had no admittance into the great houses, nor could they approach the politicians. Their part simply consisted in running over the town and picking up what they heard or saw in the streets. They carefully noted theatrical chit-chat, inquired about actors who had been hissed and gladiators who had been beaten, described minutely handsome funerals, noted the rumours and ill-natured gossip, and especially the scandalous tales they could catch.[1] All this chatter amused for a moment, but did not satisfy those political personages who wished above all to be kept abreast of affairs, and, in order to become acquainted with them, they naturally applied to some one who was in a position to know them. They chose a few trustworthy and well-informed friends of good position, and through them learnt the reason and the real character of the facts reported dryly and without comment by the journals; and while their paid correspondents gave them only the talk of the town, the others introduced them into the cabinets of the high politicians, and made them listen to their most private conversations.

[1] See Cicero's *Epist. ad fam.* ii. 8 and viii. 1. I shall quote Orelli's edition of Cicero's works in the course of this work.

No one felt this need of being kept informed of everything, and, so to say, of living in the midst of Rome after
he had left it, more than Cicero. No one liked that excitement of public life which statesmen complain of when they
possess it, and never cease to regret when they have lost it,
more than he. We must not believe him too readily when
he says that he is tired of the stormy discussions of the
senate ; that he seeks a country where they have not heard
of Vatinius or Caesar, and where they do not trouble themselves about agrarian laws; that he has an anxious craving
to go and forget Rome under the agreeable shades of
Arpinum, or in the delightful neighbourhood of Formiae. As
soon as he is settled down at Formiae or Arpinum, or in
some other of those handsome villas which he proudly calls
the gems of Italy, *ocellos Italiae*, his thoughts naturally return
to Rome, and couriers are constantly starting to go and
learn what people are thinking and doing there. He could
never take his eyes off the Forum, whatever he may say.
Far or near he must have what Saint-Simon calls "that
smack of business that politicians cannot do without."
He wished by all means to know the position of parties,
their secret agreements, their internal discords, all those
hidden intrigues that lead up to events and explain them.
This is what he was continually demanding of Atticus,
Curio, Caelius, and so many other great men mixed up
in these intrigues either as actors or spectators, and what he
himself narrates to his absent friends in the most lively
manner, and thus the letters that he received or sent contain,
without his intending it, all the history of his time.[1]

[1] I have attempted to clear up some of the questions to which the
publication of Cicero's letters has given rise in a treatise entitled,
*Recherches sur la manière dont furent recueillies et publiées les lettres de
Cicéron*, Paris, Durand, 1863.

The correspondence of political men of our time, when it is published, is far from having the same importance, because the exchange of sentiment and thought is not made so much by means of letters now as it was then. We have invented new methods. The immense publicity of the press has advantageously replaced those cautious communications which could not reach beyond a few persons. Now-a-days the newspapers keep a man informed of what is doing in the world, whatever unfrequented place he may have retired to. As he learns events almost as soon as they happen, he receives the excitement as well as the news of them, and has no need of a well-informed friend to apprise him of them. To seek for all that the newspapers have destroyed and replaced among us would be an interesting study. In Cicero's time letters often took their place and rendered the same services. They were passed from hand to hand when they contained news men had an interest in knowing ; and those of important persons which made known their sentiments were read, commented on, and copied. A politician, who was attacked, defended himself by them before people whose esteem he desired to preserve, and through them men tried to form a sort of public opinion in a limited public when the Forum was silent, as in Caesar's time. The newspapers have taken up this duty now and make a business of politics, and as they are incomparably more convenient, rapid, and diffused, they have taken from correspondence one of its principal subjects.

It is true that private affairs remain for it, and we are tempted to think at first that this subject is inexhaustible, and that with the sentiments and affections of so many kinds that fill our home life it would always be rich enough. Nevertheless, I think that private correspondence becomes every day shorter and less interesting, where it is only a question of feeling and affection. That constant and agreeable intercourse which filled so large a place in the life of former times, tends almost to disappear, and one would say that by a strange chance the facility and rapidity of intercourse, which ought to give it more animation, have been injurious to it. Formerly, when there was no post, or when it was reserved for the emperor's use, as with the Romans, men were obliged to take advantage of any opportunity that occurred, or to send their letters by a slave. Then writing was a serious affair. They did not want the messenger to make a useless journey; letters were made longer and more complete to avoid the necessity of beginning again too often; unconsciously they were more carefully finished, by the thought we naturally give to things that cost trouble and are not very easy. Even in the time of Madame de Sévigné, when the mails started only once or twice a week, writing was still a serious business to which every care was given. The mother, far from her daughter, had no sooner sent off her letter than she was thinking of the one she would send a few days later. Thoughts, memories, regrets gathered in her mind during this interval, and when she took up her pen " she could no longer govern this torrent." Now, when we know that we can write when we will, we do not collect material as Madame de Sévigné did, we do not write a little every day, we no longer seek to " empty our budget," or torment ourselves in order to forget nothing, lest forgetfulness should make the news stale by coming too late. While the periodical return of the post formerly brought more order and regularity into correspondence, the facility we have now for writing when we will causes us to write less often. We wait to have something to say, which is seldomer than one thinks. We write no more than is necessary; and this is very little for a correspondence whose chief pleasure lies in the superfluous, and we are threatened with a reduction of that little. Soon, no doubt, the telegraph will have replaced the post; we shall only communicate by this breathless instrument, the image of a matter-of-fact and hurried society, which, even in the style it employs, tries to use a little less than what is necessary. With this new progress the pleasure of private correspondence, already much impaired, will have disappeared for ever.

But when people had more opportunities for writing letters, and wrote them better, all did not succeed equally. Some dispositions are fitter for this work than others. People whose minds move slowly, and who have need of much reflection before writing, make memoirs and not letters. The sober-minded write in a regular and methodical manner, but they lack grace and warmth. Logicians and reasoners have the habit of following up their thoughts too closely; now, one ought to know how to pass lightly from one subject to another, in order that the interest may be sustained, and to leave them all before they are exhausted. Those who are solely occupied with one idea, who concentrate themselves on it, and will not leave it, are only eloquent when they speak of it, which is not enough. To be always agreeable, and on all subjects, as a regular correspondence demands, one must have a lively and active imagination which receives the impressions of the moment and changes abruptly with them. This is the first quality of good letter writers; I will add to it, if you like, a little artifice. Writing always requires a certain effort. To succeed in writing we must aim at success, and the disposition to please must precede the wish to do so. It is natural enough to wish to please that great public for whom books are written, but it is the mark of a more exacting vanity to exert one's powers for a single person. It has often been asked since

La Bruyère, why women succeed better than men in this kind of writing? Is it not because they have a greater desire to please and a natural vanity which is, so to say, always under arms, which neglects no conquest, and feels the need of making efforts to please everybody?

I think nobody ever possessed these qualities in the same degree as Cicero. That insatiable vanity, that openness to impressions, that easiness in letting himself be seized and mastered by events, are found in his whole life and in all his works. It seems, at first sight, that there is a great difference between his letters and his speeches, and we are tempted to ask ourselves how the same man has been able to succeed in styles so opposed; but astonishment ceases as soon as we look a little closer. When we seek the really original qualities of his speeches they are found to be altogether the same that charm us in his letters. His commonplaces have got rather old, his pathos leaves us cold, and we often find that there is too much artifice in his rhetoric, but his narrations and portraits remain living in his speeches. It would be difficult to find a greater talent than his for narrative and description, and for representing to the life as he does both events and men. If he shows them to us so clearly, it is because he has them himself before his eyes. When he shows us the trader Cherea " with his eyebrows shaved, and that head which smells of tricks, and in which malignity breathes,"[1] or the praetor Verres taking an airing in a litter with eight bearers, like a king of Bithynia, softly lying on Malta roses,[2] or Vatinius rushing forth to speak, " his eyes starting, his neck swollen, his muscles stretched,"[3] or the Gallic witnesses, who walk about the Forum with an air of triumph and head erect,[4] or the Greek

---

[1] *Pro. Rosc. com.* 7.　　　　[2] *In Verrem. act. sec.* v. 11.
[3] *In Vatin.* 2.　　　　[4] *Pro Font.* 11.

witnesses who chatter without ceasing and gesticulate with
the shoulders,[1] all those characters, in fine, that when once
they have been met with in his works are never forgotten,
his powerful and mobile imagination sees them before paint-
ing them.   He possesses in a wonderful degree the faculty
of making himself the spectator of what he narrates.   Things
strike him, persons attract or repel him with an incredible
vivacity, and he throws himself entirely into the pictures he
makes of them.   What passion there is in his narratives !
What furious bursts of anger in his attacks !   What frenzy of
joy when he describes some ill fortune of his enemies !
How one feels that he is penetrated and overwhelmed with
it, that he enjoys it, that he delights in it and gloats over it,
according to his energetic expressions : *his ego rebus pascor,
his delector, his perfruor !*[2]   Saint-Simon, intoxicated with
hatred and joy, expresses himself almost in the same terms
in the famous scene of the "bed of justice," when he sees
the Duke of Maine struck down and the bastards discrowned.
" I, however," says he, "was dying with joy, I was even fearing a swoon.   My heart, swelled to excess, found no room
to expand . . . . I triumphed, I avenged myself, I swam in
my vengeance."   Saint-Simon earnestly desired power, and
twice he thought he held it ; "but the waters, as with Tan-
talus, retired from his lips every time he thought to touch
them."   I do not think, however, that we ought to pity
him.   He would have ill filled the place of Colbert and
Louvois, and even his good qualities perhaps would have
been hurtful to him.   Passionate and irritable, he feels
warmly the slightest injury, and flies into a passion at
every turn.   The smallest incidents excite him, and we
feel that when he relates them he does so with all his heart.
This ardent sensitiveness which warms all his narratives

---

[1] *Pro Rabir. post.* 13.   [2] *In Pison.* 20.

has made him an incomparable painter, but as it would always have confused his judgment it would have made him an indifferent politician. Cicero's example shows this well.

We are right then in saying that we find the same qualities in Cicero's speeches as in his letters, but they are more evident in his letters, because he is freer and gives more play to his feelings. When he writes to any of his friends, he does not reflect so long as when he is to address the people ; he gives his first impressions, and gives them with life and passion as they rise in him. He does not take the trouble to polish his style; all that he writes has usually such a graceful air, something so easy and simple that we cannot suspect preparation or artifice. A correspondent who wished to please him, having spoken to him one day of the thunders of his utterance, *fulmina verborum,* he answered : " What do you think then of my letters ? Do you not think that I write to you in the ordinary style ? One must not always keep the same tone. A letter cannot resemble a pleading or a political speech . . . one uses every-day expressions in it." [1] Even if he had wished to give more care to them he could not have found leisure. He had so many to write to content everybody ! Atticus alone sometimes received three in the same day. So he wrote them where he could—during the sitting of the senate, in his garden, when he is out walking, on the high-road when he is travelling. Sometimes he dates them from his dining-room, where he dictates them to his secretaries between two courses. When he writes them with his own hand he does not give himself time to reflect any the more. " I take the first pen I find," he tells his brother, "and use it as if it were good." [2] Thus it was not always easy to decipher him. When any one complains he does not lack excuses. It is the fault of his friends'

---

[1] *Ad fam.* ix. 21.   [2] *Ad Quint.* ii. 15, 6.

messengers, who will not wait. "They come all ready to start, with their travelling caps on, saying that their companions are waiting for them at the door."[1] Not to keep them waiting, he must write at random all that comes into his mind.

Let us thank these impatient friends, these hurried messengers who did not give Cicero time to make eloquent essays. His letters please us precisely because they contain the first flow of his emotions, because they are full of graceful negligence and naturalness. As he does not take time to disguise himself we see him as he is. His brother said to him one day, "I saw your own self in your letter."[2] We are inclined to say the same thing ourselves every time we read him. If he is so lively, earnest, and animated when he addresses his friends, it is because he so easily transports himself in imagination to the places where they are. "I feel as though I were talking to you,"[3] he writes to one of them. "I don't know how it happens," he says to another, "that I think I am near you while writing to you."[4] He gives way to his passing emotions in his letters even more than in his speeches. When he arrives at one of his fine country houses that he likes so much, he gives himself up to the pleasure of seeing it again ; it has never seemed to him so fine. He visits his porticoes, his gymnasia, his garden seats; he runs to his books, ashamed of having left them. Love of solitude seizes him so strongly that he never finds himself sufficiently alone. He ends by disliking his house at Formiae because there are so many intruders. "It is not a villa," he says, "it is a public lounge."[5] There he finds again the greatest bores in the world, his friend Sebosus and his friend Arrius, who persists in not returning to Rome, however much

---

[1] *Ad fam.* xv. 17.   [2] *Ibid.* xvi. 16.   [3] *Ad Att.* xiii. 18.
[4] *Ad fam.* xv. 16.   [5] *Ad Att.* ii. 14.

he may entreat him, in order to keep him company and
philosophize with him all day long. "While I am writing
to you," he says to Atticus, "Sebosus is announced. I have
not finished lamenting this when I hear Arrius saluting me.
Is this leaving Rome? What is the use of flying from others
to fall into the hands of these?" I wish, he adds, quoting
a fine verse very likely borrowed from his own works, "I
wish to fly to the mountains of my birthplace, the cradle of
my infancy. *In montes patrios et ad incunabula nostra.*" [1]
He goes in fact to Arpinum; he extends his journey to
Antium, the wild Antium, where he passes the time counting
the waves. This obscure tranquillity pleases him so much
that he regrets he was not duumvir in this little town rather
than consul at Rome. He has no higher ambition than to
be rejoined by his friend Atticus, to walk with him in the
sun, or to talk philosophy "seated on the little bench
beneath the statue of Aristotle." At this moment he seems
disgusted with public life, he will not hear speak of it. "I
am resolved to think no more about it," [2] he says. But we
know how he kept this sort of promise. As soon as he is
back in Rome he plunges into the thick of politics; the
country and its pleasures are forgotten. We only detect
from time to time a few passing regrets for a calmer life.
"When shall we live then?" *quando vivemus?* says he sadly
in this whirlwind of business that hurries him on. [3] But
these timorous complaints are soon stifled by the noise and
movement of the combat. He enters and takes part in it
with more ardour than anybody. He is still excited by it
when he writes to Atticus, its agitation is shown by his letters
which communicate it to us. We imagine ourselves looking
on at those incredible scenes that take place in the senate
when he attacks Clodius, sometimes by set speeches, some-

[1] *Ad Att.* ii. 15.   [2] *Ibid.* ii. 4.   [3] *Ad Quint.* iii. 1, 4.

times by impetuous questions, employing against him by turns the heaviest arms of rhetoric and the lightest shafts of raillery. He is still more sprightly when he describes the popular assemblies and recounts the scandals of the elections. " Follow me to the Campus Martius, corruption is rampant, *sequere me in Campum; ardet ambitus.*" [1] And he shows us the candidates at work, purse in hand, or the judges in the Forum shamelessly selling themselves to whoever will pay them, *judices quos fames magis quam fama commovit.*

As he has the habit of giving way to his impressions and changing with them, his tone varies from letter to letter. Nothing is more desponding than those he writes in exile ; they are a continual moan ; but his sentences suddenly become majestic and triumphant immediately after his return from exile. They are full of those flattering superlatives that he distributes so liberally to those who have served him, *fortissimus, prudentissimus, exoptatissimus,* etc., he extols in magnificent terms the marks of esteem given him by people of position, the authority he enjoys in the Curia, the credit he has so gloriously reconquered in the Forum, *splendorem illum forensem, et in senatu auctoritatem et apud viros bonos gratiam.*[2] Although he is only addressing his faithful Atticus, we think we hear an echo of the set orations he has just pronounced in the senate and before the people. It sometimes happens that on the gravest occasions he smiles and jokes with a friend who amuses him. In the thick of his conflict with Antony he writes that charming letter to Papirius Poetus, in which he advises him in such a diverting manner to frequent again the good tables, and to give good dinners to his friends.[3] He does not defy dangers, he forgets them ; but let him meet some timorous person, he soon partakes his fear, his tone changes at once ; he becomes

---

[1] *Ad Att.* iv. 15.   [2] *Ibid.* iv. 1.   [3] *Ad fam.* ix. 24.

animated, heated ; sadness, fear, emotion carry him without effort to the highest flights of eloquence. When Caesar threatens Rome, and insolently places his final conditions before the senate, Cicero's courage rises, and he uses, when writing to a single person, those energetic figures of speech which would not be out of place in a public oration. "What a fate is ours! Must we then give way to his impudent demands! for so Pompey calls them. In fact has a more shameless audacity ever been seen?—You have occupied for ten years a province that the senate has not given you, but which you have seized yourself by intrigue and violence. The term has arrived which your caprice alone and not the law has fixed for your power.—But let us suppose it was the law—the term having arrived, we name your successor, but you resist and say, ' Respect my rights.' And you, what do you do to ours? What pretext have you for keeping your army beyond the term fixed by the people, in spite of the senate?—You must give way to me or fight.—Well then ! let us fight, answers Pompey, at least we have the chance of conquering or of dying free men." [1]

If I wished to find another example of this agreeable variety and these rapid changes, I should not turn to Pliny or to those who, like him, wrote their letters for the public, I should come down to Madame de Sévigné. She, like Cicero, has a very lively and versatile imagination ; she gives way to her first emotions without reflection ; she is caught by things present, and the pleasure she is enjoying always seems the highest. It has been remarked that she took pleasure everywhere, not through that indolence of mind that attaches us to the place where we are, to avoid the trouble of changing, but by the vivacity of her character which gave her up entirely to the pleasures of the moment.

[1] *Ad Att.* vii. 9.

Paris does not charm her so much as to prevent her liking
the country, and no one of that age has spoken about
nature better than this woman of fashion who was so
much at ease in drawing-rooms, and seemed made for
them. She escapes to Livry the first fine day to enjoy
"the triumph of May," to "the nightingale, the cuckoo, and
the warbler that begin the spring in the woods." But Livry
is still too fashionable, she must have a more complete
solitude, and she cheerfully retires under her great trees in
Brittany. This time her Paris friends think she will be
wearied to death, having no news to repeat or fine wits to
converse with. But she has taken some serious moral
treatise by Nicole with her; she has found among those
neglected books whose last refuge, like that of old furniture,
is the country, some romance of her young days which
she reads again secretly, and in which she is astonished
still to find pleasure. She chats with her tenants, and just
as Cicero preferred the society of the country people to that
of the provincial fashionables, she likes better to talk with
her gardener Pilois than with "several who have preserved
the title of esquire in the parliament of Rennes." She
walks in her Mall, in those solitary alleys where the trees
covered with fine-sounding mottoes almost seem as though
they were speaking to each other; she finds, in fact, so
much pleasure in her desert that she cannot make up her
mind to leave it; nevertheless no woman likes Paris better.
Once back there she surrenders herself wholly to the
pleasures of fashionable life. Her letters are full of it.
She takes impressions so readily that we might almost tell
in perusing them what books she has just been reading,
at what conversations she has been present, what drawing-
rooms she has just left. When she repeats so pleasantly to
her daughter the gossip of the court we perceive that she

has just been conversing with the graceful and witty
Madame de Coulanges, who has repeated it to her.   When
she speaks so touchingly of Turenne she has just left the
Hôtel de Bouillon, where the prince's family are lamenting
his broken fortunes as well as his death.   She lectures, she
sermonizes herself with Nicole, but not for long.   Let her
son come in and tell her some of those gay adventures of
which he has been the hero or the victim, she recounts
boldly the most risky tales on condition of saying a little
later, " Pardon us, Monsieur Nicole ! "   When she has been
visiting La Rochefoucauld everything turns to morality ;
she draws lessons from everything, everywhere she sees
some image of life and of the human heart, even in the
viper broth that they are going to give Madame de la
Fayette who is ill.   Is not this viper, which though opened
and skinned still writhes, like our old passions ?   " What
do we not do to them ?   We treat them with insult,
harshness, cruelty, disdain ; we wrangle, lament, and storm,
and yet they move.   We cannot overcome them.   We
think, when we have plucked out their heart, that they are
done with and we shall hear no more of them.   But no ;
they are always alive, they are always moving."   This ease
with which she receives impressions, and which causes her
to adopt so quickly the sentiments of the people she visits,
makes her also feel the shock of the great events she looks
on at.   The style of her letters rises when she narrates them,
and, like Cicero, she becomes eloquent unconsciously.
Whatever admiration the greatness of the thoughts and the
liveliness of expression in that fine piece of Cicero upon
Caesar that I quoted just now may cause me, I am still
more touched, I admit, by the letter of Madame de
Sévigné on the death of Louvois, and I find more boldness
and brilliancy in that terrible dialogue which she imagines

between the minister who demands pardon and God who refuses it.

These are admirable qualities, but they bring with them certain disadvantages. Such hasty impressions are often rather fleeting. When people are carried away by a too vivid imagination, they do not take time to reflect before speaking, and run the risk of often having to change their opinion. Thus Madame de Sévigné has contradicted herself more than once. But being only a woman of fashion, her inconsistency has not much weight, and we do not look on it as a crime. What does it matter to us that her opinions on Fléchier and Mascaron have varied, that after having unreservedly admired the *Princesse de Clèves* when she read it alone, she hastened to find a thousand faults in it when her cousin Bussy condemned it? But Cicero is a politician, and he is expected to be more serious. We demand that his opinions should have more coherency; now, this is precisely what the liveliness of his imagination least permits. He never boasted of being consistent. When he judges events or men he sometimes passes without scruple, in a few days, from one extreme to the other. In a letter of the end of October Cato is called an excellent friend (*amicissimus*), and the way in which he has acted is declared to be satisfactory; at the beginning of November he is accused of having been shamefully malevolent in the same affair,[1] because Cicero seldom judges but by his impressions, and in a mobile spirit like his, very different but equally vivid impressions follow each other very quickly.

Another danger, and one still greater, of this excess of imagination which cannot control itself is that it may give us the lowest and most false opinion of those who yield to

---

[1] *Ad Att.* vii. 1, 2.

C

it. Perfect characters are only found in novels. Good
and evil are so intermingled in our nature that the one is
seldom found without the other. The strongest characters
have their weaknesses, and the finest actions do not spring
only from the most honourable motives. Our best affections
are not entirely exempt from selfishness; doubts and
wrongful suspicions sometimes trouble the firmest friendships, and it may happen at certain moments that cupidity
and jealousy, of which one is ashamed the next day, flit
rapidly through the mind of the most honourable persons.
The prudent and clever carefully conceal all those feelings
which cannot bear the light; those whose quick impressions
carry them away, like Cicero, speak out, and they are very
much blamed. The spoken or written word gives more
strength and permanence to these fugitive thoughts; they
were only flashes; they are fixed and accentuated by
writing; they acquire a clearness, a relief and importance
that they had not in reality. Those momentary weaknesses,
those ridiculous suspicions which spring from wounded
self-esteem, those short bursts of anger, quieted as soon as
reflected on, those unjust thoughts that vexation produces,
those ambitious fits that reason hastens to disavow,
never perish when once they have been confided to a
friend. One of these days a prying commentator will study
these too unreserved disclosures, and will use them, to
draw a portrait of the indiscrete person who made them, to
frighten posterity. He will prove by exact and irrefutable
quotations that he was a bad citizen and a bad friend, that
he loved neither his country nor his family, that he was
jealous of honest people, and that he betrayed all parties.
It is not so, however, and a wise man will not be deceived
by the artifice of misleading quotations. Such a man well
knows that we must not take these impetuous people

literally or give too much credence to what they say. We must save them from themselves, refuse to listen to them when they are led astray by passion, and especially must we distinguish their real and lasting feelings from all those exaggerations which are merely passing. For these reasons every one is not fitted to thoroughly understand these letters, every one cannot read them as they should be read. I mistrust those learned men who, without any acquaintance with men or experience of life, pretend to judge Cicero from his correspondence. Most frequently they judge him ill. They search for the expression of his thought in that commonplace politeness which society demands, and which no more binds those who use it than it deceives those who accept it. Those concessions that must be made if we wish to live together they call cowardly compromises. They see manifest contradictions in those different shades a man gives to his opinions, according to the persons he is talking with. They triumph over the imprudence of certain admissions, or the fatuity of certain praises, because they do not perceive the fine irony that tempers them. To appreciate all these shades, to give things their real importance, to be a good judge of the drift of those phrases which are said with half a smile, and do not always mean what they seem to say, requires more acquaintance with life than one usually gets in a German university. If I must say what I think, I would rather trust a man of the world than a scholar in this matter, for a delicate appreciation.

Cicero is not the only person whom this correspondence shows us. It is full of curious details about all those who had friendly or business relations with him. They were the most illustrious persons of the time, and they played the chief parts in the revolution that put an end to the Roman Republic. No one deserves to be studied more than they. It must be remarked here, that one of

Cicero's failings has greatly benefited posterity. If it were a question of some one else, of Cato for instance, how many people's letters would be missing in this correspondence! The virtuous alone would find a place in it, and Heaven knows their number was not then very great. But, happily, Cicero was much more tractable, and did not bring Cato's rigorous scruples into the choice of his friends. A sort of good-nature made him accessible to people of every opinion; his vanity made him seek praise everywhere. He had dealings with all parties, a great fault in a politician, for which the shrewd people of his time have bitterly reproached him, but a fault that we profit by; hence it happens that all parties are represented in his correspondence. This obliging humour sometimes brought him into contact with people whose opinions were the most opposite to his, and he found himself at certain times in close relations with the worst citizens whom he has at other times lashed with his invectives. Letters that he had received from Antony, Dolabella, and Curio still remain, and these letters are full of expressions of respect and friendship. If the correspondence went further back we should probably have some of Catiline's, and, frankly, I regret the want of them; for if we wish to judge of the state of a society as of the constitution of a man, it is not enough to examine the sound parts, we must handle and probe to the bottom the unsound parts. Thus, all the important men of that time, whatever their conduct may have been, or to whatever party they may have belonged, had dealings with Cicero. Memorials of all are found in his correspondence. A few of their letters still exist, and we have a large number of those that Cicero wrote to them. The private details he gives us about them, what he tells us of their opinions, their habits, and character, allows us to enter freely into their life. Thanks to him, all those persons indistinctly depicted by history resume their original appearance ; he seems to bring them nearer to us and to make us acquainted with them ; and when we have read his correspondence we can say that we have just visited the whole Roman society of his time.

The end we have in view in this book is to study closely a few of these personages, especially those who were most involved in the great political events of that period. But before beginning this study it is necessary to make a firm resolution not to bring to it considerations which belong to our own time. It is too much the custom now-a-days to seek arms for our present struggles in the history of the past. Smart allusions and ingenious parallels are most successful. Perhaps Roman antiquity is so much in fashion only because it gives political parties a convenient and less dangerous battle-field where, under ancient costumes, present-day passions may struggle. If the names of Caesar, Pompey, Cato, and Brutus are quoted on all occasions, these great men must not be too proud of the honour. The curiosity they excite is not altogether disinterested, and when they are spoken of it is almost always to point an epigram or set off a flattery. I wish to avoid this mistake. These illustrious dead seem to me to deserve something better than to serve as instruments in the quarrels that divide us, and I have sufficient respect for their memory and their repose not to drag them into the arena of our every-day disputes. It should never be forgotten that it is an outrage to history to subject it to the changing interest of parties, and that it should be, according to the fine expression of Thucydides, a work made for eternity.

These precautions being taken, let us penetrate with Cicero's letters into the Roman society of that great period, and let us begin by studying him who offers himself so gracefully to do us the honours.

CICERO IN PUBLIC AND PRIVATE LIFE

I

CICERO'S PUBLIC LIFE

CICERO'S public life is usually severely judged by the historians of our time. He pays the penalty of his moderation. As this period is only studied now with political intentions, a man like him who tried to avoid extremes fully satisfies nobody. All parties agree in attacking him; on all sides he is laughed at or insulted. The fanatical partisans of Brutus accuse him of timidity, the warmest friends of Caesar call him a fool. It is in England and amongst us[1] that he has been least abused, and that classical traditions have been more respected than elsewhere; the learned still persist in their old habits and their old admirations, and in the midst of so many convulsions criticism at least has remained conservative. Perhaps also the indulgence shown to Cicero in both countries comes from the experience they have of political life. When a man has lived in the practice of affairs and in the midst of the working of parties, he can better understand the sacrifices that the necessities of the moment, the interest of his friends and the safety of his cause may demand of a statesman, but he who only judges his conduct by inflexible

[1] Forsyth, *Life of Cicero*. London, Murray, 1864. Merivale, *History of the Romans under the Empire*, vols. i., ii.

22

theories thought out in solitude and not submitted to the test of experience becomes more severe towards him. This, no doubt, is the reason why the German scholars use him so roughly. With the exception of M. Abeken,[1] who treats him humanely, they are without pity. Drumann [2] especially overlooks nothing. He has scrutinized his works and his life with the minuteness and sagacity of a lawyer seeking the grounds of a law-suit. He has laid bare all his correspondence in a spirit of conscientious malevolence. He has courageously resisted the charm of those confidential disclosures which makes us admire the writer and love the man in spite of his weaknesses, and by opposing to each other detached fragments of his letters and discourses he has succeeded in drawing up a formal indictment, in which nothing is omitted and which almost fills a volume. M. Mommsen [3] is scarcely more gentle, he is only less long. Taking a general view of things he does not lose himself in the details. In two of those compact pages full of facts, such as he knows how to write, he has found means to heap on Cicero more insults than Drumann's whole volume contains. We see particularly that this pretended statesman was only an egotist and a short-sighted politician, and that this great writer is only made up of a newspaper novelist and a special-pleader. Here we perceive the same pen that has just written down Cato a Don Quixote and Pompey a corporal. As in his studies of the past he always has the present in his mind, one would say that he looks for the squireens of Prussia in the Roman aristocracy, and that in Caesar he salutes in advance that popular despot whose firm hand can alone give unity to Germany.

[1] Abeken, *Cicero in seinen Briefen.* Hannover, 1835.
[2] Drumann, *Geschichte Roms,* etc., vols. v., vi.
[3] Mommsen, *Römische Geschichte,* vol. iii.

How much truth is there in these fierce attacks? What confidence can we place in this boldness of revolutionary criticism? What judgment must we pronounce on Cicero's political conduct? The study of the facts will teach us.

I.

Three causes generally contribute to form a man's political opinions—his birth, his personal reflections, and his temperament. If I were not speaking here of sincere convictions only, I would readily add a fourth, which causes more conversions than the others, namely interest, that is to say, that leaning one has almost in spite of oneself to think that the most advantageous course is also the most just, and to conform one's opinion to the position one holds or wishes for. Let us try and discover what influence these causes had upon Cicero's conduct and political preferences.

At Rome, for a long time past, opinions had been decided by birth. In a city where traditions were so much respected the ideas of parents were inherited as well as their property or their name, and it was a point of honour to follow their politics faithfully; but in Cicero's time these customs were beginning to decay. The oldest families had no scruple in failing in their hereditary engagements. At that time many names which had become illustrious by defending popular interests are found in the senatorial party, and the most audacious demagogue of that time bore the name of Clodius. Besides, Cicero would never at any time have found political direction in his birth. He belonged to an unknown family, he was the first of his race to engage in public affairs, and the name he bore did not commit him in advance to any party. In fact, he was not born at

Rome. His father lived in one of those little country municipia of which the wits readily made fun, because doubtful Latin was spoken and fine manners were not well known in them, but which, none the less, were the strength and honour of the Republic. That rude but brave and temperate people who inhabited the neglected cities of Campania, Latium, and the Sabine country, and among whom the habits of rural life had preserved something of the ancient virtue,[1] was in reality the Roman people. That which filled the streets and squares of the great city, spent its time in the theatre, took part in the riots of the Forum, and sold its votes in the Campus Martius, was only a collection of freedmen and foreigners among whom only disorder, intrigue, and corruption could be learnt. Life was more honest and healthy in the municipia. The citizens who inhabited them remained for the most part strangers to the questions that were debated in Rome, and the rumour of public affairs did not reach them. They were sometimes seen on the Campus Martius or the Forum, when it was a question of voting for one of their fellow-citizens, or of supporting him by their presence before the tribunals; but usually they troubled themselves little about exercising their rights, and stayed at home. They were none the less devoted to their country, jealous of their privileges, even when they made no use of them, proud of their title of Roman citizens, and much attached to the Republican Government that had given it them. For them the Republic had preserved its prestige because, living at a distance, they saw less of its weaknesses and always recalled its ancient glory. Cicero's childhood was spent in the midst of these rural populations, as backward in their ideas as in their manners. He learnt from them to love

[1] *Pro Rosc. Amer.* 16.

the past more than to know the present. This was the
first impression and the first teaching he received from the
places as from the people among whom his early years were
passed. Later, he spoke with emotion of that humble
house that his father had built near the Liris, and which
recalled the house of the old Curius [1] by its stern simplicity.
I fancy that those who lived in it must have thought themselves carried back a century, and that in causing them to
live among the memorials of the past, it gave them the
inclination and taste for old-fashioned things. If Cicero
owed anything to his birth it was this. He may have
gained in his family respect for the past, love of his country,
and an instinctive preference for the Republican Government, but he found in it no precise tradition, no positive
engagement with any party. When he entered political life
he was obliged to decide for himself, a great trial for an
irresolute character! And in order to choose among so
many conflicting opinions it was necessary early to study
and reflect.

Cicero has embodied the results of his reflections and
studies in political writings, of which the most important,
The Republic, has only reached us in a very imperfect state.
What remains of it shows that he is here, as everywhere
else, a fervent disciple of the Greeks. He attaches himself
by preference to Plato, and his admiration for him is so
strong that he often almost makes us think that he is
content with translating him. In general Cicero does not
appear to care much for the glory of originality. This is
almost the only vanity he lacks. In his correspondence
there is a singular admission on this subject, which has
been freely used against him. In order to make his friend
Atticus understand how his works cost him so little trouble,

---

[1] *De leg.* ii. 1.

he says: "I only furnish the words, of which I have no lack";[1] but Cicero, contrary to his usual custom, calumniates himself here. He is not such a servile translator as he wishes to make believe, and the difference between him and Plato is great, especially in his political works. Their books bear, indeed, the same title, but as soon as they are opened we perceive that in reality they are quite unlike. It is the characteristic of a speculative philosopher like Plato to consider the absolute end in everything. If he wants to form a constitution, instead of studying the people to be governed by it, he begins with some principle which reason lays down, and follows it up with inflexible rigour to its logical consequences. Thus he succeeds in forming one of those political systems where everything is bound and held together, and which by their admirable unity delight the mind of the sage who studies them as the regularity of a fine building pleases the eye of those who look at it. Unfortunately this kind of constitution, thought out in solitude and cast all of a piece, is difficult of application. When it comes to be put in practice unexpected resistance crops up on all sides. National traditions, character, and recollections, all those social forces which have been overlooked, will not submit to the severe laws imposed on them. It is then perceived that these things cannot be moulded at will, and since they absolutely refuse to give way, one must be prepared to modify this constitution which seemed so fine when it was not put into use. But here again the difficulty is great. It is not easy to change anything in these compact and logical systems, where everything is so skilfully arranged that one piece being disturbed throws the rest out of gear. Besides, philosophers are naturally imperious and absolute; they do not like to be thwarted. To avoid that

[1] *Ad Att.* xii. 52.

opposition that provokes them, to escape as much as possible the demands of reality, they imitate the Athenian of whom Aristophanes speaks, who, despairing of finding here below a republic to suit him, went to look for one in the clouds. They also build castles in the air, ideal republics governed by imaginary laws. They frame admirable constitutions, but they have the defect of not applying to any particular country because they are made for the whole human race.

Cicero did not act thus. He knew the public he addressed ; he knew that that grave and sensible race, so quick to seize the practical side of things, would be ill-satisfied with these fancies, and so he does not lose himself in these dreams of the ideal and the absolute. He does not presume to make laws for the universe ; he is thinking especially of his own country and his own times, and although he appears to be drawing up the plan of a perfect republic, that is to say, one that cannot exist, it is plain that his eyes are fixed on a constitution which does really exist. The following are very nearly his political theories. Of the three forms of government usually distinguished, none altogether pleases him when it is isolated. I need not speak of the absolute government of a single man, he died in order to oppose that.[1]

---

[1] It has been remarked that, in his *Republic*, Cicero speaks of kingship with much esteem, and even a sort of emotion which may easily surprise us in a republican like him ; but he understands by it a kind of primitive and patriarchal government, and he demands so many virtues in the king and his subjects that we see very well that he does not think that this royalty was easy or even possible. We cannot therefore admit, as has been done by some, that Cicero meant to announce beforehand, and to approve of the revolution that Caesar accomplished some years later. On the contrary, he indicates in very clear terms what he will think of Caesar and his government when he attacks those tyrants who, in their greed for rule, wish to govern alone, in contempt of the rights of the people. " The tyrants many be clement," he adds ; " but what does

The other two, government by all or by a few, that is to say democracy and aristocracy, do not seem to him faultless either. It is difficult to be quite contented with the aristocracy when one has not the advantage of belonging to a great family. The Roman aristocracy, notwithstanding the great qualities it displayed in the conquest and government of the world, was supercilious and exclusive like others. The checks it had suffered for a century, its visible decline, and the feeling it must have had of its approaching end, far from curing its pride, rendered it more intractable. Prejudices seem to become narrower and more inflexible when they have but a short time to live. We know how our *émigrés*, face to face with a victorious revolution, used up their last strength in foolish struggles for precedence. In the same way the Roman nobility, at the moment when the power was slipping from it, seemed to make a point of exaggerating its defects, and of discouraging by its disdain the respectable people who offered themselves to defend it. Cicero felt himself drawn towards it by his taste for refinement of manners and elegant pleasures ; but he could not endure its insolence. Thus he always kept up the ill-will of the discontented plebeian against it, even while serving it. He knew very well that his birth was not overlooked, and that he was called an upstart (*homo novus*), and in return he was never tired of jesting about those fortunate people who do not need to have any merit, who do not require to take trouble, and to whom the highest places in the republic come while they are sleeping (*quibus omnia populi romani beneficia dormientibus deferuntur*).[1]

But if aristocracy pleased him little, he liked popular

---

it matter whether we have an indulgent or a barbarous master ? One is none the less a slave with either " (*De Rep.* i. 33).

[1] *In Verr. act. sec.* v. 70.

government still less. It is the worst of all, he said, anticipating Corneille,[1] and in saying so he followed the opinion
of the greater number of the Greek philosophers, his masters,
who have almost all shown a great aversion to democracy.
They were not only kept aloof from the multitude by the
nature of their studies, pursued in silence and solitude, but
they carefully shunned it lest they should partake of its
errors and prejudices. Their constant care was to keep
themselves outside and above it. The pride that this isolation nourished in them prevented them seeing an equal in a
man of the people, a stranger to those studies they were so
proud of. Thus the supremacy of numbers, which gives the
same importance to the unlearned as to the sage, was distasteful to them. Cicero says positively that equality understood in this way is the greatest inequality, *ipsa aequitas
iniquissima est*.[2] This was not the only nor even the greatest
reproach that the Greek philosophers, and Cicero with them,
threw on democracy. They thought it was naturally restless
and turbulent, the enemy of meditation, and that it does not
give that leisure to the learned and the sage which is needful for the works they are projecting. When Cicero thought
of popular government, he had in his mind only wrangles
and faction-fights. He recalled the plebeian riots and the
stormy scenes of the Forum. He fancied he heard those
threatening complaints of the debtors and the needy which
had troubled the repose of the rich for three hundred years.
How could any one apply himself amidst this turmoil to
studies which require peace and quietness? The pleasures
of the mind are interrupted every moment in this reign of
violence, which constantly drags people from the tranquillity
of their library into the public streets. This tumultuous and
unstable life was ill suited to such a firm friend of study, and

[1] *De Rep.* i. 26. [2] *Ibid* i. 34.

if the arrogance of the nobles sometimes threw him towards the popular party, dislike of violence and noise did not allow him to remain in it.

What form of government then seemed to him the best ? That which unites them all in a just equilibrium—he says so very plainly in his *Republic*. " I should wish that there be in the state a supreme and royal power, that another part be reserved for the authority of the chief citizens, and that certain things be left to the judgment and will of the people." [1] Now this mixed and limited government is not, according to him, an imaginary system, like the republic of Plato. It is in actual existence and working ; it is that of his own country. This opinion has been much contested. M. Mommsen thinks it agrees as little with philosophy as with history. Taking it strictly, it is certainly more patriotic than true. It would be going very far to consider the Roman constitution as a faultless model, and to close our eyes to its defects at the very moment when it perished through those very defects ; yet it must be admitted that, with all its imperfections, it was one of the wisest of ancient times, and that none, perhaps, had made so many efforts to satisfy the two great needs of society—order and liberty. Nor can it be denied that its chief merit consisted in its effort to unite and reconcile the different forms of government, notwithstanding their obvious antagonisms. Polybius had perceived this before Cicero, and it derives this merit from its origin and the way in which it was formed. The constitution of Greece had almost all been the work of one man, the Roman constitution was the work of time. That skilful balance of powers that Polybius admired so much, had not been contrived by ône foreseeing mind. We do not find in the early times of Rome a single legislator

[1] *De Rep*. i. 45.

who regulated in advance the part each social element was
to play in the general combination ; these elements combined by themselves. The seditions of the plebeians, the
desperate struggles of the tribunate with the patricians,
which terrified Cicero, had contributed more than all the
rest to complete that constitution that he admired. After a
struggle of nearly two hundred years, when the opposing
forces perceived that they were not able to destroy each
other, they resigned themselves to unite, and from the efforts
they made to agree together there resulted a government,
imperfect doubtless—can there be a perfect one ?—but which
is none the less the best, perhaps, of the ancient world. We
remember, of course, that Cicero did not bestow this praise
on the Roman constitution as it was in his time. His
admiration went further back. He recognized that it had been
profoundly modified since the time of the Gracchi, but he
thought that before it had undergone these alterations it was
irreproachable. Thus the studies of his riper age carried
him back to those first impressions of his childhood, and
strengthened his love of ancient times and his respect for
ancient customs. As he advanced in life all his mistakes
and all his misfortunes threw him back to that time. The
more the present was sad and the future threatening the
more he looked back with regret on the past. If he had
been asked in what time he would have wished to have been
born, I think he would have unhesitatingly chosen the
period that followed the Punic wars, that is to say, the
moment when Rome, proud of her victory, confident in the
future and dreaded by the world, caught a glimpse for the
first time of the beauties of Greece, and began to feel
the charm of letters and the arts. Cicero considers this
Rome's best time, and places in it by preference the scene
of his dialogues. He would certainly have liked to live

among those great men whom he causes to speak so well, in the company of Scipio, Fabius, and Cato the Elder, by the side of Lucilius and Terence ; and in this illustrious group, the personage whose life and career would most have tempted him, he that he would have wished to be, if a man could choose his time and order his destiny, was the wise and learned Laelius.[1] To unite, like him, a high political situation to the cultivation of literature, to add to the supreme authority of eloquence some military successes, which the greatest preachers of pacific triumphs do not disdain, to reach the highest dignities of the republic in quiet and orderly times, and after an honourable life to enjoy a respected old age—this was Cicero's ideal. What regrets and sadness does he not experience, when he wakes from this fine dream to the disappointments of reality, and instead of living in a tranquil republic, and in free intercourse with the Scipios, he must be the rival of Catiline, the victim of Clodius, and the subject of Caesar.

Cicero's temperament, I think, had still more to do with his political preferences than his birth or his reflections. There is no more to learn about the weaknesses of his character ; they have been laid bare with delight, they have even been wilfully exaggerated, and since Montaigne it is the usual thing to laugh at them. I need not repeat, then, what has been said so often, that he was timid, hesitating, and irresolute. I admit with everybody that nature made him a man of letters rather than a politician, but I do not think that this admission does him so much harm as might be thought. The mind of the man of letters is often more perfect, more comprehensive, broader than that of the

[1] In that curious letter that he wrote to Pompey after his consulship (*ad fam.* v. 7), in which he seems to propose a kind of alliance, he attributes to him the part of Scipio and takes for himself that of Laelius.

D

politician, and it is precisely this breadth that cramps and thwarts him when he undertakes public affairs. We ask ourselves what qualities are necessary for a statesman; would it not be wiser to seek those it is good for him to lack, and does not political capacity show itself sometimes in its limitations and exclusions? A man of action who ought to decide quickly may be hampered by the number of contradictory reasons a too close and penetrating view of things may present to him. A too vivid imagination, showing him many plans at once, prevents him fixing on any. Determination often comes from narrowness of mind, and is one of the greatest virtues in a politician. A very sensitive conscience, by making him too particular in the choice of his allies, would deprive him of powerful support. He must distrust those generous impulses which lead him to do justice even to his enemies : in the furious struggle for power a man runs the risk of disarming himself and allowing an advantage to be taken if he has the misfortune to be just and tolerant. There is nothing that may not become a danger for him, even to that natural uprightness, the first quality of a statesman. If he is too sensitive to the excesses and acts of injustice of his party he will serve it feebly, if his fidelity is to be unshaken he must not only excuse, he should be able to shut his eyes to them. These are some of the imperfections of heart and mind by which he gains his successes. If it be true, as I believe it is, that the politician often succeeds in the government of a state through his defects, and that the literary man fails by his very qualities, it is paying the latter almost a compliment to say he is not fit for the management of affairs.

We may say then without discrediting Cicero, that he was not altogether fit for public life. The causes which made him an incomparable writer did not allow him to be a good politician. That openness to impressions, that delicate and irritable sensitiveness, the principal sources of his literary talent, did not leave him sufficiently master of his will. Particular events had too great a hold on him, and a man must be able to detach himself from these in order to control them. His versatile and fertile imagination, by drawing his attention to all sides at once, rather incapacitated him for forming well-connected plans. He could not delude himself enough about men or enterprises, and thus he was subject to sudden fits of irresolution. He often boasted of having foreseen and predicted the future. It was certainly not in his position of augur, but by a kind of troublesome perspicacity, that showed him the consequences of events, and the bad ones rather than the good. On the nones of December, when he executed Catiline's accomplices, he did not forget the vengeance to which he exposed himself, and he foresaw his exile : that day then, notwithstanding the irresolution he has been reproached with, he had more courage than another who in a moment of excitement would not have seen the danger. One cause of his inferiority and weakness was that he was moderate, moderate by constitution rather than principle, that is to say, with that nervous and irritable impatience which at last employs violence to defend moderation. In political struggles all excess can seldom be avoided. Usually parties are unjust in their complaints when they are beaten, cruel in their reprisals when they conquer, and ready to do without scruple, as soon as they are able, what they blame in their enemies. If any in the victorious party perceive they are going too far and dare to say so, they inevitably irritate everybody against them. They are accused of timidity and vacillation, they are called weak and changeable ; but is this reproach well deserved? Did Cicero contradict himself when, after defending the unfortunate men whom the aristocracy oppressed under Sulla, he defended, thirty years later, the victims of the democracy under Caesar? Was he not, on the contrary, more consistent than those who, after bitterly complaining of being exiled, exiled their enemies as soon as they had the power? We must, however, admit that if this lively sense of justice is honourable in a private man it may become dangerous in a politician. Parties do not like those who refuse to join in their excesses, and in the midst of general licence set up the claim of alone remaining within bounds. It was Cicero's misfortune not to have that firm resolution which fixes a man in his opinions, and to pass from one opinion to another, because he saw clearly the good and evil of all. A man must be very self-reliant to try and do without others. This isolation takes for granted a decision and energy that were wanting in Cicero. If he had resolutely attached himself to one party he would have found in it traditions and fixed principles, firm friends and steady leading, and need only have allowed himself to be led. On the other hand, by endeavouring to walk alone he risked making all the rest his enemies while he himself had no clearly marked out line of conduct. A glance at the chief events of his political life is sufficient to show that this was the origin of a part of his misfortunes and his faults.

II.

What I have just said of Cicero's character explains his early political opinions. He first appeared in the Forum under the government of Sulla. The aristocracy was then all-powerful, and strangely abused its power. Having been conquered for a moment by Marius its reprisals had been terrible. Tumultuous and indiscriminate massacres could not appease its rage. Applying its cold and orderly spirit to murder itself, it had invented proscription, which was only another way of organizing assassination. After having thus satisfied its vengeance it began to strengthen its authority. It had dispossessed the richest municipia of Italy of their property, excluded the knights from the tribunals, lessened the privileges of the popular comitia, deprived the tribunes of the right of intervention, that is, it had levelled everything around itself. When it had broken down all resistance by the death of its enemies, and concentrated all power in itself, it solemnly declared that the revolution was ended, that legal government would re-commence, and that "killing would cease after the kalends of June." Notwithstanding these pompous declarations, massacres still continued for a long time. Assassins, protected by the freedmen of Sulla, who shared the profits with them, went out by night into the dark and crooked streets of the old city, even to the foot of the Palatine. They murdered rich men returning home, and under some pretext or other obtained their property from the courts of justice, no one daring to complain. Such was the government under which men lived at Rome when Cicero pleaded his first causes. A moderate man like him, to whom excess was distasteful, must have had a horror of this violence. An aristocratic tyranny did not suit him better than a popular tyranny. Before this abuse of authority that the nobility allowed itself he felt himself naturally drawn to aid the democracy, and he began his career in the ranks of its defenders.

He made a bold and splendid beginning. In the midst of that silent terror that the memory of the proscriptions kept up, he dared to speak out, and the universal silence

gave a louder echo to his words. His political importance
dates from the defence of Roscius. This unfortunate man,
whose property had been first taken, and who had then been
accused of murdering his father, could find no defender.
Cicero undertook his defence. He was young and unknown, two great advantages in undertaking these bold
strokes, for obscurity diminishes the danger which a man
runs, and youth prevents the seeing it. He had no trouble
in proving the innocence of his client, who was accused
without evidence ; but this success was not enough for
him. It was known that one of the most powerful freedmen of Sulla, the rich and voluptuous Chrysogonus, was the
hidden mover of the accusation. No doubt he thought
the dread his name inspired was a sufficient protection
against the boldness of the defence. Cicero dragged him
into the case. Traces of the dismay that seized the audience
when they heard this dreaded name are perceptible in his
speech. The accusers were dumfoundered, the multitude
remained silent. The young orator alone seemed tranquil
and self-possessed. He smiled, he joked, he dared to jeer
at those terrible men whom no one else dared look in
the face, because in doing so they thought of the two
thousand heads of knights and senators they had cut off.
He does not altogether respect the master himself. That
surname, "the happy," that his flatterers had given him gave
rise to a pun. "What man is *happy* enough," says he, "not
to have some rascal in his train ? " [1] This rascal is no
other than the all-powerful Chrysogonus. Cicero does not
spare him. He depicts his vulgar luxury and arrogance.
He shows him heaping up in his house on the Palatine all
the precious objects that he had taken from his victims,
annoying the neighbourhood with the noise of his singers and

---

[1] *Pro. Rosc. Amer.* 8.

musicians, " or hovering about the Forum with his hair well combed and shining with unguents." [1] More serious accusations are mingled with these jests. The word proscriptions is sometimes pronounced in this speech, the memory and impression they have left is found everywhere. We feel that the speaker, who has seen them, has his mind full of the subject, and that the horror that he feels and that he cannot master prevents him keeping silence whatever danger there may be in speaking. This generous emotion shows itself every moment, in spite of the reticence the neighbourhood of the proscribers imposes. Speaking of their victims, he dares to say that they have been cruelly murdered, though it was usual to attribute to them every kind of crime. He holds up to public scorn and hatred the wretches who have enriched themselves by these massacres, and with a successful pun calls them "cut-heads and cut-purses." [2] He then demands formally that an end should be put to these proceedings, of which humanity was ashamed; "otherwise," he adds, "it would be better to go and live among wild beasts than to remain in Rome." [3]

Cicero spoke thus at a few paces from the man who had ordered the proscriptions, and in the presence of those who had carried them out and profited by them. We can imagine the effect his words must have produced. They expressed the secret feelings of all, they relieved the public conscience, forced to keep silence, and humiliated by its silence. Thus the democratic party showed the most lively sympathy, from that time, for the eloquent young man who protested so courageously against a hateful rule. The remembrance of this preserved the popular favour for him so faithfully even to the time of his consulship. Every time he sought an office the citizens hastened in crowds to

[1] *Pro. Rosc. Amer.* 46.   [2] *Ibid.* 29.   [3] *Ibid.* 52.

the Campus Martius to record their votes for him. No politician of that time, and there were many more eminent than he, so easily reached the highest dignities. Cato suffered more than one check, Caesar and Pompey needed coalitions and intrigues to succeed. Cicero is almost the only one whose candidatures succeeded the first time, and who never had to recur to the means usually required for success. In the midst of those scandalous bargains which gave honours to the richest, notwithstanding those deep-rooted traditions which seemed to reserve them for the noblest, Cicero, who had no claims of birth and but a small fortune, always defeated all the rest. He was appointed quaestor, aedile ; he obtained the urban praetorship, which was the most honourable ; he attained the consulship the first time he sought for it, as soon as the law permitted him to aspire to it, and none of these dignities cost anything either to his honour or his fortune.

It is worthy of remark, that when he was appointed praetor he had not delivered any political speech. Up to the age of forty years he was only what we call an advocate, and had not felt the need of being anything else. Forensic eloquence then led to everything ; a few brilliant successes before the tribunals were sufficient to carry a man to public dignities, and nobody thought of asking Cicero for any other proof of his capacity for public business, when they were about to commit the highest interests of his country to his charge, and to invest him with the supreme authority. However, if this long time passed at the bar was not detrimental to his political career, I think it caused some injury to his talents. All the reproaches we may address to the advocate of to-day, wrongly, no doubt, were well deserved by the advocate of those times. It may be said of him with truth, that he took all cases indifferently, that he changed his opinion with each suit, that he used all his art in and made his fame by finding good reasons for supporting every sophism. The young man who devoted himself to oratory in the ancient schools, never heard it said that it was necessary to be convinced, and proper only to speak conscientiously. He was taught that there are different kinds of cases, those which are honest and those which are not so (*genera causarum sunt honestum, turpe*, etc.).[1] It was not thought necessary to add that the latter were to be avoided. On the contrary, by exaggerating the merit of success in these, he acquired the taste for undertaking them by preference. After he had been taught how to defend and save the guilty, he was, without hesitation, also taught how to bring discredit on an honest man. Such was the education received by the pupil of the rhetoricians, and when he had quitted their schools he did not lack opportunity of applying their precepts. For instance, he did not make the mistake of being moderate and restrained in his attacks. By constraining himself to be just he would have deprived himself of an element of success with that fickle and passionate mob which applauded satirical portraits and violent invective. He was not more prejudiced in favour of truth than of justice. It was a precept of the schools to invent, even in criminal causes, racy and imaginary details that diverted the audience (*causam mendaciunculis adspergere*).[2] Cicero quotes with great commendation some of these agreeable little lies which perhaps cost the honour or the life of some unfortunate people who were unlucky enough to have too witty opponents, and as he had himself a fertile imagination in this way, he did not stint himself in having recourse to this easy means of success. Nothing was more indifferent to the ancient advocate than being incon-

[1] *Ad Herenn.* i. 3.   [2] *De Orat.* ii. 59.

sistent with himself. It was said that the orator Antonius never would write any of his speeches, lest some one should take it into his head to compare his late with his present opinion. Cicero had not these scruples. He contradicted himself all his life, and was never uneasy about it. One day, when he too openly stated the contrary to what he had formerly upheld, as he was pressed to explain these sudden changes, he answered without perturbation : "You are mistaken if you think that you find the expression of our personal opinions in our speeches ; they are the language of the cause and the case, and not that of the man and the orator." [1] This at least is a sincere avowal ; but how much do the orator and the man not lose by thus suiting their language to circumstances ! They learnt to be careless of putting order and consistency in their lives, to dispense with sincerity in their opinions, and conviction in their speech, to make the same expenditure of talent for untruth as for truth, to consider only the needs of the moment, and the success of the case in hand. These are the lessons that the bar of that age taught Cicero. He remained at it too long, and when he quitted it at forty to make his first essay in political oratory, he could not shake off the bad habits acquired there.

Does this mean that Cicero should be struck off the list of political orators ? If this name is given to every man whose speech has some influence on the affairs of his country, who sways the mob, or convinces honest people, it seems difficult to refuse it to Cicero. He knew how to talk to the multitude and make himself listened to. At times he mastered it in its most furious outbursts. He made it accept and even applaud opinions contrary to its preferences. He seemed to drag it out of its apathy, and

[1] *Pro Cluent.* 50.

to call up in it for a short time an appearance of energy and patriotism. He is not to blame if his successes were not followed up, if after these grand triumphs of eloquence brute force remained master. At least he did with his words all that words could then do. I admit, however, that what was wanting in his character was wanting also in his political eloquence. It is nowhere sufficiently resolute, decided, practical. It is too much taken up with itself, and not enough with the questions it is treating. It does not attack them boldly on their salient points. It is involved in pompous phrases, instead of trying to speak that clear and precise language which is the language of public business. When we examine it closely, and begin to analyze it, we find that it is chiefly composed of a good deal of rhetoric and a little philosophy. All those agreeable and smart arguments, all those artifices of debate, and also all that ostentation of pathos that we find in it, come from rhetoric. Philosophy has furnished those grand commonplaces developed with talent, but not always germane to the subject. There is too much artifice and method about it. A concise and simple statement would be more suitable to the discussion of affairs than these subtleties and emotions ; these long philosophical tirades would be advantageously replaced by a clear and judicious exposition of the orator's principles and of the general ideas that regulate his conduct. Unfortunately, as I have said, Cicero preserved, on reaching the rostrum, the habits he had acquired at the bar. He attacks, with the arguments of an advocate, that agrarian law, so honest, moderate, and wise, which was proposed by the tribune Rullus. In the fourth Catilinarian Oration he had to discuss this question, one of the gravest that can be placed before a deliberative assembly, namely, how far is it permitted to deviate from legality in order to save one's country? He has not even approached it. It is painful to see how he hangs back from it, how he flies from and avoids it, to develop small reasons and lose himself in a vulgar pathos. The grave and serious kind of eloquence evidently was not that which Cicero preferred, and in which he felt most at ease. If you wish to know the real tendency of his talents, read, immediately after the fourth Catilinarian Oration, the speech for Muraena, delivered at the same time. There is none more agreeable in the collection of his speeches, and we wonder how a man who was consul, and who had then so many affairs on his hands, found his mind sufficiently free to joke with so much ease and point ; the truth is, there he was in his element. Accordingly, although he was consul or consular, he returned to the bar as often as he could. It was to oblige his friends, he said. I think that he wished still more to please himself ; he appears happy, and his animation and wit expand so freely, when he has some agreeable and lively case to plead. Not only did he never miss an opportunity of appearing before the judges, but as much as possible he threw his political discourses into the form of ordinary pleadings. Everything turned into personal questions with him. The discussion of ideas usually leaves him cold. He had to contend against some one in order to let us see him at his best. The finest speeches he delivered in the Forum or the senate are eulogies or invectives. In them he is unrivalled ; in them, according to one of his expressions, his eloquence rises and triumphs ; but however fine invectives and eulogies may be, they are not altogether our ideal of political eloquence, and we demand something else of it now-a-days. All that can be said in justification of Cicero's speeches is, that they were perfectly appropriate to his time, and that their character is explained by the circumstances in which they were delivered. Eloquence did not then guide the state as in the best times of the republic. Other influences had replaced it ; in the elections, money and the intrigues of the candidates, in out-door discussions, the occult and terrible power of the popular societies, and above all the army, which, since Sulla, raised or overthrew every government. Eloquence feels itself powerless in the midst of these forces which overpower it. How can it still preserve the commanding accent, the imperious and resolute tone of one who knows his power ? Need it appeal to reason and logic, and try and force itself upon men's convictions by a close and forcible argument, when it knows that the questions it is treating are decided otherwise ? M. Mommsen maliciously remarks, that in most of his great political speeches Cicero pleads causes already victorious. When he published the Verrine Orations, the laws of Sulla on the composition of the tribunals had just been abolished. He well knew that Catiline had decided to leave Rome when he pronounced the first Catilinarian Oration, in which he so feelingly adjures him to go away. The second Philippic, which seems so bold when we think of it as spoken to the face of the all-powerful Antony, was only made public at the moment when Antony was flying to Cisalpine Gaul. Of what use then were all these fine speeches ? They did not cause decisions to be taken, since these decisions were already taken ; but they caused them to be accepted by the multitude, they stirred public opinion and excited it in their favour : this was something. It was necessary to accept the facts of the situation ; speech no longer governed, eloquence could no longer hope to direct events, but it acted on them indirectly, it tried to produce those great movements of opinion that prepare or complete them ; "it does not secure votes and acts, it arouses the emotions." [1]   If this moral effect is the only end it had in view at the time, Cicero's eloquence, by its copiousness and splendour, by its brilliancy and pathos, was well calculated to attain it.

At first he had put his eloquence at the service of the popular party ; we have seen that it was in the ranks of this party that he made his first political appearance ; but although he faithfully served it for seventeen years, I am inclined to think that he did not always do so heartily. The excesses of the aristocratic government threw him towards democracy, but he must have found democracy not much wiser, especially when it was victorious.   It sometimes gave him terrible clients to defend.   He had to plead the cause of factious and seditious persons who were always troubling the public peace.   One day he even pleaded, or was on the point of pleading, for Catiline.   It is probable that all this was painful to him, and that the violent excesses of democracy tempted him more than once to separate from it.   Unfortunately he did not know where to go if he left it, and if the plebeians offended him by their violence, the aristocracy, by its arrogance and prejudices, did not any more attract him.   Since in existing parties he did not find any which exactly corresponded to his convictions, and which altogether suited his disposition, he had no other resource than to form one for himself.   This is what he

---

[1] I here employ the phrases of M. Havet, who has set this idea in a clear light in one of the too scanty writings he has published on Cicero. Speaking of this, we may be permitted to regret that M. Berger and he have not given to the public the excellent series of lectures which they delivered at the Collège de France and at the Sorbonne, of which Cicero was so often the subject. If they had acceded to the wishes of their auditors, and the entreaties of all friends of letters, France would have nothing to envy Germany on this important question.

tried to do. When he felt that the brilliancy of his eloquence, the offices he had filled, the popularity that surrounded him, made him an important person, in order to assure his future, to take a higher and more permanent position in the republic, to free himself from the requirements of his former protectors, in order not to be forced to stretch out his hand to his old enemies, he sought to create a new party, composed of the moderate men of all parties, and of which he was to be the head. But he very well understood that he could not create this party in a moment and produce it from nothing. It was necessary first to find a nucleus around which the new recruits that he expected should group themselves. He thought he had found it in that class of citizens to which he belonged by his birth, and who were called the knights.

Rome always lacked what we now call the middle and citizen class. In proportion as the small farmers left their friends to go and live in the city, and "as those hands which had worked at the corn and the vine were only occupied in applauding at the theatre and the circus,"[1] the gap became greater between the opulent aristocracy which possessed almost all the public wealth, and that indigent and famished people that was continually recruited from the slaves. The sole intermediaries were the knights. This name, at the time we are considering, was not only used to describe the citizens to whom the state gave a horse (*equites equo publico*), and who voted separately in the elections; it was also given to all those who possessed the equestrian income qualification, that is to say, those whose fortune exceeded 400,000 sesterces (£3200). We may well believe that the nobility behaved haughtily to these obscure plebeians whom chance or economy had enriched; it kept these

[1] Varro, *De re rust.* ii. I.

parvenus at a distance; dealt out its disdain to them as liberally as to the poor people of the plebs, and obstinately closed the entrance to public dignities to them. When Cicero was appointed consul it was thirty years since a new man, whether knight or plebeian, had attained the consulship. Removed from political life by the jealousy of the great nobles, the knights were obliged to turn their energies elsewhere. Instead of wasting time in useless candidatures, they busied themselves in making their fortunes. When Rome had conquered the world, it was the knights especially who profited by these conquests. They formed an industrious and enlightened class, they were already in easy circumstances, and able to make loans, and thought they could speculate in the conquered countries for their own profit. Penetrating wherever the Roman arms were carried, they became merchants, bankers, farmers of the taxes, and amassed immense riches. As Rome was no longer the Rome of the Curii and the Cincinnati, and dictators were no longer taken from the plough, their wealth gave them consideration and importance. From that time they were spoken of with more respect. The Gracchi, who wished to make them allies in the struggle they were waging with the aristocracy, caused it to be decided that the judges should be taken from their ranks. Cicero went further; he tried to make them the foundation of the great moderate party he wished to create. He knew that he could count on their devotedness. He belonged to them by birth; he had shed over them the splendour that surrounded his name; he had never neglected to defend their interests before the tribunals or in the senate. He also reckoned that they would be grateful to him for wishing to augment their importance and call them to a great political future.

All these combinations of Cicero seemed at first to succeed very happily; but, to tell the truth, the merit of this success was chiefly due to circumstances. This great coalition of the moderates upon which he congratulated himself as his finest work, almost succeeded under the influence of fear. A social revolution seemed imminent. The dregs of all the old parties, wretched plebeians and ruined nobles, old soldiers of Marius, and proscribers of Sulla, had united under the leadership of a bold and able chief, who promised them a new distribution of public wealth. The existence of this party compelled those whom it threatened to unite also in order to defend themselves. Fear was more efficacious than the finest speeches would have been, and in this sense we may say that Cicero was perhaps more indebted for this union which he regarded as the main point of his policy to Catiline rather than to himself. Community of interests, then, brought about, at least for a time, a reconciliation of the aims of various classes. The richest, and consequently the most seriously endangered, namely the knights, were naturally the soul of the new party. By their side the honest plebeians who did not wish political reforms to be exaggerated took their stand, as well as those nobles whose threatened pleasures drew them from their apathy, who would have allowed the republic to perish without defending it, but who did not wish their lampreys and fish-ponds touched. The new party had not to look about long for a head. Pompey was in Asia, Caesar and Crassus secretly favoured the conspiracy. Besides these there was no greater name than Cicero's. This explains that great wave of public opinion which carried him into the consulship. His election was almost a triumph. I shall say nothing of his consulship, of which he has had the misfortune to speak too much himself. I do not wish to

E

underrate the victory that he gained over Catiline and
his accomplices. The danger was serious; even his enemy
Sallust affirms it. Behind the plot were hidden ambitious
politicians ready to profit by events. Caesar knew well
that the reign of anarchy could not last long. After some
pillaging and massacres, Rome would have recovered from
her surprise, and honest folks, being driven to activity by
despair, would have again got the upper hand. Only it is
probable that then one of those reactions that usually follow
great anarchy would have taken place. The remembrance
of the ills from which they had escaped with such difficulty
would have disposed many people to sacrifice the liberty
which exposed them to so many perils, and Caesar held
himself ready to offer them the sovereign remedy of absolute
power. By cutting the evil at the root, by surprising and
punishing the conspiracy before it broke out, Cicero perhaps
delayed the advent of monarchical government at Rome for
fifteen years. He was not wrong, then, in boasting of the
services he rendered at that time to his country's liberty,
and we must acknowledge, with Seneca, that if he has
praised his consulship without measure he has not done so
without reason.[1]

Coalitions of this kind, unfortunately, seldom long survive the circumstances that give rise to them. When the
interests that a common danger had united began to feel
themselves secure, they recommenced their old quarrels.
The plebeians, who were no longer afraid, felt their old
animosity against the nobility revive. The nobles began
again to envy the wealth of the knights. As to the
knights, they had none of those qualities that were necessary to make them the soul of a political party, as Cicero
had hoped. They were more occupied with their private

---

[1] *De brevit. vitæ*, 5. *Non sine causa, sed sine fine laudatus.*

affairs than with those of the republic. They had not the strength of numbers, like the plebeians, and were wanting in those great traditions of government that maintained so long the authority of the nobility. Their only guiding principle was that instinct usual with men of large fortunes, which led them to prefer order to liberty. They sought, before all things, a strong power which could defend them, and Caesar had in the end no more devoted followers than they. In this break-up of his party, Cicero, who could not stand alone, asked himself on which side he ought to place himself. The fright that Catiline had given him, the presence of Caesar and Crassus in the ranks of the democracy, prevented his return to that party, and he finally attached himself to the nobility, notwithstanding his repugnance. From the date of his consulship he resolutely turned towards this party. We know how the democracy avenged itself for what it considered a betrayal. Three years after it condemned its old head, now become its enemy, to exile, and only consented to recall him to cast him at the feet of Caesar and Pompey, whose union had made them masters of Rome.[1]

III.

The gravest political crisis that Cicero passed through, after the great struggles of his consulship, was certainly that which terminated in the fall of the Roman republic at Pharsalia. We know that he did not willingly engage in this terrible conflict, of which he foresaw the issue, and that he hesitated for nearly a year before deciding on his course.

[1] On the exile of Cicero, and the policy that he followed after his return, see the study on *Caesar and Cicero*, Part I.

It is not surprising that he hesitated so long. He was no longer young and obscure as when he pleaded for Roscius. He had a high position and an illustrious name that he did not wish to compromise, and a man may be allowed to reflect before he risks fortune, glory, and perchance life on a single cast. Besides, the question was not so simple nor the right so clear as they seem at first sight. Lucan, whose sympathies are not doubtful, yet said that it could not be known on which side justice lay, and this obscurity does not seem to be altogether dissipated, since, after eighteen centuries of discussion, posterity has not yet succeeded in coming to an agreement. It is curious that, among us, in the seventeenth century, at the height of monarchical government, the learned all pronounced against Caesar without hesitation. Magistrates of the high courts, men cautious and moderate by their offices and character, who approached the king and were not sparing of flattery, took the liberty of being Pompeians and even furious Pompeians in private. "The First President," says Guy-Patin, "is so much on Pompey's side, that one day he expressed his joy that I was so, I having said to him, in his fine garden at Bâville, that if I had been in the senate when Julius Caesar was killed, I would have given him the twenty-fourth stab." On the contrary, it is in our own days, in a democratic epoch, after the French Revolution, and in the name of the revolution and the democracy, that the side of Caesar has been upheld with the greatest success, and that the benefit humanity has reaped from his victory has been set in its clearest light.

I have no intention to re-open this debate, it is too fertile in stormy discussions. I only wish here to deal with so much of it as is indispensable to explain Cicero's political life. There are, I think, two very different ways of looking

at the question : our own first, namely, that of people unconcerned in these quarrels of a former age, who approach
them as historians or philosophers, after time has cooled
them, who judge them less by their causes than by their
results, and who ask themselves, above all, what good or
evil they have done in the world ; then that of contemporaries, who judge of them with their passions and prejudices,
according to the ideas of their time, in their relation to
themselves, and without knowing their remote consequences.
I am going to place myself solely at this latter point of view,
although the other seems to me grander and more profitable ;
but as my only design is to ask from Cicero an explanation
of his political actions, and as one cannot reasonably require
of him that he should have divined the future, I shall confine myself to showing how the question was stated in his
time, what reasons were alleged on both sides, and in what
manner it was natural for a wise man who loved his country
to appreciate those reasons. Let us forget, then, the eighteen
centuries that separate us from these events, let us suppose
ourselves at Formiae or Tusculum during those long days of
anxiety and uncertainty that Cicero passed there, and let us
hear him discuss, with Atticus or Curio, the reasons that the
two parties urged to draw him into their ranks.

What shows plainly that the judgment of contemporaries
on the events which pass before them is not the same as
that of posterity is, that the friends of Caesar, when they
wished to gain over Cicero, did not employ the argument
that seems the best to us. The chief reason that is appealed
to now to justify Caesar's victory is that, on the whole, if by
it Rome lost some of her privileges, it was for the advantage
of the rest of the world that she was despoiled. What does
it matter that a few thousand men, who did not make a very
good use of their political liberty, were deprived of it, if by

the same stroke almost the entire world was rescued from
pillage, slavery, and ruin? It is certain that the provinces
and their inhabitants, so roughly treated by the pro-consuls
of the republic, found themselves better off under the *régime*
inaugurated by Caesar. His army was open to all foreigners;
he had with him Germans, Gauls, and Spaniards. They
helped him to conquer, and naturally profited by his victory:
and this was, without his wishing it perhaps, the revenge of
the conquered nations. These nations were not anxious to
recover their independence; they had lost the taste for it with
their defeat. Their ambition was quite the reverse: they
wished to be allowed to become Romans. Up till then,
however, that proud and greedy aristocracy, who held
power, and who meant to use the human race for the
benefit of their pleasures or their grandeur, had obstinately
refused to raise them to a level with themselves, no doubt
in order to preserve the right of treating them according to
their caprice. In overthrowing the aristocracy, Caesar overthrew the barrier that closed Rome to the rest of the nations.
The empire made the entire world Roman; it reconciled,
says a poet, and blended under one name, all the nations of
the universe. These are surely great things, and it does not
become us to forget them, us the sons of the vanquished, called
by Caesar to partake in his victory. But who, in Cicero's
time, thought it would be thus? who could foresee and indicate these remote consequences? The question did not
present itself then as it does to us who study it from a distance. Caesar does not anywhere allege the interest of the
conquered among the reasons he gives for his enterprise.
The senate never claimed to be the representative of the
Roman nationality, threatened by an invasion of the barbarians, and it does not appear that the provinces rose in
favour of him who came to defend them; on the contrary,

they were almost equally divided between the two rivals. If the West fought on Caesar's side, all the East repaired to Pompey's camp, which proves that when the struggle commenced its consequences were unknown even to those who were to profit by them, and whose interest should have made them clear-sighted. Besides, even if Cicero had suspected the benefits that the world was going to draw from Caesar's triumph, can we think that this reason would have sufficed to decide him? He was not one of those whose love for the whole of humanity excuses them from serving their country. He would have resigned himself with difficulty to the sacrifice of his liberty, under the pretence that this sacrifice would profit the Gauls, the Britons, and the Sarmatians. No doubt he was not indifferent to the interest of the world, but that of Rome touched him closer. His temple was gentle and humane, he had written in beautiful works that all nations are only one and the same family, he had made himself loved in the province he had governed; nevertheless, when Caesar opened the city and even the senate to the strangers who accompanied him, he showed himself very discontented, and attacked these barbarians with his most cruel raillery. He saw plainly that those Spaniards and Gauls who were walking proudly about the Forum were triumphing over Rome. His Roman pride revolted at this sight, and I see no reason to blame him for it. If he could divine or even catch a glimpse of the general emancipation of the conquered nations which was preparing, he understood also that this emancipation would bring with it the loss of the original, distinct, and independent existence of his country. It was natural that a Roman should not wish to pay this price even for the prosperity of the world.

Putting aside this reason, another, specious if not true, was much used to entice the irresolute. They were told that the republic and liberty were not interested in the war, that it was simply a struggle between two ambitious men who were contending for power. In this assertion there was a certain amount of truth capable of misleading thoughtless minds. Personal questions certainly held a large place in this contest. The soldiers of Caesar fought solely for him, and Pompey had in his suite many friends and creatures whom thirty years of prosperity and power had gained for him. Cicero himself gives us to understand, several times, that it was his old friendship for Pompey that led him into his camp. "It is to him and to him alone that I sacrifice myself," said he, when he was preparing to leave Italy.[1] There are moments in which he seems to take pleasure in limiting the subject of this quarrel he is about to engage in, and when, writing to his friends, he repeats to them what Caesar's partisans said—"It is a conflict of ambition, *regnandi contentio est.*"[2] But we must be careful when reading his correspondence of this period, and must read it with caution. Never was he more irresolute. He changes his opinion every day, he attacks and defends all parties, so that by skilfully putting together all the words let fall in this discontent and uncertainty, one may find in his letters grounds for charges against everybody. These are only the sallies of a restless and frightened mind, of which we must not make too much use either against others or against himself. Here, for instance, when he asserts that the republic has nothing to do in the contest, he does not say what he really thinks. It is only one of those pretexts that he invents to justify his hesitation in his friends' eyes and his own. So rare is it to be quite sincere, I do not say with others only but with oneself! We are so ingenious in proving to ourselves that we have a thousand

[1] *Ad Att.* ix. 1.   [2] *Ibid.* x. 7.

reasons for doing what we do without reason, or through interest or caprice ! But when Cicero wishes to be frank, when he has no motive to delude himself or deceive others, he speaks in another manner. Then the cause of Pompey becomes really that of justice and right, that of honest men and of liberty. Without doubt, Pompey had rendered very indifferent services to the republic before being led by circumstances to defend it. He could not be trusted entirely, and his ambition was to be feared. In his camp he affected the airs of a sovereign ; he had his flatterers and his ministers. "He is a little Sulla," said Cicero, " who dreams also of proscriptions, *sullaturit, proscripturit.*" [1] The republican party would certainly have taken another defender if it had been free to choose ; but at the time when Caesar assembled his troops, this party, which had neither soldiers nor generals, was really forced to accept Pompey's aid. It accepted it as that of an ally whom one distrusts and watches, who, perhaps, will become an enemy after the victory, but with whom one cannot dispense during the fight. Besides, although Pompey might not altogether secure liberty, it was known that it ran fewer risks with him than with Caesar. He was ambitious doubtless, but more ambitious of honours than of power. Twice he had been seen to arrive at the gates of Rome with an army. The democracy called him, to make himself king, he had only to will it, and twice he had disbanded his troops and laid down the fasces. He had been made sole consul, that is to say, almost dictator, and at the end of six months he had voluntarily taken a colleague. These precedents made sincere republicans believe that after the victory he would content himself with sonorous titles and pompous eulogies, and that his services would be repaid, without danger to

[1] *Ad Att.* ix. 10.

any one, with laurels and the purple. In any case, if he had demanded something else, we may be certain that he would have been refused, and that he would have found adversaries in the greater number of those who had become his allies. There were in his camp many persons who were not his friends, and who cannot be suspected of having taken arms to win a throne for him. Cato distrusted him, and had always opposed him. Brutus, whose father he had killed, hated him. The aristocracy did not pardon him for having restored the power of the tribunes, and for having united with Caesar against it. Is it likely that all these eminent persons, experienced in affairs, were the dupes of this indifferent politician who never deceived anybody, and that, without knowing it, they worked for him alone? or must we admit, which is still less likely, that they knew it, and that they voluntarily abandoned their country, risked their fortunes, and gave their lives to serve the interests and the ambition of a man whom they did not love? Assuredly, for them, something else was in question. When they went over sea, when they decided, notwithstanding their repugnance, to begin a civil war, when they came to put themselves under the orders of a general against whom they had so many reasons for ill-will, they did not intend to intervene solely in a personal quarrel, but to come to the help of the republic and of that liberty which were threatened. " But here," people say, " you are deceived again. These names, liberty and republic, delude you. It was not liberty that was defended in Pompey's camp, it was the oppression of the people by a caste. They wished to maintain the privileges of a burdensome and unjust aristocracy. They fought to preserve for it the right to oppress the plebs, and to crush the world." At that rate the friends of liberty ought to keep for Caesar the sympathies they generally accord to Pompey, for he is the liberal and the democrat, the man of the people, the successor of the Gracchi and of Marius. This is indeed the part he assumed from the day when, almost a child, he had braved Sulla. Praetor and consul, he had appeared to serve the popular cause with devotion, and at the moment when he marched on Rome, abandoned by the senate, he still said, " I come to deliver the Roman people from a faction that oppresses it." [1]

How much truth is there in this pretence that he makes of being the defender of the democracy? What ought to be thought of it, I do not say by a patrician, who naturally thought much ill of the people, but by an enemy of the nobility, by a new man like Cicero? Whatever anger the disdain of the aristocracy had caused to Cicero, whatever impatience he had felt at always finding in his way, in his candidatures, one of those nobles to whom " *honours came while they slept,*" I do not find that his ill-humour had ever led him to pretend that the people was oppressed ; [2] and I suppose that when it was asserted before him that Caesar took up arms to restore him his liberty, he asked how long it was since he had lost it, and what new privileges they wished to add to those he already possessed? He called to mind that the people possessed a legal organization, had their own magistrates to whom they appealed from the decisions of others, magistrates inviolable and sacred, whom the law armed with the enormous power of staying the action of the government by their interference, and of interrupting political life ; that they had the liberty of

[1] *De bello civ.* i. 22.

[2] He even seems to say several times that the position of the plebeians in the republic was, on the whole, better than that of the patricians (*Pro Cluent.* 40. *Pro domo sua,* 14).

speech and of the rostrum, the right of voting, in which they trafficked for a living, and finally, free access to all grades of the magistracy, and he had only to cite his own case to demonstrate that it was possible for a man without birth and almost without fortune to attain even the consulship. Such success in truth was rare. The equality laid down in the law disappeared in practice. The consular records of that period contain scarcely any but illustrious names. A few great families seem to have established themselves in the highest dignities of the state; they guarded the avenues to them, and allowed no one to approach; but was it necessary, in order to break down the obstacles that the cleverness of a few ambitious men opposed to the regular working of the institutions, to destroy these institutions themselves? was the evil so great that it was necessary to have recourse to the radical remedy of absolute power? Was it impossible to think that it would be more surely cured by liberty than by despotism? Had it not been seen by recent examples that a strong current of popular opinion was sufficient to overturn all this aristocratic resistance? The laws gave the people the means of recovering their influence if they willed it energetically. With the liberty of voting and of speaking in the public assembly, with the intervention of the tribunes and the invincible strength of numbers, they must always end in being masters. It was their own fault if they left the power to others, and they deserved the degradation in which the nobility held them, since they made no effort to free themselves. Cicero had small esteem for the common people of his time; he thought them careless and apathetic by nature. "They demand nothing," said he, "they desire nothing";[1] and every time he saw them stirring in the

---

[1] *Pro Sext.* 49.

Forum he suspected that the liberality of some ambitious men had worked this miracle. He was not, therefore, led to think it necessary to accord them new rights when he saw them use their ancient rights so little or so ill, and so he did not regard the pretext put forth by Caesar for taking up arms as serious. He never consented to look upon him as the successor of the Gracchi coming to emancipate the oppressed plebs; the war which was preparing never seemed to him to be the renewal of the ancient struggles between the people and the aristocracy, of which Roman history is full. In fact, an assembly of ruined nobles, like Dolabella, Antony, and Curio, marching under the leadership of him who boasted of being the son of the gods and of kings, little deserved the name of the popular party, and there was something else at stake than the defence of the privileges of birth in a camp to which so many knights and plebeians had repaired, and which reckoned among its chiefs Varro, Cicero, and Cato, that is to say, two burgesses of small fortune of Arpinum and Reate, and the descendant of the peasant of Tusculum.

Caesar, however, does not seem to have been very much prepossessed with this part of champion of the democracy. We do not find, on reading his memoirs, that he speaks very much of the people's interests. The phrase just quoted is almost the only one in which they are mentioned. Elsewhere he is more frank. At the beginning of the civil war, when he set forth his reasons for commencing it, he complained that he was refused the consulship, that his province was taken from him, that he was torn from his army; he says not a word of the people, of their unrecognized rights, of their crushed liberty. This was, however, the moment to speak of them in order to justify an enterprise that so many people, and those the most honest, condemned. What did he demand in the final conditions he laid before the senate before marching on Rome ? His consulship, his army, his province; he defended his personal interests, he bargained for himself, it never came into his mind to demand any guarantee for that people whose defender he called himself. Around him, in his camp, one thought no more of the people than they did of themselves. His best friends, his bravest generals, had no pretension to be reformers or democrats. They did not think, in following him, that they were going to give liberty to their fellow-citizens ; they wished to avenge their outraged chief, and to win power for him. "We are the soldiers of Caesar," said they with Curio.[1] They had no other title, they knew no other name. When some one came to speak to those old centurions who had seen Germany and Britain, who had taken Alesia and Gergovia, of abandoning Caesar and passing over to the side of the laws and the republic, they did not reply that they were defending the people and their rights. "We," said they, "shall we quit our general who has given all of us our ranks, shall we take arms against an army in which we have served and been victorious for thirty-six years? We will never do it ! "[2] These men were no longer citizens but soldiers. After thirty-six years of victories, they had lost the traditions of civil life and the taste for it ; the rights of the people had become indifferent to them, and for them glory took the place of liberty. Cicero and his friends thought that these surroundings were not those of a popular chief who came to restore liberty to his fellow-citizens, but those of an ambitious man who came to establish absolute power by arms, and they were not mistaken. Caesar's conduct after the war proves this more than all the rest.

[1] *De bello afric.* 45.   [2] *De bello civ.* ii. 32.

How did he use his victory? What benefits did he confer on the people whose interests he pretended to defend? I do not speak of what he was able to do for their comfort and their pleasures, the sumptuous feasts, the public meals that he gave, the corn and oil that he so generously distributed to the poorest, the 400 sesterces (£3 4*s.*) that he paid each citizen on the day of his triumph : if these alms satisfied the plebeians of that time, if they consented to sacrifice their liberty at that price, I pardon Cicero for not having more esteem for them, and for not putting himself on their side ; but if they demanded something else, if they wished for a more complete independence, for a larger share in the affairs of their country, for new political rights, they did not obtain them, and Caesar's victory, notwithstanding his promises, rendered them neither freer nor more powerful. Caesar humiliated the aristocracy, but only for his own advantage. He took the executive power out of the hands of the senate, but only to put it in his own. He established equality between all the orders, but it was an equality of servitude, and all were henceforth reduced to the same level of obedience.

I know that after he had silenced the public speakers, deprived the people of the right of voting, and united in himself all public authority, the senate that he had appointed, having exhausted flattery, solemnly awarded to him the name of Liberator, and voted the erection of a Temple of Liberty. If it is against this liberty that Cicero and his friends are accused of having taken up arms, I do not think it is worth the trouble to defend them from this charge.

Let us call things by their real name. It was for himself and not for the people that Caesar worked, and Cicero, in opposing him, thought he was defending the republic and not the privileges of the aristocracy.

But did this republic deserve to be defended? Was there any hope of preserving it? Was it not manifest that its ruin was inevitable? This is the greatest charge that is made against those who followed Pompey's party. I admit it is not easy to answer it. The evil that Rome suffered, and which showed itself in those disorders and that violence of which Cicero's letters give us such a sad picture, was not of a kind to be averted by a few wise reforms. It was ancient and profound. It became worse every day without any law being able to prevent or arrest it. Could one hope to cure it with those slight changes that the boldest proposed? Of what use was it to diminish, as was wished, the privileges of the aristocracy and to augment the rights of the plebeians? The sources of public life themselves were seriously impaired. The evil came from the way in which the citizenship was acquired.

For a long time Rome had drawn her strength from the country people. It was from the rustic tribes, the most honoured of all, that those valiant soldiers who had conquered Italy and subdued Carthage had come; but this agricultural and warlike people, who had so well defended the republic, could not defend themselves against the encroachments of the great estates. Enclosed little by little by those immense domains where cultivation is easiest, the poor peasant had for a long time struggled against misery and the usurers; then, discouraged in the struggle, he had ended by selling his field to his rich neighbour, who coveted it to round off his estate. He had tried then to become a tenant-farmer, a metayer, a hired labourer on the property where he had been for so long the master, but there he met with the competition of the slave, a more frugal worker, who did not stand out for his wages, who did not make terms, who might be treated as one liked.[1] Thus, driven twice from his fields, both as owner and as tenant farmer, without work or resources, he had been forced to migrate to the city. At Rome, however, life was not more easy for him. What could he do there? There was little trade, and usually it was not in the hands of the free men. In countries where slavery flourishes, work is looked down upon. To die of hunger without doing anything, is regarded by the free man as a privilege and an honour. Besides, each noble had men of all trades among his slaves, and as such a number of workmen were too many for himself alone, he hired them out to those who had none, or made them keep shop in a corner of his house for his own profit. Here again slave competition killed free labour. Happily at this time Marius opened the ranks of the army to the poorest citizens (*capite censi*). These unfortunate men, finding no other resource, became soldiers. For lack of something better to do, they achieved the conquest of the world, subjugated Africa, Gaul, and the East, visited Britain and Germany, and the greater number of them, the bravest and best, were killed in these distant expeditions. During this time, the vacancies left in the city by those who departed and did not return were ill filled. Since Rome had become powerful, people from all parts of the world came to her, and we may well suppose they were not always the most respectable.

Several times she had endeavoured to defend herself against these invasions of foreigners; but it was useless to make severe laws to remove them, they always returned to hide themselves in that immense city without a police, and, once settled there, the more prosperous, by means of their

[1] See the *Histoire de l'esclavage dans l'antiquité* of M. Wallon, Vol. II. ch. ix.

F

money, the others by means of base services or cunning, succeeded in obtaining the title of citizens. Those who received it more naturally, and without needing to demand it, were the freedmen. No doubt the law did not grant them all political rights at once; but after one or two generations all these reservations disappeared, and the grandson of him who had ground at the mill and who had been sold in the slave-market voted the laws and elected the consuls like a Roman of the old stock. It was of this mixture of freedmen and foreigners, that was formed what at this time was called the Roman people, a wretched people who lived on the bounty of private persons or the alms of the state, who had neither memories nor traditions, nor political capacity, nor national character, nor even morality, for they were ignorant of that which makes up the honour and dignity of life in the lower classes, namely, work. With such a people a republic was no longer possible. This is, of all governments, that which demands the greatest integrity and political judgment in those who enjoy it. The more privileges it confers the more devoted-ness and intelligence it demands. People who did not use their rights, or only used them to sell them, were not worthy to preserve them. That absolute power which they had invited by their votes, which they had received with applause, was made for them; and one understands that the historian who studies from afar the events of the past, when he sees liberty disappear from Rome, consoles himself for its fall by saying that it was deserved and inevitable, and that he pardons or even applauds the man who, in overturning it, was only an instrument of necessity or justice.

But the men who lived then, who were attached to the republican government by tradition and memories, who recalled the great things it had done, who owed to it their dignities, position, and renown, could they think like us and resign themselves as easily to its fall? Firstly, this government existed. They were familiarized to its defects, since they had lived with them so long. They suffered less from them, through the long habit of enduring them. On the other hand, they did not know what this new power that wished to replace the republic would be. Royalty inspired the Romans with an instinctive repugnance, especially since they had conquered the East. They had found there, under this name, the most odious of governments, the most complete slavery in the midst of the most refined civilization, all the pleasures of luxury and the arts, the finest expansion of intellect with the heaviest and basest tyranny; princes accustomed to play with the fortune, honour, and life of men, a species of cruel spoilt children, such as are only now to be found in the African deserts. This picture did not attract them, and whatever disadvantages the republic had, they asked themselves if it was worth while to exchange them for those that royalty might have. Besides, it was natural that the fall of the republic should not appear to them so near and so sure as it does to us. It is with states as with men, for whom we find, after their death, a thousand causes of death which nobody suspected during their lifetime. While the machinery of this ancient government was still working it could not be seen how disorganized it was. Cicero has, sometimes, moments of profound despair, in which he announces to his friends that all is lost; but these moments do not last, and he quickly regains his courage. It seems to him that a firm hand, an eloquent voice, and the agreement of good citizens can repair all, and that liberty will easily remedy the abuses and faults of liberty. He never perceives the whole gravity of danger. In the worst days, his thoughts never go beyond the schemers and the ambitious men who disturb the public repose; it is always Catiline, Caesar, or Clodius whom he accuses, and he thinks that all will be saved if one can succeed in overcoming them. He was mistaken, Catiline and Clodius were only the symptoms of a deeper evil that could not be cured; but is he to be blamed for entertaining this hope, chimerical as it was? Is he to be blamed for having thought that there were other means of saving the republic than the sacrifice of liberty? An honest man and a good citizen ought not to accept these counsels of despair at first. It is useless to tell him that the decrees of destiny condemn to perish the constitution that he prefers and that he has promised to defend, he does well not to believe it entirely lost until it is actually overthrown. We may call such men, if we like, blind or dupes; it is honourable in them not to be too perspicacious, and there are errors and illusions that are worth more than a too easy resignation. Real liberty existed no longer at Rome, as I believe, the shadow only remained, but the shadow was still something. One cannot bear a grudge against those who attached themselves to it and made desperate efforts not to allow it to perish, for this shadow, this semblance, consoled them for lost liberty and gave them some hope of regaining it. This is what honest men like Cicero thought, who, after mature reflection, without enthusiasm, without passion, and even without hope, went to find Pompey again; this is what Lucan makes Cato say in those admirable lines which seem to me to express the feelings of all those who, without concealing from themselves the sad state of the republic, persisted in defending it to the last : "As a father who has just lost his child takes pleasure in conducting his obsequies, lights with his own hands the funeral pyre, leaves it with regret, as tardily as he can ; so, Rome, I will not forsake thee until that I have held thee dead in my arms.

I will follow to the end thy very name, O Liberty, even when thou shalt be no more than a vain shadow!"[1]

IV.

Pharsalia was not the end of Cicero's political career, as he had thought. Events were to lead him back once more to power and replace him at the head of the republic. His retired life, his silence during the early days of Caesar's dictatorship, far from injuring his reputation, on the contrary enhanced it. Statesmen do not lose so much as they think by remaining for a time outside of affairs. Retirement, supported with dignity, increases their importance. That they are no longer in power suffices for people to find some inclination to regret them. There are fewer reasons to be severe towards them when their place is not coveted, and as people no longer suffer from their faults the memory of them is easily lost, and their good qualities only are remembered. This is what happened to Cicero. His disgrace disarmed all the enemies that his power had made him, and his popularity was never so great as when he kept himself voluntarily from the public eye. A little later, when he thought he ought to draw nearer to Caesar, he conducted himself with so much tact, he adjusted so cleverly submission and independence, he knew so well how to preserve an appearance of opposition even in his eulogies and flatteries, that public opinion did not cease to favour him. Besides, the most illustrious defenders of the

[1] Luc., *Phars.* ii. 300 :

> *Non ante revellar*
> *Exanimem quam te complectar, Roma, tuumque*
> *Nomen, libertas, et inanem prosequar umbram.*

vanquished cause, Pompey, Cato, Scipio, Bibulus, were dead. Of all those who had occupied with honour the highest posts under the old government, he alone remained; consequently it was usual to regard him as the last representative of the republic. We know that on the Ides of March, Brutus and his friends, after having struck down Caesar, while brandishing their bloody swords, called for Cicero. They seemed to recognize him as the head of their party, and to give him the credit of the bloodshed that they had just committed.

It was, then, circumstances rather than his own will that caused him to play so great a part in the events which followed the death of Caesar.

I shall narrate later[1] how he was led to engage in that struggle with Antony, in which he was to perish. I shall show that it was not of himself and voluntarily that he began it. He had quitted Rome and did not wish to return. He thought that the time for resistance under legal forms had passed, that it was necessary to oppose to Antony's veterans good soldiers rather than good reasons, and he was not wrong. Convinced that his part was finished, and that that of the men of war was about to begin, he set out for Greece, when a gale cast him on the coast of Rhegium. Thence he repaired to the port of Velia, where he found Brutus, who was also preparing to leave Italy, and it was he who, always scrupulous, always the enemy of violence, asked him to make once again an effort to rouse the people, and once more to attempt the struggle on the basis of law. Cicero yielded to the request of his friend, and although he had little hope of success, he hastened to return to Rome there to offer this last battle.

[1] In the study on Brutus.

This was the second time that he came, like Amphiaraüs, "to throw himself alive into the gulf."

Brutus did him a good service that day. The desperate enterprise in which he engaged him, almost in spite of himself, could not be useful to the republic, but was serviceable to Cicero's glory. This was perhaps the grandest moment in his political life. In the first place, we have the pleasure and almost the surprise of finding him firm and decided. He seems to have freed himself from all that hesitation that usually troubled his conduct; and besides, it was scarcely possible to hesitate then, for the question had never been so clearly stated. At each new development of events, the parties stood out more clearly. For the first time, the ambition of Caesar, of which everybody knew, by rallying round the Roman aristocracy all those who wished, like it, to preserve the ancient institutions, had enlarged the limits of this party and modified its programme. By taking into itself new elements it changed in name as in character; it became the party of order, the party of honest men, of the "optimates." It is thus that Cicero loves to name it. The meaning of this name was at first rather vague, after Pharsalia it became more precise. As at this moment there was no longer any doubt of the intentions of the conqueror, as he was seen to openly substitute his authority for that of the senate and people, the party that resisted him took the name proper to it, and which nobody could any longer refuse it; it became the republican party. The struggle was fairly begun between the republic and despotism. And, that doubt might be still less possible, despotism after Caesar's death showed itself to the Romans under its least disguised and, so to say, most brutal form. A soldier without political genius, without distinction of manners, without greatness of soul, at once coarse, debauched

and cruel, asserted by force his right to the inheritance of
the great dictator.   He did not take the trouble to hide
his designs, and neither Cicero nor anybody else could be
deceived any longer.   It must have been a great relief to
that mind usually so undecided and uncertain to see the
truth so clearly, to be no longer perplexed by shadows, to
have such a complete confidence in the justice of his cause,
and after so much doubt and obscurity at last to fight in
clear daylight.   We feel that his mind is at ease ! how much
freer and more lively he is ! what ardour there is in this old
man, and what eagerness for the fight !   None of the young
men about him show so much decision as he, and he himself
is assuredly younger than when he strove against Catiline
or Clodius.   Not only does he begin the struggle resolutely,
but, what is more unusual with him, he pursues it to the end
without giving way.   By a strange contrast, the most dangerous enterprise that he had ever undertaken, and which was
to cost him his life, was precisely that in which he best
resisted his usual fits of discouragement and weakness.

Immediately on his return to Rome, while he was still
inspired by the ardour that he had acquired at Velia from
his conversations with Brutus, he went to the senate and
ventured to speak there.   The first Philippic, compared
with the others, appears timid and colourless ; what courage,
however, did it not need to pronounce it in that unconcerned
city, before those frightened senators, at a few paces from
the furious and threatening Antony, who by his spies heard
all that was said against him !   Cicero ended then as he
had begun.   Twice, at an interval of thirty-five years, he
raised his voice alone, in the midst of a general silence,
against a dreaded power which would not tolerate resistance.
Courage, like fear, is contagious.   The courage that Cicero
showed in his speech awakened that of others.   This

freedom of speech surprised at first, then shamed those who
kept silence. Cicero took advantage of this first revival,
which was still rather hesitating, to assemble a few persons
round him and find some defenders of the almost forgotten
republic. Here was the difficulty. There were scarcely any
republicans left, and the most determined had gone to join
Brutus in Greece. All that could be done was to appeal
to the moderates of all parties, to all those whom Antony's
excesses had shocked. Cicero adjured them to forget their
old enmities and to reunite. " Now," said he, " there is only
one vessel for all honest men." [1]   Here we recognize his
usual policy. It is again a coalition that he tries to form
as at the time of his consulship. This part is clearly that
for which he has most taste and which suits him best. By
the pliability of his character and his principles he was fitter
than anybody to reconcile opinions, and the habit he had of
approaching all parties made him not a stranger to any, and
he had friends everywhere. Thus his undertaking appeared
at first to succeed very well. Several of Caesar's generals
readily listened to him, those especially who thought that,
in the main, they lost less by remaining citizens of a free
state, than by becoming subjects of Antony ; and ambitious
subalterns, like Hirtius and Pansa, who, after the master's
death, did not feel themselves strong enough to aim at the
first place, and who would not be contented with the
second. Unfortunately it was still but a collection of
chiefs without soldiers, and never had there been more
need of soldiers than at that moment. Antony was at
Brundusium, where he was waiting for the legions he had
sent for to Macedonia. Enraged by the unexpected resistance that he had met with, he proclaimed that he would
avenge himself by pillage and slaughter, and he was

[1] *Ad fam.* xii. 25.

known to be the man to do so. Every one thought that
already he saw his house sacked, his estate parcelled out,
his family proscribed. Fear reigned everywhere, men
trembled, hid themselves and fled. The most courageous
sought on all sides for some one who might be called upon
to defend the republic. No aid was to be hoped for but
from Decimus Brutus, who occupied Cisalpine Gaul with
some legions, or from Sextus Pompey, who was reorganizing
his troops in Sicily, but this aid was distant and doubtful,
and ruin was near and sure. In the midst of this general
panic, the nephew of Caesar, the young Octavius, whom
the jealousy of Antony, and the distrust of the republicans
had up till then kept away, and who impatiently awaited
the opportunity of making himself known, thought that this
opportunity had come. He went through the environs of
Rome calling to arms his uncle's veterans who were settled
there. His name, his liberality, the promises he lavished
soon brought him soldiers. At Calatia, at Casilinum, he
found three thousand in a few days. Then he addressed
the leaders of the senate, offered them the support of his
veterans, demanding for sole recompense that they would
acknowledge him in the efforts he was about to make to
save them. In such distress there was no means of refusing
this help without which they would perish, and Cicero himself, who had at first shown some distrust, let himself be
seduced at last by this young man who consulted him,
flattered him, and called him father. When, thanks to him,
they had been saved, when they saw Antony, abandoned
by some of his legions, obliged to leave Rome where
Octavius held him in check, the gratitude of the senate was
as lavish as their fear had been great. The liberator was
loaded with dignities and honours. Cicero, in his eulogies,
raised him much above his uncle ; he called him a divine

young man raised up by heaven for the defence of his country : he stood surety for his patriotism and fidelity ; imprudent words for which Brutus reproached him severely, and which the event was not long in falsifying !

The events that followed are too well known for me to have need of repeating them. Never had Cicero played a greater political part than at this moment ; never had he better deserved that name of statesman that his enemies denied him. For six months he was the soul of the re-publican party, which was re-constituted at his call. "It was I, said he proudly, who gave the signal for this awaken-ing,"[1] and he was right in saying so. His voice seemed to restore some patriotism and some energy to this unconcerned people. He made them once more applaud those grand names of country and liberty that the Forum would soon hear no more. From Rome, the ardour gained the neighbouring townships, and gradually all Italy was roused. This, however, was not enough for him, he went still further to raise up enemies for Antony and defenders for the republic. He wrote to the proconsuls of the pro-vinces and to the generals of the armies. From one end of the world to the other he chid the lukewarm, flattered the ambitious, and congratulated the energetic. He it was who incited Brutus, always undecided, to seize Greece. He applauded the bold stroke of Cassius, which made him master of Asia ; he urged Cornificius to drive Antony's soldiers from Africa ; he encouraged Decimus Brutus to resist in Modena. The promises of support that he invited with so much earnestness arrived from all sides. Even enemies and traitors dared not openly refuse him their co-operation. Lepidus and Plancus made emphatic protestations of fidelity. Pollio wrote to him in a

---

[1] *Philipp.* xiv. 7.

solemn tone "that he swears to be the enemy of all tyrants."[1] On all sides his friendship is demanded, his support solicited, men put themselves under his protection. His Philippics, which, happily, he had not time to revise, are scattered through the whole world, very nearly as he spoke them, and with the vivacity of the first sketch, preserve traces of the interruptions and applause of the people. These passionate harangues carry everywhere the passion of these grand popular scenes. They are read in the provinces, they are devoured in the armies, and from the most distant countries evidence of the admiration they excite arrives to Cicero! "Your robe is even more fortunate than our arms," says a victorious general to him, and adds, "In you the consular has conquered the consul."[2] "My soldiers are yours," wrote another to him.[3] The credit of all the good fortune of the republic was attributed to him. It was he who was congratulated and thanked for all the successes that were obtained. On the evening that the victory of Modena was known at Rome, the whole people went to his house to seek him, conducted him in triumph to the Capitol, and wished to hear from his own mouth an account of the battle. "This day, he wrote to Brutus, has repaid me for all my trouble."[4]

This was the last triumph of Cicero and the republic. Success is sometimes more fatal to coalitions than reverses. When the common enemy, hatred of whom has united them, has been conquered, private dissensions break out. Octavius wished to weaken Antony in order to obtain from him what he wanted; he did not wish to destroy him. When he saw him flying towards the Alps, he made overtures to him, and both together marched on Rome. From that time

---

[1] *Ad fam.* x. 31.　　　[2] *Ibid.* xii. 13.
[3] *Ibid.* xii. 12.　　　[4] *Ad Brut.* 3.

nothing remained for Cicero but "to imitate brave gladiators, and seek like them to die honourably."[1] His death was courageous, whatever Pollio, who, having betrayed him, had an interest in calumniating him, may have asserted. I would rather believe the testimony of Livy, who was not one of his friends, and who lived at the court of Augustus : "Of all his misfortunes, says he, death is the only one that he bore like a man."[2] This, it must be confessed, was something. He might have fled, and at one moment he tried to do so. He wished to set out for Greece, where he would have found Brutus ; but after some days' sailing with contrary winds, suffering from the sea, tormented above all by regrets and sadness, he lost heart for life, and was landed at Gaeta, and went back to his house at Formiæ to die there. He had often thanked the gale that took him back to Velia, the first time that he wished to flee to Greece. This it was that gave him the opportunity to deliver his Philippics. The storm which drove him ashore at Gaeta has not been less serviceable to his fame. His death seems to me to redeem the weaknesses of his life. It is much for a man like him, who did not boast of being a Cato, to have been so firm at this terrible moment ; the more timid he was by temperament the more I am touched at finding him so resolute in dying. Thus, when, in studying his history, I am tempted to reproach him with his irresolution and weakness, I think of his end, I see him as Plutarch has so well depicted him, " his beard and hair dirty, his countenance worn, taking his chin in his left hand as his manner was, and looking steadily at his murderers,"[3] and I no longer dare to be severe. Notwithstanding his defects he was an honest man, " who loved his country well," as Augustus himself said on a

---

[1] *Philipp.* iii. 14.   [2] Apud Senec., *Suas*, 6.
[3] Plut. *Cic.* 48.

day of sincerity and remorse. If he was sometimes too
hesitating and feeble, he always ended by defending what
he regarded as the cause of justice and right, and when that
cause had been for ever conquered, he rendered it the last
service it could claim from its defenders, he honoured it by
his death.

II

CICERO'S PRIVATE LIFE

I

THOSE who have read Cicero's correspondence with Atticus, and know what place questions of money occupy in these private communications, will not be surprised that I begin the study of his private life by endeavouring to estimate the amount of his fortune. The men of those days were as much concerned about money as the men of to-day, and it is perhaps in this that these two periods, which men have so often taken pleasure in comparing, most resemble each other.

It would be necessary to have at hand the account-books of Eros, Cicero's steward, in order to set down with exactness the expenses of his household. All that we know with certainty on this subject is, that his father left him a very moderate fortune only, and that he increased this greatly, while we cannot say precisely to how much it amounted. His enemies were in the habit of exaggerating it in order to throw suspicion on the means by which it had been acquired, and it is indeed probable that if we knew the total it would appear to us considerable; but we must take care not to judge of it according to the ideas of our own time. Wealth is not an absolute thing; a man is rich or poor according to

79

the position in which he lives, and it is possible that what would be wealth in one place would scarcely be a competency elsewhere. Now we know that at Rome wealth was far from being so evenly distributed as it is among us. Forty years before the consulship of Cicero, the tribune Philip said that, in that immense city, there were not two thousand persons who had a patrimony; [1] but these possessed all the public wealth. Crassus asserted that, in order to call himself rich, it was necessary for a man to be able to support an army out of his revenues, and we know that he was in a position to do so without inconvenience. Milo contrived to get into debt in a few years to the amount of more than seventy million sesterces (£560,000). Caesar, while still a private person, expended, at one time, one hundred and twenty million sesterces (£960,000) in order to make a present of a new Forum to the Roman people. This outrageous extravagance implies immense fortunes. In comparison with these, we can understand that Cicero's, which scarcely sufficed for the purchase of a house on the Palatine, and which the adornment of his Tusculan villa almost exhausted, must have appeared very moderate.

In what manner had he gained it? It is not without interest to know this in order to reply to the ill-natured reports that his enemies circulated. He says somewhere that the means by which a fortune was honestly made at Rome were commerce, contracting for public works and farming the taxes; [2] but these means, very convenient for people in haste to enrich themselves, could only be used by

[1] *De offic.* ii. 21 : Things had not changed when Cicero was consul. We see that his brother, in a letter that he addressed to him then, says that there were few knights in Rome, *pauci equites*, that is, few men possessing more than £3200.

[2] *Parad.* 6. *Qui honeste rem quaerunt mercaturis faciendis, operis dandis publicis sumendis*, etc.

those who had no political ambition ; they excluded from public honours, and consequently did not suit a man who aspired to govern his country. We do not see, either, that he acted like Pompey, who invested his funds in an important bank and shared in the profits ; at least there remains no trace in his letters of undertakings of this nature. Nor could he think of making money out of his works. It was not the custom then for an author to sell his works to a bookseller ; or rather, the trade of a bookseller, as we understand it now, scarcely existed. Usually those who wished to read or possess a book borrowed it of the author or of his friends, and had it copied by their slaves. When they had more copyists than they needed for their own use, they made them work for the public and sold the copies they did not want ; but the author had nothing to do with the profits they drew from them. And finally, public offices could not have enriched Cicero ; we know that they were less a means of making money than an occasion of expense and ruin, either by the price it was sometimes necessary to pay for them, or by the games and entertainments that were expected from those who had obtained them. It was only in the government of provinces that immense gains were made. It was on these gains that the ambitious nobles usually counted to repair the waste of their fortunes that the luxury of their private life and the profusion of their public life had caused. Now Cicero deprived himself of this opportunity by yielding to his colleague Antony the province that, according to custom, he ought to have governed after his consulship. It has been suspected, indeed, that he then made with him some bargain by which he reserved to himself a share in the handsome profits that he relinquished. If this bargain existed, which is doubtful, it is certain it was not kept. Antony pillaged

G

his province, but he pillaged it for himself alone, and Cicero drew nothing from it. Twelve years later, without having desired it, he was appointed pro-consul of Cilicia. We know that he remained there only a year, and that, without doing any illegal act, and while securing the happiness of his subjects, he contrived to take back two million two hundred thousand sesterces (£17,600), which gives us an idea of what might be gained in the provinces when they were pillaged without scruple. Besides, this money did not profit Cicero; he lent part of it to Pompey, who did not return it, and it is probable that the civil war caused him to lose the rest, since he found himself without means at its close. We must seek, then, elsewhere for the origin of his fortune. If he had lived in our days we should have no trouble in learning whence it came. It would be sufficiently explained by his ability as an advocate. With an eloquence such as his, he would not fail now-a-days to enrich himself quickly at the bar; but at that time there was a law forbidding orators to accept any fee or present from those for whom they had pleaded (*lex Cincia, de donis et muneribus*). Although it was the work of a tribune, who had made it, says Livy, in the interest of the people,[1] it was at bottom an aristocratic law. By not allowing the advocate to draw a legitimate profit from his talent, it kept away from the bar those who had nothing, and reserved the exercise of this profession for the rich as a privilege, or rather it prevented it becoming really a profession. I think, however, that this law was always very imperfectly obeyed. As it could not provide against everything, it was scarcely possible for it to prevent the gratitude of clients finding some ingenious method to escape its severity. If they were really determined to pay in some manner for the services which they

[1] *Hist.* xxxiv. 4.

had received, it seems to me that the law could only
with difficulty prevent it. In Cicero's time, they did not
fail to violate it openly. Verres told his friends that he
had divided the money he brought back from Sicily into
three parts ; the most considerable was to corrupt his judges,
the second to pay his advocates, and he contented himself
with the third.[1] Cicero, who on this occasion laughed at
Verres' advocate, Hortensius, and at the sphynx that he had
received on account, took care not to imitate him. His
brother affirms that up to the time when he was a candidate
for the consulship he had never asked anything from his
clients.[2] Nevertheless, whatever scruples we may suppose
him to have had, it is very difficult to admit that he had
never profited by their good-will. No doubt he refused the
presents that the Sicilians wished to make him when he had
avenged them on Verres ; perhaps it would not have been
prudent to accept them after such a notorious trial, which
had drawn all eyes upon him, and made him powerful
enemies ; but some years afterwards I see that he allowed
himself to accept the present made him by his friend Papirius Poetus, for whom he had just pleaded.[3] It consisted
of some fine Greek and Latin books, and Cicero loved
nothing so much as books. I notice also that when he had
need of money, which happened sometimes, he preferred
to apply to rich men whom he had defended. These were
less harsh and more patient creditors to him than others,
and it was natural that he should profit by their influence
after having aided them by his eloquence. He tells us himself that he bought the house of Crassus with the money of
his friends. Among them, P. Sylla, for whom he had just
pleaded, alone lent him two million sesterces (£16,000).

---

[1] *In Verrem, act. prim.* 14. [2] *De petit cons.* 5 and 9.
[3] *Ad Att.* i. 20.

When he was attacked for this in the senate, Cicero got out
of it with a joke; which proves that the *lex Cincia* was no
longer much respected, and that those who infringed it had
no great fear of being prosecuted.[1] It is very possible, then,
that those nobles whose honour or fortune he had saved,
that those towns or provinces that he had protected against
greedy governors, that those foreign princes whose interests
he had defended in the senate, above all, those rich societies
of farmers of the taxes, through whose hands passed all the
money that the world sent to Rome, and whom he served
so vigorously by his reputation or his eloquence, had often
sought and sometimes found an opportunity of testifying
their gratitude. This generosity appears to us now-a-days so
natural that we should scarcely blame Cicero for not having
always rejected it; but we may be sure that, if he sometimes
thought that he might accept it, he always did so with more
moderation and reserve than the greater number of his
contemporaries.

We know one of the most usual forms, and, as it seems,
one of the most legal by which this generosity showed
itself. It was the custom at Rome to pay, after death
and by will, all debts of gratitude and affection contracted
during life. This was a means that offered itself to the
client of discharging his obligations to the advocate who
had defended him, and it does not appear that the *lex
Cincia* threw any obstacle in the way. We have nothing
like it among ourselves. At that time, the father of a family
who had natural heirs might withdraw from his fortune any
amount that he wished, and give his relations, his friends,
and all who had been useful or agreeable to him, a good
share of his estate. This custom had become an abuse.
Fashion and vanity had come to have a large share in it.

[1] A. Gell. xii. 12.

A man wished to appear to have many friends by inscribing the names of many persons in his will, and naturally the most illustrious were inscribed by preference. Sometimes people were brought together in it who seldom met anywhere else, and who must have been surprised to find themselves there. Cluvius, a rich banker of Puteoli, left his estate to Cicero and Caesar after Pharsalia.[1] The architect Cyrus placed among his heirs both Clodius and Cicero, that is to say, the two persons who most heartily detested each other in Rome.[2] This architect, no doubt, regarded it as an honour to have friends among all parties. It even happened that a man set down in his will people whom he had never seen. Lucullus augmented his immense wealth by bequests which unknown persons left him while he governed Asia. Atticus received a good number of legacies from people of whom he had never heard, and who only knew him by reputation. How much more then must a great orator like Cicero, to whom so many were under obligation, and of whom all Romans were proud, have been often the object of this posthumous liberality! We see in his letters that he was the heir of many persons who do not seem to have held a large place in his life. In general, the amounts left to him are not very large. One of the largest is that which he inherited from his old master the Stoic Diodotus, whom he had kept at his house till his death.[3] In recompense of this long-continued affection, Diodotus left him all his savings as a philosopher and teacher. They amounted to a hundred thousand sesterces (£800). The union of all these small legacies no doubt made up a considerable sum. Cicero himself values it at more than twenty million sesterces (£160,000).[4] It seems to me, therefore, that there is no

---

[1] *Ad Att.* xiii. 45 *et seq.*   [2] *Pro Mil.* 18.
[3] *Ad Att.* ii. 20.   [4] *Philipp.* ii. 16.

doubt that these legacies, with the presents he may have received from the gratitude of his clients, were the chief sources of his wealth.

This wealth was composed of property of different kinds. He possessed, firstly, houses in Rome. Besides that which he inhabited on the Palatine, and that which he had from his father at Carinae, he had others in Argiletum and on the Aventine which brought him in an income of eighty thousand sesterces (£640).[1] He possessed numerous villas in Italy. We know of eight very important ones belonging to him,[2] without reckoning those small houses (*diversoria*) that the nobles bought along the principal roads to have somewhere to rest when they went from one domain to another. He had also sums of money of which he disposed in different manners, as we see in his correspondence. We cannot estimate this part of his wealth with exactness; but according to the practice of the rich Romans of that time, it may be affirmed that it was not less than his houses or estates. One day when he is asking Atticus to buy him some gardens that he wishes, he says to him, in an offhand way, that he thinks he may have about six hundred thousand sesterces (£4800) in his own hands.[3] We have here perhaps one of the most curious differences that distinguish that state of society from ours. Now-a-days scarcely any but bankers by profession handle such considerable sums of money. Our aristocracy has always affected to look down upon questions of finance. The Roman aristocracy, on the

[1] *Ad Att.* xvi. 1.

[2] His villa at Tusculum particularly had cost him very dear. What proves it to have been of great value is that on his return from exile the senate allowed him 500,000 sesterces (£4000) to repair the damage it had suffered in his absence, and that he thought they were far from having given him enough.

[3] *Ad Att.* xii. 25.

contrary, understood them well, and thought much about them. Their great wealth was used to further political ambition, and they did not hesitate to risk a part of it to gain adherents. The purse of a candidate for public honours was open to all who could be of use to him. He gave to the poorest, he lent to others, and sought to form with them bonds of interest which would attach them to his cause. Success usually followed those who had put the greatest number of men under obligations. Cicero, although less rich than the majority of them, imitated them. In his letters to Atticus he is almost always writing about bills and dates of maturity, and we see in them that his money circulated on all sides. He is in constant business relations, and as we should now say, has a running account with the greatest personages. Sometimes he lends to Caesar, and sometimes borrows of him. Among his numerous debtors are found persons of all ranks and fortunes, from Pompey to Hermogenes, who seems to have been a simple freedman. Unfortunately, counting them all, his creditors are still more numerous. Notwithstanding the example and advice of Atticus, he ill understood how to manage his fortune. He constantly had costly fancies. He would have at any price statues and pictures to adorn his galleries and give them the appearance of the gymnasia of Greece. He ruined himself to embellish his country houses. Generous out of season, we see him lending to others when he is constrained to borrow for himself. It is always when he is deepest in debt that he has the greatest desire to buy some new villa. He does not hesitate, then, to apply to all the bankers of Rome ; he goes to see Considius, Axius, Vectenus, Vestorius ; he would even try to soften Caecilius, the uncle of his friend Atticus, if he did not know that he was inflexible. Nevertheless he bears his troubles with a light heart. The prudent Atticus tells him in vain that it is disgraceful to be in debt; but as he shares this disgrace with a great many people it seems light, and he is the first to joke about it. One day he told one of his friends that he was so much in debt that he would willingly enter into some conspiracy, if any one would receive him, but that since he had punished Catiline's he inspired no confidence in others;[1] and when the first day of the month arrives, when payments become due, he is content to shut himself up at Tusculum and leave Eros or Tiro to argue with the creditors.

These embarrassments and troubles, of which his correspondence is full, make us think, almost in spite of ourselves, of certain passages in his philosophical works which appear rather surprising when we compare them with his mode of living, and which may easily be turned against him. Is it really this thoughtless prodigal, always ready to spend without consideration, who exclaimed one day in a tone of conviction that moves us : " Ye immortal gods, when will men understand what treasures are found in economy ! "[2] How dared this ardent lover of works of art, this impassioned friend of magnificence and luxury, how dared he treat as madmen people who love statues and pictures too well, or build themselves magnificent houses? He stands self-condemned, and I do not wish to entirely absolve him ; but while we pronounce on him a severe sentence, let us remember the times in which he lived, and let us think of his contemporaries. I will not compare him with the worst men, his superiority would be too evident ; but among those who are regarded as the most honourable, he still holds one of the foremost places. He did not owe his wealth to usury like Brutus and his friends ; he did not augment it by that sordid avarice with which Cato is reproached ; he did

[1] *Ad fam.* v. 6.   [2] *Parad.* 6.

not pillage the provinces like Appius or Cassius; he did
not consent like Hortensius to take his share of this pillage.
We must then acknowledge that, notwithstanding the blame
we may lay upon him, he was more scrupulous and disinterested in money matters than others. In the main, his
irregularities only injured himself, [1] and if he had too much
taste for ruinous prodigality, at least he did not have
recourse to scandalous gains in order to satisfy it. These
scruples honour him so much the more as they were then
very rare, and few people have passed, without stain, through
that greedy and corrupt society in the midst of which he
lived.

II.

He does not deserve less praise for having been honourable and regular in his family life. These were virtues of
which his contemporaries did not set him an example.

It is probable that his youth was austere.[2] He had
firmly resolved to become a great orator, and that was not
to be done without trouble. We know from himself how
hard the apprenticeship to oratory then was. " To succeed
in it, he tells us, a man must renounce all pleasures, avoid
all amusements, say farewell to recreation, games, entertainments, and almost to intercourse with one's friends." [3] This
was the price he paid for his success. The ambition by which

[1] It is not probable that Cicero wronged his creditors like Milo, who
only gave them 4 per cent. When he left Rome after the death of
Caesar, Cicero wrote to Atticus that the money that was owing him
would suffice to pay his debts; but as at that moment money was scarce
and debtors held off, he ordered him to sell his goods, if necessary, and
added : " Consult only my reputation." *Ad Att.* xvi. 2.

[2] *Ad fam.* ix. 26 : *Me nihil istorum ne juvenem quidem movit
unquam.*

[3] *Pro Caelio,* 19.

he was devoured preserved him from the other passions, and sufficed him. His youth was completely taken up with study. When once these early years were passed the danger was less; the habit of work that he had formed, and the important affairs in which he was engaged might suffice to preserve him from all dangerous impulses. Writers who do not like him have vainly tried to find in his life traces of that licentiousness which was so common around him. The most ill-disposed, like Dio,[1] banter him about a clever woman, named Caerellia, whom he somewhere calls his intimate friend.[2] She was so in fact, and it appears that she was not wanting in influence over him. His correspondence with her was preserved and published. This correspondence was, it is said, rather free in tone, and seemed at first to give some occasion to the malicious; but it must be remarked, that Caerellia was much older than he; that, far from being a cause of dissension in his household, we only see her intervening to reconcile him with his wife,[3] in fact that their acquaintance seems to have begun in a common liking for philosophy;[4] a sedate origin which does not forebode unpleasing consequences. Caerellia was a learned lady whose conversation must have been very pleasing to Cicero. Her age, her education which was not that of ordinary women, put him at ease with her, and, as he was naturally quick at repartee, as, once excited by the animation of conversation, he could not always govern and restrain his wit, and as, besides, by patriotism as by taste, he put nothing above that free and daring gaiety of which Plautus seemed to him the model, it may have happened that he wrote to her without ceremony those pleasantries "more spicy than those of the Attic

---

[1] *Dio Cass*. xlvi. 18.   [2] *Ad fam*. xiii. 72.
[3] *Ad Att*. xiv. 19.   [4] *Ibid*. xiii. 21.

writers, and yet truly Roman." [1]   Later, when these rustic
and republican manners were no longer in fashion, when,
under the influence of the gradually developing court life,
the rules of politeness were being refined, and manners
were becoming more ceremonious, the freedom of these
remarks no doubt shocked some fastidious minds, and may
have given rise to ill-natured remarks.   For our own part,
of all that correspondence of Cicero which is now lost, the
letters to Caerellia are those perhaps that we most regret.
They would have shown us better than all the rest the
habits of society, and the life of the fashionable world at
that time.

It is thought that he was about thirty when he married.
It was towards the end of Sulla's rule, at the time of his
first oratorical successes.   His wife, Terentia, belonged to a
rich and distinguished family.   She brought him in dowry,
according to Plutarch,[2] 120,000 drachmae (£4440), and
we see that she possessed houses in Rome, besides a forest
near Tusculum.[3]   It was an advantageous marriage for a
young man just beginning political life with more talent
than fortune.   Cicero's correspondence does not give a
very good impression of Terentia.   We imagine her as
an economical and orderly, but sharp and disagreeable
housewife, with whom it was difficult to live at ease.   She
did not agree very well with her brother-in-law Quintus,
and still less with Pomponia her sister-in-law, who, however, did not agree with anybody.   She had that influence
over her husband that a determined and obstinate woman
always has over a careless and irresolute mind.   For a long
time Cicero left her absolute mistress of the household, he

---

[1] *Ad fam.* ix. 15: *Non attici, sed salsiores quam illi Atticorum,
romani veteres atque urbani sales.*

[2] Plut. *Cic.* 8.　　　　　[3] *Ad Att.* ii. 4.

was very glad to shift on to somebody else those occupations that did not suit him. She was not without influence on his political life. She advised him to take energetic measures at the time of the great consulship, and later she embroiled him with Clodius, from dislike to Clodia, whom she suspected of wishing to allure him. As no gain came amiss to her, she succeeded in entangling him in some financial affairs, that Atticus himself, who was not over scrupulous, did not think very honourable; but there her power ended. She seems to have remained a stranger, and perhaps to have been indifferent to her husband's literary glory. In none of Cicero's works, in which the names of his daughter, his brother, and his son recur so frequently, is there any mention of his wife. Terentia had no influence on his mind. He never confided to her his private opinions on the most serious affairs of life; he never admitted her to share in his opinions and beliefs. We have a curious proof of this in his correspondence. Terentia was devout, and devout to excess. She consulted soothsayers, she believed in prodigies, and Cicero did not take the trouble to cure her of this eccentricity. He seems even, somewhere, to make a singular distribution of labours between her and himself; he shows her respectfully serving the gods, while he is occupied in working for men.[1] Not only did he not disturb her devotion, but he showed a consideration for her which surprises us. When he was about to start for Pompey's camp, he wrote to her: "At last I am free from that uneasiness and suffering that I experienced, and which caused you so much concern. The day after my departure I recognized the cause. During the night I threw off pure bile, and felt myself relieved as if

[1] *Ad fam.* xiv. 4: *Neque Dii, quos tu castissime coluisti, neque homines, quibus ego semper servivi,* etc.

some god had been my doctor. Evidently it was Apollo
and Aesculapius. I beg you to return thanks to them with
your usual piety and zeal." [1] This is strange language in
the mouth of that sceptic who wrote the treatise *On the
Nature of the Gods ;* but Cicero was, no doubt, one of those
people, like Varro and many others, who while they make
little use themselves of religious practices, think that they
are not bad for the common people and for women. There
has survived a whole book of letters from Cicero to Terentia,
which contains the history of his household. What strikes
one on opening it is that, as we get further on, the letters
become shorter, the last are no more than short notes.
And not only does the length of the letters diminish, but
their tone is no longer the same, and marks of affection
become more and more rare. We may then conclude
that this affection was not of the kind that increases with
time ; that common life, which strengthens true personal
unions, enfeebled this one. Instead of being strengthened,
it was worn out by length of time. The earlier letters show
an incredible passion, and this in spite of the fact that
Cicero had been married nearly twenty years; but he was
then very unfortunate, and it seems that misfortune makes
people more tender, and that families feel the need of
drawing closer when heavy blows fall on them. Cicero
had just been condemned to exile. He departed very
sorrowfully from Rome, where he knew that his house was
burnt, his friends persecuted, his family ill-treated. Terentia
had behaved very energetically, she had suffered for her
husband, and suffered with courage. On learning the
manner in which she had been treated, Cicero wrote to
her despairingly : " How wretched I am ! And must a
woman so virtuous, so honourable, so gentle, so devoted,

[1] *Ad fam.* xiv. 7.

be thus tormented for my sake!"[1] "Be assured, he tells her elsewhere, that I have nothing dearer than you. At this moment I think I see you, and cannot restrain my tears!"[2] He added with still more effusion, "Oh, my life, I would wish to see you again, and die in your arms!"[3] The correspondence then ceases for six years. It re-commences at the time Cicero left Rome, to go and govern Cilicia, but the tone is very much changed. In the single letter remaining to us of this date, affection is replaced by business. It has to do with a legacy that had fallen in very opportunely for Cicero's fortunes, and of the means of turning it to the best account. It is true he still calls Terentia his very dear and much-desired wife, *suavissima atque optatissima*, but these words have the appearance of polite phrases. However, he shows a great desire to see her again, and asks her to come as far as she can and wait for him.[4] She went as far as Brundusium, and, by a lucky chance, she entered the town at the same time that her husband arrived in the harbour; they met and embraced on the Forum. It was a happy moment for Cicero. He returned with the title of *imperator* and the hope of a triumph; he found his family united and joyous. Unfortunately the civil war was just about to break out. During his absence parties had broken with each other; they were about to come to blows, and immediately after his arrival Cicero was obliged to make choice between them, and to take his side. This war not only injured his political position, it was fatal to his private happiness. When the correspondence recommences, after Pharsalia, it becomes extremely matter-of-fact. Cicero returns to Italy, and lands again at Brundusium, no longer triumphant and

[1] *Ad fam.* xiv. 1.   [2] *Ibid.* xiv. 3.
[3] *Ibid.* xiv. 4.   [4] *Ibid.* xiv. 5.

happy, but vanquished and desperate. This time he does not wish to see his wife again, although he never had more need of consolation. He keeps her at a distance, and that without much ceremony. "If you come, he tells her, I do not see how you can be useful to me." [1] What makes this answer more cruel is, that, at the same time, he sent for his daughter, and consoled himself with her conversation. As to his wife she gets nothing more from him than short notes, and he has the courage to tell her that he does not make them longer because he has nothing to say. [2] At the same time he refers her to Lepta, Trebatius, Atticus, and Sicca, to learn what decisions he has taken. This shows clearly enough that she no longer enjoyed his confidence. The only mark of interest he still gives her is to ask her, from time to time, to take care of her health, a superfluous recommendation, since she lived more than a hundred years! The last letter he addressed to her is just what a man would write to his steward to give an order. "I expect to be at Tusculum the 7th or 8th of the month, he says ; be careful to prepare everything. I shall, perhaps, have several persons with me, and very likely we shall remain some time. Let the bath be ready, and let nothing be wanting that is necessary to comfort and health." [3] A few months afterwards, the separation which this tone foreshadows, took place between the couple. Cicero divorced Terentia after more than thirty years of marriage, and when they had children and grandchildren.

What motives drove him to this disagreeable extremity ? Probably we do not know them all. Terentia's disagreeable temper must have often caused those little quarrels in the household which, repeated continually, end by wearing out the most steadfast affection. About the time that Cicero

[1] *Ad fam.* xiv. 12. [2] *Ibid.* xiv. 17. [3] *Ibid.* xiv. 20.

was recalled from exile, and a very few months after he had
written those passionate letters of which I have spoken, he
said to Atticus: "I have some domestic troubles of which I
cannot write to you," and added, so that he might be understood: "My daughter and my brother love me still." [1]   We
must think that he had good reason to complain of his
wife, to leave her thus out of the list of persons by whom he
thought himself loved.   It has been suspected that Terentia
was jealous of the affection Cicero showed to his daughter.
This affection was somewhat excessive and so exclusive as
possibly to wound her, and she was not a woman to endure
this without complaint.   We may believe that these dissensions prepared and led up to the divorce, but they were
not the final cause of it.   The motive was more prosaic
and vulgar.   Cicero justified it by the waste and misuse of
his money by his wife, and several times he accused her of
having ruined him for her own benefit.   One of the most
curious characteristics of that age was that the women
appear as much engaged in business and as interested in
speculations as the men.   Money is their first care.   They
work their estates, invest their funds, lend and borrow.
We find one among Cicero's creditors, and two among his
debtors.   Only, as they could not always appear themselves
in these financial undertakings, they had recourse to some
obliging freedman, or some shady business man, who watched
their interests and profited by their gains.   Cicero, in his
speech for Caecina, coming across a character of this sort,
whose business was to devote themselves to the fortune of
women, and often to make their own at their expense,
depicts him in these terms: "There is no man one finds
oftener in ordinary life.   He is the flatterer of women, the
advocate of widows, a pettifogging lawyer by profession, a

[1] *Ad Att.* iv. I.

lover of quarrels, a constant attendant at trials, ignorant and stupid among men, a clever and learned lawyer among women, expert in alluring by the appearance of a false zeal and a hypocritical friendship, eager to render services sometimes useful but rarely faithful." [1] He was a marvellous guide for women tormented with the desire of making a fortune; so Terentia had one of these men about her, her freedman, Philotimus, a clever man of business, but not very scrupulous, who had succeeded at this trade, since he was rich and himself possessed slaves and freedmen. In early days Cicero often made use of him, doubtless at the request of Terentia. It was he who got for him at a low price some of the property of Milo when he was exiled. It was a profitable piece of business, but not in very good taste, and Cicero, who felt it to be so, speaks of it with some shame. On his departure for Cilicia he left the administration of part of his property to Philotimus, but he was not long in repenting of it. Philotimus, like the steward of a great house, paid less attention to his master's interests than to his own. He kept for himself the profits he had made on the property of Milo, and on Cicero's return presented him an account in which he figured as his creditor for a considerable amount. " He is a marvellous thief!" [2] said Cicero, in a rage. At this time his suspicions did not go beyond Philotimus; when he returned from Pharsalia he saw clearly that Terentia was his accomplice. " I have found my household affairs, said he to a friend, in as bad a state as those of the republic." [3] The distress in which he found himself at Brundusium made him distrustful. He looked more closely into his accounts, a thing that was not usual with him, and it was not difficult for him to discover that Terentia had often

[1] *Pro Caecin.* 5.   [2] *Ad Att.* vii. 1, 3.   [3] *Ad fam.* iv. 14.

H

deceived him. At one time she had retained sixty thousand sesterces [1] (£480) out of her daughter's dowry. This was a handsome profit, but she was not negligent of small gains. Her husband caught her one day pocketing two thousand sesterces (£16) out of a sum he had asked her for.[2] This rapacity completed the irritation of Cicero, whom other causes no doubt had soured and hurt for a long time. He resigned himself to the divorce, but not without sorrow. We do not break with impunity the bonds that habit, in the absence of affection, ought to draw closer. At the moment of separation, after so many happy days have been passed together, so many ills supported in common, there must always be some memory which troubles us. What adds to the sadness of these painful moments is, that when we wish to withdraw and isolate ourselves in our sorrow, business people arrive; we must defend our interests, reckon and discuss with these people. These discussions, which had never suited Cicero, made him then suffer more than usual. He said to the obliging Atticus, when asking him to undertake them for him : " The wounds are too recent, I could not touch them without making them bleed." [3] And as Terentia continued making difficulties, he wished to put an end to the discussion by giving her all she asked. " I would rather," he wrote, " have cause to complain of her than become discontented with myself." [4]

We can well understand that the wags did not fail to make merry on the subject of this divorce. It was a just retaliation after all, and Cicero had too often laughed at others to expect to be spared himself. Unfortunately he gave them, a short time after, a new opportunity of amusing

---

[1] *Ad Att.* xi. 2.　　　　　[2] *Ibid.* xi. 24.
[3] *Ibid.* xii. 22.　　　　　[4] *Ibid.* xii. 21.

themselves at his expense. Notwithstanding his sixty-three years he thought of marrying again, and he chose a very young girl, Publilia, whom her father, when dying, confided to his guardianship. A marriage between guardian and ward is a real stage marriage, and the guardian generally has the worst of it. How did it happen that Cicero, with his experience of the world and of life, allowed himself to be drawn into this imprudent step? Terentia, who had to revenge herself, repeated everywhere that he had fallen violently in love with this young girl; but his secretary, Tiro, asserted that he had only married her in order to pay his debts with her fortune, and I think we must believe Tiro, although it is not usual that, in this kind of marriage, the elder is also the poorer. As might be foreseen, trouble was not long in appearing in the household. Publilia, who was younger than her step-daughter, did not agree with her, and, it appears, could not conceal her joy when she died. This was an unpardonable crime in Cicero's eyes, and he refused to see her again. It is strange that this young woman, far from accepting with pleasure the liberty that he wished to restore to her, made great efforts to re-enter the house of this old man who divorced her,[1] but he was inflexible. This time he had had enough of marriage, and it is said that, when his friend Hirtius came to offer him the hand of his sister, he refused her, under the pretence that it is difficult to attend at the same time to a wife and to philosophy. It was a wise answer, but he would have done well to have thought of it sooner.

[1] *Ad Att.* xii. 32.

III.

Cicero had two children by Terentia. His daughter Tullia was the elder. He had brought her up in his own way, initiating her into his studies, and giving her the taste for those intellectual things that he loved so much himself, and which, it appears, his wife did not care for. " I find in her, he said, my features, my words, my mind; " [1] accordingly he loved her tenderly. While she was still very young her father could not refrain from making allusion in one of his pleadings to the affection he had for her.[2] This affection, certainly the deepest he ever felt, was the great anxiety of his life. A sadder fate than that of this young woman it is impossible to imagine. Married at thirteen to Piso, then to Crassipes, and separated from them by death and divorce, she re-married for the third time while her father was absent governing Cilicia. Suitors were numerous, even among young men of illustrious family, and it was not only the renown of the father-in-law that attracted them, as we might think. He tells us that they supposed he would return from his government very rich. By marrying his daughter these young men thought to make an advantageous match which would allow them to pay their debts.[3] Among them were the son of the consul Sulpicius and Tiberius Nero, who was the father of Tiberius and Drusus. Cicero favoured the latter, who even went to Cilicia to seek his consent, but his wife and daughter, to whom on leaving he had given the right of choosing, decided without him for Cornelius Dolabella. He was a young man of high family, a friend of Curio, of Caelius and Antony, who till then had lived like them, that

---

[1] *Ad Quint.* i. 3.   [2] *In Verr. act. sect.* i. 44.
[3] *Ad Att.* vii. 4.

is to say in risking his reputation and wasting his fortune; he was, besides, a man of wit and fashion. This husband was not much to the taste of Atticus; but it seems that Terentia was gained over by his great name, and perhaps Tullia was not insensible to his fine manners. At first the marriage seemed a happy one. Dolabella charmed his mother-in-law and his wife by his good-nature and kindness. Cicero himself, who had been at first surprised at the haste with which the affair had been carried through, thought that his son-in-law had a good deal of wit and refinement. "For the rest, he added, we must be resigned." [1] He referred to the frivolous and dissipated habits that Dolabella did not give up notwithstanding his marriage. He had promised to reform, but kept his promise badly, and, however willingly Cicero would have shut his eyes to his dissoluteness, ended by making resignation very difficult. He continued to live like the youth of that time, making an uproar in the streets at night under the windows of fashionable women, and his debaucheries seemed scandalous in a city accustomed to debauch. He attached himself to a fashionable woman, celebrated by her amorous adventures, Caecilia Metella, wife of the consular Lentulus Sphinther. She was the same woman who afterwards ruined the son of the great tragic actor Æsopus, that madman who, not knowing what to invent to ruin himself most quickly, had the strange caprice, at a dinner that he gave to his mistress, to dissolve and swallow a pearl worth a million sesterces [2] (£8000). With a woman like Metella, Dolabella soon squandered his fortune, he then dissipated his wife's, and not content with betraying and ruining her, threatened to divorce her when she dared to complain. It seems that Tullia loved him very much, and for a long time resisted those who advised

---

[1] *Ad Att.* vii. 3.   [2] Horace, *Sat.* II. 3, 239.

a divorce. Cicero blames, somewhere, what he calls his daughter's[1] folly, but she had at last to decide for this after fresh outrages, and leave her husband's house to return to her father's. She was enceinte. The confinement that followed in these painful circumstances carried her off at Tusculum at the age of thirty-one.

Cicero was inconsolable for her death, and his grief at losing her was certainly the greatest of his life. As his affection for his daughter was well known, letters came to him from all sides, of the sort that usually console those only who have no need of consolation. The philosophers, to whom his name gave credit, tried by their exhortations to make him support his loss more courageously. Caesar wrote to him from Spain, where he had just vanquished Pompey's sons. The greatest personages of all parties, Brutus, Lucceius, Dolabella himself, shared his sorrow; but none of these letters must have touched him more sensibly than that which he received from one of his old friends, Sulpicius, the great lawyer, who at that time governed Greece. Fortunately it has been preserved. It is worthy of the great man who wrote it and of him to whom it was addressed. The following passage has often been quoted : " I must tell you a reflection that has consoled me, perhaps it will succeed in diminishing your affliction. On my return from Asia, as I was sailing from Aegina towards Megara, I began to look at the country surrounding me. Megara was in front of me, Aegina behind, the Piraeus on the right, Corinth on the left. Formerly these were very flourishing cities, now they are but scattered ruins. At this sight I said to myself : How dare we, poor mortals that we are, complain of the death of our friends, whose life nature has made so short, when we see at one glance the mere corpses

[1] *Ad Att.* xi. 25.

of so many great cities lying around!"[1] The thought is new and grand. This lesson drawn from the ruins, this manner of drawing moral ideas from nature, this grave melancholy mingled with the contemplation of a fine landscape, are sentiments little known to pagan antiquity. This passage seems inspired by the spirit of Christianity. We should say it was written by a man familiar with the sacred writings, and "who was already sitting, with the prophet, on the ruins of desolate cities." This is so true that Saint Ambrose, wishing to write a letter of condolence, imitated this one, and it was thought, quite naturally, to be Christian. Cicero's reply was not less noble. We see in it a most touching picture of his sadness and isolation. After having described the sorrow he felt at the fall of the republic, he adds: "My daughter at least was left me. I had a place to which to retire and rest. The charm of her conversation made me forget my cares and sorrows; but the dreadful wound I received in losing her has re-opened in my heart all those wounds that I thought closed. Formerly I retired into my family to forget the misfortunes of the state, but can the state now offer me any remedy to make me forget the misfortunes of my family? I am obliged to shun, at the same time, both my home and the Forum, for my home no longer consoles me for the trouble the republic causes me, and the republic cannot fill the void that I find in my home."[2]

Tullia's sad fate, and the grief that her death caused her father, attract us towards her. When we see her lamented so much we wish to know her better. Unfortunately, not a single letter of hers remains in Cicero's correspondence; when he lavishes compliments on her mind, we are obliged to take it upon trust, and a father's compliments are always

---

[1] *Ad fam.* iv. 5. [2] *Ad Att.* iv. 6.

open to suspicion. From what we know, we can easily admit that she was an accomplished woman ; _lectissima femina_, is the praise Antony, who did not like her family, gives her.[1] We should like to know, however, how she bore the education that her father gave her. We rather mistrust this sort of education, and we cannot help fearing that Tullia suffered somewhat from it. The very manner in which her father bewailed her is, to our way of thinking, prejudicial to her memory. In composing on her death, that treatise " On Consolation " which was filled with her praises, he has not, perhaps, done her a great service. A young woman so unfortunate deserved an elegy ; a philosophic treatise seems to weigh on her memory. Is it not possible that her father rather spoilt her in wishing to make her too learned ? It was quite the custom at that time. Hortensius had made his daughter an orator, and it is asserted that, one day, she pleaded an important case better than a good advocate. I suspect that Cicero wished to make his a philosopher, and I am afraid he succeeded only too well. Philosophy presents many dangers for a woman, and Madame de Sévigné had not much reason to congratulate herself on having put her daughter under the system of Descartes. That dry and pedantic figure is not calculated to make us like women philosophers.

Philosophy succeeded still less with Cicero's son Marcus than with his daughter. His father was completely mistaken about his tastes and abilities, which is not very extraordinary, for parental tenderness is often more warm than enlightened. Marcus had only the instincts of a soldier, Cicero wished to make him a philosopher and an orator, but he lost his labour. These instincts, repressed for a moment, always broke out again with added force. At eighteen, Marcus

[1] _Ad Att._ x. 8.

lived like all the young men of that time, and it was necessary to remonstrate with him on his expenditure. He was bored with the lessons of his master, Dionysius, and with the rhetoric that his father tried to teach him. He wished to set out for the Spanish war with Caesar. Instead of listening to him, Cicero sent him to Athens to finish his education. He had an establishment like a nobleman's son. They gave him freedmen and slaves that he might make as good a figure as the young Bibulus, Acidinus and Messala who studied with him. About a hundred thousand sesterces (£800) were assigned to him for his annual expenses, which seems a reasonable allowance for a student in philosophy; but Marcus went away in a bad humour, and his stay at Athens did not have the results that Cicero expected. No longer under his father's eyes he indulged his tastes without restraint. Instead of following the lectures of the rhetoricians and philosophers, his time was taken up with good dinners and noisy entertainments. His life was so much the more dissolute as, to all appearance, he was encouraged in his dissipation by his master himself, the rhetorician Gorgias. This rhetorician was a thorough Greek, that is to say, a man ready to do anything to make his fortune. In studying his pupil he saw that he should gain more by flattering his vices than by cultivating his good qualities, and he accordingly flattered his vices. In this school, Marcus, instead of paying attention to Plato and Aristotle, as his father recommended him, acquired the taste for Falernian and Chian wine, a taste that continued with him. The only reputation that he was proud of afterwards was that of being the hardest drinker of his time; he sought and obtained the glory of conquering the triumvir Antony, who enjoyed a great reputation in this line, that he was very proud of. This was his way of avenging his father, whom Antony had put to death.

Later, Augustus, who wished to pay the son the debt he had contracted with his father, made him a consul, but did not succeed in breaking him of his habits of debauchery, for the sole exploit that we are told of him is, that one day, when he was drunk, he threw his glass at Agrippa's head.[1]

We can understand what sorrow Cicero must have felt when he learnt of his son's early dissoluteness. I suppose he hesitated to believe it for a long time, for he liked to delude himself about his children. So when Marcus, lectured by all the family, dismissed Gorgias and promised to behave better, his father, who was very willing to be deceived, was eager to believe it. From this time we see him constantly engaged in begging Atticus not to let his son want for anything, and in studying the letters he receives from him to try and discover some progress. There remains just one of these letters of Marcus of the time when he seems to return to better habits. It was addressed to Tiro, and is full of protestations of repentance. He acknowledges himself so humiliated, so tormented by all his faults, " that not only his soul detests them, but he cannot bear to hear of them." To convince him thoroughly of his sincerity he draws the picture of his life; it is impossible to imagine one better occupied. He passes his days and almost his nights with the philosopher Cratippus, who treats him like a son. He keeps him to dinner in order to deprive himself of his society as little as possible. He is so charmed with the learned conversation of Bruttius that he wishes to have him near him, and pays his board and lodging. He declaims in Latin, he declaims in Greek with the most learned rhetoricians. He only visits well-informed men; he only sees learned old men, the wise Epicrates, the venerable Leonidas, all the Areopagus in fact, and this edifying narration ends

[1] Plin. *Hist. nat.* xiv. 22.

with these words : " Above all, take care to keep in good health, that we may be able to talk science and philosophy together." [1]

It is a very pleasing letter, but in reading it a certain suspicion comes into our mind. These protestations are so exaggerated that we suspect Marcus had some design in making them, especially when we remember that Tiro possessed the confidence of his master, and disposed of all his liberalities. Who knows if these regrets and high-sounding promises did not precede and excuse some appeal for funds ?

It must be said in favour of Marcus that, after having grieved his father by his dissipation, at least he consoled his last moments. When Brutus passed through Athens, calling to arms the young Romans who were there, Marcus felt his soldierly instincts revive. He remembered that at seventeen he had successfully commanded a cavalry corps at Pharsalia, and he was one of the first to respond to the call of Brutus. He was one of his most skilful, most devoted and most courageous lieutenants, and often deserved his praise. "I am so pleased, wrote Brutus to Cicero, with the valour, activity and energy of Marcus, that he seems always to recall to me the father whose son he has the honour to be." [2] We can well understand how pleased Cicero must have been with this testimony. It was while rejoicing over this awakening of his son that he wrote and dedicated to him his treatise *De Officiis,* which is perhaps his finest work, and which was his last farewell to his family and his country.

[1] *Ad fam.* xvi. 21.   [2] *Brut. ad Cic.* ii. 3.

IV.

This study of Cicero's family life is not yet complete ; there remain a few details to add. We know that a Roman family was not only composed of the persons united by relationship, but that it also comprised the slaves. Servant and master were then more closely connected than they are now, and they had more community of life. In order to know Cicero thoroughly, then, in his family, we must say a few words about his relations with his slaves.

In theory, he did not hold opinions upon slavery different from those of his time. Like Aristotle, he accepted the institution, and thought it legitimate. While proclaiming that a man has duties to fulfil towards his slaves, he did not hesitate to admit that they must be held down by cruelty when there was no other means of managing them ;[1] but in practice he treated them with great mildness. He attached himself to them so far as to weep for them when he had the misfortune to lose them. This, probably, was not usual, for we see that he almost begs pardon for it of his friend Atticus. " My mind is quite troubled, he writes to him ; I have lost a young man named Sositheus, who was my reader, and I am more grieved perhaps than I ought to be at the death of a slave." [2] I only see one, in all his correspondence, with whom he seems to be very angry; this was a certain Dionysius whom he sought for even in the depths of Illyria, and whom he wished to have again at any price ;[3] but Dionysius had stolen some of his books, and this was a crime that Cicero could not forgive. His slaves also loved him very much. He boasts of the fidelity they showed towards him in his misfortunes, and we know that

[1] *De offic.* ii. 7. [2] *Ad Att.* i. 12.
[3] *Ad fam.* xiii. 77.

at the last moment they would have died for him if he had not prevented them.

We know better than the rest one of them, who had a greater share in his affection, namely, Tiro. The name he bears is Latin, which makes us suspect that he was one of those slaves born in the master's house (*vernae*), who were looked upon as belonging to the family more than the rest, because they had never left it. Cicero became attached to him early, and had him carefully instructed. Perhaps he even took the trouble to finish his education himself. He calls himself, somewhere, his teacher, and likes to rally him about his way of writing. He had a very lively affection for him, and at last could not do without him. He played a great part in Cicero's house, and his powers were very various. He represented in it order and economy, which were not the ordinary qualities of his master. He was the confidential man through whose hands all financial matters passed. On the first of the month he undertook to scold the debtors who were in arrears, and to get too pressing creditors to have patience; he revised the accounts of the steward Eros, which were not always correct; he went to see the obliging bankers whose credit supported Cicero in moments of difficulty. Every time there was some delicate commission to be executed he was applied to, as for instance when it was a question of demanding some money of Dolabella without displeasing him too much. The care he gave to the most important affairs did not prevent him being employed on the smallest. He was sent to overlook the gardens, spur on the workmen, superintend the building operations: the dining-room, even, fell within his province, and I see that he is entrusted with the sending out the invitations to a dinner, a thing not always without its difficulties, for one must only bring together guests who are

mutually agreeable, "and Tertia will not come if Publius is
invited." [1] But it is as secretary, especially, that he rendered
Cicero the greatest services. He wrote almost as quickly
as one speaks, and he alone could read his master's writing,
that the copyists could not decipher. He was more than a
secretary for him, he was a confidant, and even a col-
laborator. Aulus Gellius asserts that he helped him in the
composition of his works, [2] and the correspondence does not
belie this opinion. One day when Tiro had remained ill in
some country house, Cicero wrote to him that Pompey, who
was then on a visit to him, asked him to read him something, and that he had answered that all was mute in the
house when Tiro was not there. " My literature, he added,
or rather ours, languishes in your absence. Come back as
quickly as possible to re-animate our muses." [3]   At this time
Tiro was still a slave. It was not till much later, about the
year 700, that he was manumitted. Every one about Cicero
applauded this just recompense for so many faithful services.
Quintus, who was then in Gaul, wrote expressly to his
brother to thank him for having given him a new friend.
In the sequel, Tiro bought a small field, no doubt out of
his master's bounty, and Marcus, in the letter he wrote him
from Athens, rallies him pleasantly on the new tastes this
acquisition will develop in him. " Now you are a land-
owner ! says he, you must leave the elegance of the town
and become quite a Roman peasant. How much pleasure
I have in contemplating you from here under your new
aspect !   I think I see you buying agricultural imple-
ments, talking with the farmer, or saving seeds for your
garden in a fold of your robe at dessert ! " [4]   But, proprietor

---

[1] *Ad fam.* xvi. 22.   [2] A. Gell. vii. 3.
[3] *Ad fam.* xvi. 10.   .   [4] *Ibid.* xvi. 21.

and freedman, Tiro was no less at his master's service than when he was a slave.

His health was poor, and not always sufficiently attended to. Everybody liked him, but under this pretext everybody made him work. They seemed to agree in abusing his good-nature, which they knew to be inexhaustible. Quintus, Atticus, and Marcus insisted upon his constantly giving them news of Rome and of Cicero. Tiro so readily took his share of each addition to the business that came upon his master, that at last he fell ill. He fatigued himself so much during Cicero's governorship of Cilicia that, on the return journey, he had to be left at Patras. Cicero very much regretted the separation from him, and to testify the sorrow he felt at leaving him, he wrote to him as often as three times in the same day. The care that Cicero took on every occasion of this delicate and precious health was extreme; he became a doctor in order to cure him. One day, when he had left him indisposed at Tusculum, he wrote to him : "Take care of your health, which you have heretofore neglected in order to serve me. You know what it demands : a good digestion, no fatigue, moderate exercise, amusement, and keeping the body open. Come back a good-looking fellow, I shall like you all the better for it, you and Tusculum." [1] When the illness was graver the advice was given at greater length. All the family joined in writing, and Cicero, who held the pen, said to him, in the name of his wife and children : "If you love us all, and particularly me who have brought you up, you will only think of re-establishing your health. . . . I beg you not to regard expense. I have written to Curius to give you all that you want, and to pay the doctor liberally that he may be more attentive. You have rendered me numberless

[1] *Ad fam.* xvi. 18.

services at home, at the Forum, at Rome, in my province, in my public and private affairs, in my studies and my literary work; but you will put the finishing touch if, as I hope, I see you again in good health." [1]   Tiro repaid this affection by an indefatigable devotedness.   With his feeble health, he lived more than a hundred years, and we may say that all this long life was employed in his master's service.   His zeal did not flag when he had lost him, and his time was taken up with him to his last moments.   He wrote his biography, he brought out his unpublished works; that nothing should be lost, he collected his smallest notes and witty sayings, of which, it is said, he made a somewhat too large collection, for his admiration did not allow him to distinguish, and he published some excellent editions of his speeches, which were still consulted in the time of Aulus Gellius. [2]   These assuredly were services for which Cicero, who thought so much of his literary glory, would have most heartily thanked his faithful freedman.

There is one reflection that we cannot help making when we study the relations of Tiro with his master, and that is, that ancient slavery, looked at from this point of view, and in the house of such a man as Cicero, appears less repulsive. It was evidently much softened at this time, and letters have a large share in this improvement.   They had diffused a new virtue among those who loved them, one whose name often recurs in Cicero's philosophical works, namely, humanity, that is to say, that culture of mind that softens the heart.   It was by its influence that slavery, without being attacked in principle, was profoundly modified in its effects.   This change came about noiselessly.   People did not try to run counter to dominant prejudices; up to Seneca's time they did not insist on establishing the right

[1] *Ad fam.* xvi. 3, 4.   [2] A. Gell. xiii. 20.

of the slave to be reckoned among men, and he continued to be excluded from the grand theories that were made upon human brotherhood; but in reality no one profited more than he by the softening of manners. We have just seen how Cicero treated his slaves, and he was not exceptional. Atticus acted like him, and this humanity had become a sort of point of honour, on which this society of polished and lettered people prided themselves. A few years later, Pliny the younger, who also belonged to this society, speaks with a touching sadness of the sickness and death of his slaves. " I know well, he says, that many others only regard this kind of misfortune as a simple loss of goods, and in thinking thus they consider themselves great and wise men. For myself, I do not know if they are as great and wise as they imagine, but I do know that they are not men." [1] These were the sentiments of all the distinguished society of that time. Slavery, then, had lost much of its harshness towards the end of the Roman republic and in the early times of the empire. This improvement, which is usually referred to Christianity, was much older than it, and we must give the credit of it to philosophy and letters.

Besides the freedmen and slaves, who formed part of the family of a rich Roman, there were other persons who were attached to it, although less closely, namely, the clients. Doubtless the ancient institution of clientage had lost much of its grave and sacred character. The time had gone by when Cato said that the clients should take precedence of kinsmen and neighbours in the house, and that the title of patron came immediately after that of father. These ties were much slackened,[2] and the obligations they

---

[1] Plin. *Epist.* viii. 16.
[2] Virgil, however, always faithful to ancient traditions, places, in

imposed had become much less rigid. Almost the only one still respected was the necessity the clients were under of going to salute the patron early in the morning. Quintus, in the very curious letter that he addressed to his brother on the subject of his candidature for the consulship, divides them into three classes : first, those who content themselves with the morning visit; these are, in general, lukewarm friends or inquisitive observers who come to learn the news, or who even sometimes visit all the candidates that they may have the pleasure of reading in their faces the state of their hopes; then, those who accompany their patron to the Forum and form his train while he takes two or three turns in the basilica, that everybody may see that it is a man of importance who arrives; and lastly, those who do not leave him all the time he is out of doors, and who conduct him back to his house as they had gone to meet him there. These are the faithful and devoted followers, who do not haggle about the time they give, and whose unwearied zeal obtains for the candidate the dignities he desires.[1]

When a man had the good fortune to belong to a great family, he possessed by inheritance a ready-made clientage. A Claudius or a Cornelius, even before he had taken the trouble to oblige anybody, was sure to find his hall half filled every morning with people whom gratitude attached to his family, and he produced a sensation in the Forum by the number of those who accompanied him the day he went there to plead his first cause. Cicero had not this advantage; but, although he owed his clients to himself alone, they were none the less very numerous. In that

Tartarus, the patron who had deceived his client beside the son who had struck his father.

[1] *De petit. cons.* 9.

time of exciting struggles, when the quietest citizens were exposed every day to the most unreasonable accusations, many people were forced to have recourse to him to defend them. He did so readily, for he had no other means of making a clientage than by giving his services to a great many. It was this, perhaps, that made him accept so many bad cases. As he arrived at the Forum almost alone, without that train of persons whom he had obliged, which gave public importance, it was necessary for him not to be too particular in order to form and increase it. Whatever repugnance his honest mind may have felt on taking up a doubtful case, his vanity could not resist the pleasure of adding another person to the multitude of those who accompanied him. There were, in this crowd, according to his brother, citizens of every age, rank, and fortune. Important personages no doubt were mingled with those insignificant folks who usually formed this kind of retinue. Speaking of a tribune of the people, Memmius Gemellus, the protector of Lucretius, he calls him his client.[1]

It was not only at Rome that he had clients and persons who were under obligation to him; we see by his correspondence that his protection extended much further, and that people wrote to him from all parts demanding his services. The Romans were then scattered over the entire world; after having conquered it they busied themselves in making the greatest possible profit out of it. In the track of the legions and almost at their heels, a swarm of clever and enterprising men settled on the just conquered provinces to seek their fortunes there; they knew how to adapt their skill to the resources and needs of each country. In Sicily and in Gaul they cultivated vast estates, and speculated in wines and corn; in Asia, where there were so many cities

[1] *Ad fam.* xiii. 19.

opulent or involved in debt, they became bankers, that is to say, they furnished them, by their usury, a prompt and sure means of ruining themselves. In general, they thought of returning to Rome as soon as their fortune was made, and in order to return the sooner, they sought to enrich themselves as quickly as possible. As they were only encamped, and not really settled in the conquered countries, as they found themselves there without ties of affection and without root, they treated them without mercy and made themselves detested. They were often prosecuted before the tribunals and had great need of being defended, and so they sought to procure the support of the best advocates, above all that of Cicero, the greatest orator of his time. His talent and his credit were not too great to extricate them from the discreditable affairs in which they were mixed up.

If we wish to become well acquainted with one of those great merchants of Rome, who, by their character and their fate, sometimes resemble the speculators of our days, we must read the speech that Cicero delivered in defence of Rabirius Postumus. He there narrates the whole story of his client. It is a lively story, and it is not without interest to sum it up in order to know what those Roman business men, who so often had recourse to his eloquence, were like. Rabirius, the son of a rich and acute farmer of taxes, was born with the spirit of enterprise. He did not confine himself to a single branch of commerce, for he was one of those of whom Cicero said that they knew all the roads by which money could come in, *omnes vias pecuniae norunt*.[1] He transacted all kinds of business, and with equally good fortune; he undertook much himself, and often shared in the enterprises of others. He farmed the public taxes; he lent to private persons, to the provinces and to kings. As

[1] *Ad Quint.* i. I.

generous as he was rich, he made his friends profit by his good fortune. He created employment for them, gave them an interest in his business, and a share in the profits.

His popularity therefore was very great at Rome; but, as sometimes happens, his prosperity ruined him. He had lent a good deal of money to Ptolemy Auletes, King of Egypt, who probably gave him good interest. This king having got himself expelled by his subjects, Rabirius was induced to make him fresh advances in order to recover the money that was at stake. He pledged his own fortune and even that of his friends to provide for his expenses; he defrayed the cost of the magnificent royal *cortège* when Ptolemy went to Rome to demand the support of the senate, and, what must have cost him still more, gave him the means of gaining over the most influential senators. Ptolemy's business appeared safe. As people hoped much from the gratitude of the king, the most important personages strove for the honour or rather the profit of reinstating him. Lentulus, then proconsul of Cilicia, contended that they could not refuse it to him; but at the same time Pompey, who received the young prince at his house at Alba, demanded it for himself. This rivalry caused everything to miscarry. The opposing interests counteracted each other, and in order not to cause jealousy by letting one man profit by this fortunate opportunity, the senate would not grant it to anybody. It is said that Rabirius, who knew the Romans well, then gave the king the bold advice to apply to one of those adventurers of whom Rome was full and who flinched from nothing for money. A former tribune, Gabinius, governed Syria. He was promised 10,000 talents (£2,200,000) if he would openly disobey the decree of the senate. It was a large sum; Gabinius accepted the bargain, and his troops brought Ptolemy back to Alexandria. As soon as Rabirius knew that he was re-established he hastened to meet him. To make more sure of recovering his money, he consented to become his overseer of the revenue (*diaecetes*), or as we should now say, his minister of finance. He wore the Greek mantle, to the great scandal of strict Romans, and put on the insignia of his office. He had only accepted it with the idea that he should never be better paid than if he paid himself, through his own hands. This is what he tried to do, and it appears that in raising the money promised to Gabinius he also cautiously took enough to repay himself; but the people, who were being ruined, complained, and the king, to whom Rabirius had become intolerable now that he had no longer need of him, and who was no doubt delighted to find a convenient means of getting rid of a creditor, threw him into prison and even threatened his life. Rabirius fled from Egypt as soon as he could, happy to have left only his fortune there. He had only one resource left. At the same time that he administered the king's finances, he had bought on his own account Egyptian merchandise, paper, flax, glass, and had laden several vessels which unloaded at Puteoli with considerable ostentation. The report of this reached Rome, and, as people there were used to the lucky adventures of Rabirius, rumour took pleasure in exaggerating the number of the vessels and the value of their cargo. It was even said, in an undertone, that there was among these ships a smaller one that was not shown, no doubt because it was full of gold and precious objects. Unfortunately for Rabirius there was no truth in all these tales. The little ship only existed in the imagination of news-mongers, and the goods that the others carried being sold at a loss, he was quite ruined. His disaster made a sensation at Rome, and was the talk of a whole season.

The friends he had so generously obliged deserted him ; public opinion, which up to that time had been so favourable to him, turned against him. The most indulgent called him a fool, the most violent accused him of feigning poverty and of withholding a part of his fortune from his creditors. It is certain, however, that he had nothing, and only lived on the bounty of Caesar, one of that small number who remained true to him in his misfortune. Cicero did not forget him either. He remembered that, at the time of his exile, Rabirius had put his fortune at his disposal and paid men to accompany him, and therefore he hastened to plead for him when it was proposed to include him in the prosecution of Gabinius, and he succeeded at least in preserving his honour and liberty.

One trait is missing in this description. Cicero tells us in his speech that Rabirius was only moderately educated. He had done so many things in his life that he had not had time to think of learning, but this was not usual ; we know that many of his colleagues, notwithstanding their not very literary occupations, were none the less witty and lettered men. Cicero, recommending a merchant of Thespiae to Sulpicius, tells him : " He has a taste for our studies." [1] He looked upon Curius of Patras as one of those who had best preserved the turn of the ancient Roman humour. "Make haste and come back to Rome, he wrote him, lest the seed of our native humour be lost." [2] Those knights who associated themselves in powerful companies and farmed the taxes, were also men of wit and men of the best society. Cicero, who came from their ranks, had connection with almost all of them ; but it seems that he was more especially connected with the company that farmed

---

[1] *Ad fam.* xiii. 22.   [2] *Ibid.* vii. 31.

the pasturages of Asia, and he says that it put itself under his protection.

This protection was also extended to people who were not Romans by birth. Foreigners, we can well understand, regarded it as a great honour and security to be in any way connected with an illustrious personage in Rome. They could not be his clients, they wished to become his hosts. At a time when there were so few convenient hotels in the countries one passed through, it was necessary, when you wished to travel, to have obliging friends who would consent to receive you. In Italy, rich people bought little houses where they passed the night on the roads they were accustomed to travel; but, elsewhere, they journeyed from one host to another. To shelter a rich Roman in this way was often a heavy expense. He always had a large train with him. Cicero tells us that he met P. Vedius in the depths of Asia "with two chariots, a carriage, a litter, horses, numerous slaves, and, besides, a monkey on a little car, and a number of wild asses." [1] Vedius was a comparatively unknown Roman. One may judge of the suite that a proconsul and a praetor had when they went to take possession of their provinces! However, although their passage exhausted the house that received them, this ruinous honour was solicited because numberless advantages were found in securing their support. Cicero had hosts in all the great cities of Greece and Asia, and they were almost always the principal citizens. Kings themselves like Deiotarus and Ariobarzanes considered themselves honoured by this title. Important cities, Volaterrae, Atella, Sparta, Paphos frequently claimed his protection and rewarded it with public honours. He counted entire provinces, nations almost, among his clients, and after the affair of Verres, for

[1] *Ad Att.* vi. i.

instance, he was the defender and patron of Sicily. This custom survived the republic, and in the time of Tacitus orators of renown had still among their clients provinces and kingdoms. It was 'the only mark of real distinction that remained to eloquence.

These details, it seems to me, complete our knowledge of what the life of an important person was at that time. As long as we are satisfied with studying the few persons who compose what we should now-a-days call his family, and only see him with his wife and children, his life very much resembles our own. The sentiments which are the foundation of human nature have not changed, and they always lead to very nearly the same results. The cares which troubled Cicero's domestic hearth, his joys and misfortunes, are much like ours; but as soon as we leave this limited circle, when we replace the Roman among the crowd of his servants and familiar friends, the difference between that society and ours becomes manifest. Now-a-days life has become more plain and simple. We have no longer those immense riches, those extensive connections, nor that multitude of people attached to our fortunes. What we call a great retinue would scarcely have sufficed for one of those clerks of the farmers of the revenue who went to collect the taxes in some provincial town. A noble, or even a rich Roman knight, did not content himself with so little. When we think of those armies of slaves they gathered together in their houses and on their estates, of those freedmen who formed a sort of court around them, of that multitude of clients who encumbered the streets of Rome through which they passed, of those hosts they had throughout the world, of those cities and realms that implored their protection, we can better understand the authority of their speech, the haughtiness of their bearing, the breadth of their eloquence, the gravity of their deportment, the feeling of personal importance which they threw into all their actions and speeches. It is here, above all, that the perusal of Cicero's letters renders us a great service. They give us a notion of lives lived on a scale such as we no longer know, and thus help us to understand better the society of that time.

ATTICUS

Of all Cicero's correspondents, none kept up a longer or more regular intercourse with him than Atticus. Their friendly relations lasted without interruption and without a shadow till their death. They corresponded during the shortest absences, and, when it was possible, more than once a day. These letters, sometimes short to communicate a passing reflection, sometimes long and studied, when events were graver, playful or serious according to circumstances, that were written in haste wherever the writers happened to be, these letters reflect the whole life of the two friends. Cicero characterized them happily when he said "They were like a conversation between us two." Unfortunately, at present, we hear only one of the speakers and the conversation has become a monologue. In publishing his friend's letters Atticus took good care not to add his own. No doubt he did not wish his sentiments to be read too openly, and his prudence sought to withhold from the public the knowledge of his opinions and the secrets of his private life ; but in vain he sought to hide himself, the voluminous correspondence that Cicero kept up with him was sufficient to make him known, and it is easy to form from it an exact idea of the person to whom it is addressed. This person is assuredly one of the most curious of an important epoch, and deserves that we should take the trouble to study him with some care.

I.

Atticus was twenty years old when the war between Marius and Sulla began. He saw its beginnings and nearly became its victim; the tribune Sulpicius, one of the chief heads of the popular party, and his relation, was put to death with his partisans and friends by Sulla's orders, and as Atticus often visited him he ran some risk. This first danger decided his whole life. As, notwithstanding his age, he had a firm and prudent mind, he did not allow himself to be discouraged, but reconsidered his position. If he had had hitherto some slight inclination towards political ambition, and the idea of seeking public honours, he gave them up without hesitation when he saw what a price must sometimes be paid for them. He understood that a republic, in which power could only be seized by force, was lost, and that in perishing it was likely to drag down with it those who had served it. He resolved then to hold himself aloof from public affairs, and his whole policy consisted henceforth in creating for himself a safe position, outside of parties, and out of reach of danger.

Sieyès was asked one day : " What did you do during the Terror?" "What did I do?" he answered; " I lived." That was a great thing to do. Atticus did still more, he lived not only during a terror of a few months, but during a terror of several years. As if to test his prudence and ability, he was placed in the most troubled period in history. He looked on at three civil wars, he saw Rome four times invaded by different leaders, and the massacres re-commence at each new victory. He lived, not humble, unknown, allowing himself to be forgotten in some distant town, but at Rome, and in full publicity. Everything contributed to draw

attention to him ; he was rich, which was a sufficient cause
for being proscribed, he had a great reputation as a man of
wit, he willingly associated with the powerful, and, through
his connections at least, he was regarded as an important
person.   Nevertheless, he was able to escape all the dangers
that his position and his wealth created for him, and even
contrived to become greater at each of those revolutions
which, it seemed, might have ruined him.   Each change of
government, which hurled his friends from power, left him
richer and stronger, so that at last he found himself placed,
quite naturally, almost on a level with the new master.   By
what miracle of cleverness, by what prodigy of skilful combinations did he succeed in living honoured, rich and
powerful at a time when it was so difficult to live at all ?   It
was a problem full of difficulties ; this is how he solved it.

In view of the first massacres of which he had been a
witness, Atticus decided to take no part henceforth in
public affairs and parties ; but that is not so easy to do as
one might think, and the firmest resolution does not always
suffice for success.   It is useless to declare that you wish
to remain neutral; the world persists in classing you according to the name you bear, your family traditions, your
personal ties and the earlier manifestations of your preferences.   Atticus understood that, in order to escape this
sort of forced enlistment and to throw public opinion off
the scent, it was necessary to leave Rome, and to leave it
for a long time.   He hoped, by this voluntary exile, to regain
full possession of himself and break the ties that, against his
will, still bound him to the past.   But, if he wished to withdraw himself from the eyes of his fellow-citizens, he did not
intend to be forgotten by everybody.   He meant to return ;
and did not wish to return as a stranger, no longer recognized,
and lose all the benefit of his early friendships.   Thus he did

not choose for his retreat some distant estate, in an unknown
province, or one of those obscure towns on which the eyes of
the Roman people never fell.   He retired to Athens, that is to
say, to the only city that had preserved a great renown, and
which still held a place in the admiration of the nations on
a level with Rome.   There, by a few well-placed liberalities,
he drew to himself the affection of everybody.   He distributed corn to the citizens, he lent money without interest
to that city of men of letters, the finances of which were
always embarrassed.   He did more, he flattered the Athenians
on their most sensitive side.   He was the first Roman who
dared openly to declare his taste for the letters and arts of
Greece.   Up to that time it had been the fashion among his
countrymen to esteem and cultivate the Greek muses in
private, and to laugh at them in public.   Cicero himself, who
on so many occasions braved this stupid prejudice, dared
not appear to know off-hand the name of a great sculptor ;
but Cicero was a statesman for whom it was proper to show,
at least now and then, that haughty disdain for other
nations which partly constituted what is called the Roman
dignity.   It was necessary to flatter this national weakness if
one wished to please the people.   Atticus, who did not
mean to ask anything of them, was more free ; so he openly
laughed at these customs.   Immediately on his arrival he
began to speak and write Greek, to openly frequent the
studios of sculptors and painters, to buy statues and pictures,
and to compose works on the fine arts.   The Athenians
were as much delighted as surprised to see one of their conquerors partake in their most cherished tastes, and thus
protest against the unjust disdain of the rest.   Their gratitude, which was always very noisy, as we know, overwhelmed
Atticus with all sorts of flattery.   Decrees in his honour were
multiplied, he was offered all the dignities of the city ; they

even wished to raise statues to him. Atticus hastened to refuse everything; but the effect was produced, and the report of such great popularity did not fail to reach Rome, carried by those young men of high family who had just finished their education in Greece. In this manner the reputation of Atticus lost nothing by his absence; people of taste talked of this enlightened connoisseur of the arts who had made himself remarked even at Athens; and during this same time the politicians, no longer seeing him, lost the habit of classing him with a political party.

This was an important step. There remained a more important one to take. Atticus had seen betimes that to be rich is the first condition of independence. This general truth was even more evident at that time than at any other. How many people were there whose conduct during the civil wars can only be explained by the state of their fortunes! Curio had but one motive for serving Caesar, whom he did not like, namely, the pressure of his creditors; and Cicero himself puts among the chief reasons that prevented him going to Pompey's camp, whither all his sympathies called him, the money that Caesar had lent him, and which he could not repay. To escape embarrassments of this kind and gain entire liberty, Atticus resolved to become rich, and became so. It is of importance, I think, to give here a few details to show how people got rich at Rome. His father had left him a rather moderate fortune, two million sesterces (£16,000). When he left Rome he sold almost all the family property, that he might leave nothing behind to tempt the proscribers, and bought an estate in Epirus, in that country of large herds, where the land brought in so much. It is probable he did not pay much for it. Mithridates had just ravaged Greece, and, as there was no money, everything went at a low price. This domain quickly prospered under skilful management; new lands were bought every year out of the surplus revenue, and Atticus became one of the great landed proprietors of the country. But is it likely that his wealth came to him solely through the good management of his land? He would have willingly had this believed, in order to resemble somewhat in this manner Cato and the Romans of the old school. Unluckily for him, his friend Cicero betrays him. In reading this unreserved correspondence we are not long in perceiving that Atticus had many other ways of enriching himself besides the sale of his corn and herds. This skilful agriculturalist was at the same time a clever trader, who carried on all businesses successfully. He excelled in drawing a profit, not only from the follies of others, which is common, but even from his own pleasures, and his talent consisted in enriching himself where others ruin themselves. We know for instance that he was fond of fine books; then, as now, this was a very costly fancy, but he knew how to make it a source of handsome profits. He collected in his house a large number of skilful copyists whom he trained himself; after having made them work for him, when his passion was satisfied he set them to work for others, and sold the books they copied to the public very dear. He was thus a veritable publisher for Cicero, and as his friend's works sold well it happened that this friendship, which was full of charm for his heart, was not without use to his fortune.[1] This commerce might be avowed, and a friend to letters was not forbidden to become a book-seller; but Atticus engaged as well in many transactions that ought to have been more repugnant to him. As he saw the success that everywhere

[1] I have endeavoured to prove this with more detail in a memoir published by the *Revue archéologique*, entitled, *Atticus, éditeur de Cicéron.*

attended gladiatorial fights, and that no festival took place
without one of these grand butcheries, he thought of raising
gladiators on his estates. He had them carefully instructed
in the art of dying gracefully, and hired them out at a high
rate to cities that wished to amuse themselves.[1] It must be
acknowledged that this is not a suitable trade for a scholar
and a philosopher; but the profits were large, and the
philosophy of Atticus was accommodating as soon as there
was a good profit to make. Besides, he was a banker when
the opportunity offered, and lent at a high rate of interest,
as the greatest nobles of Rome did without scruple. Only,
he was more circumspect than others, and took care to
appear as little as possible in the affairs that he conducted,
and he had, no doubt, in Italy and Greece, clever agents
who made the most of his capital. His business relations
extended throughout the world; we know of his debtors in
Macedonia, Epirus, Ephesus and Delos, almost everywhere.
He lent to private persons; he lent also to cities, but quite
secretly, for this business was then as little esteemed as it
was lucrative, and persons who took to it were not considered
either honest or scrupulous. So Atticus, who thought as
much of his reputation as of his fortune, would not let
any one know that he conducted this sort of business. He
carefully concealed it even from his friend Cicero, and we
should be ignorant of it now if he had not experienced some
untoward accidents in this risky business. Although usually
great profits were gained, some dangers also were run.
After having suffered the Roman domination for two
centuries, all the cities, allied and municipal, and especially
those of Asia, were completely ruined. They all had less
revenue than debts, and the proconsuls, combined with the
farmers of the taxes, carried off their resources so completely
that there was nothing left for the creditors to take, unless

[1] *Ad Att.* iv. 4, 8.

they exerted themselves. This is what happened once to
Atticus, notwithstanding his activity. We see that Cicero
rallies him in one of his letters about the siege he is going to
lay to Sicyon ; [1] this siege was evidently that of some recal-
citrant debtors ; Atticus never made any other campaigns ;
and, in truth, this one succeeded badly. While he thus
went to war against this unfortunate indebted town, the
senate took pity on it, and protected it by a decree against
its too exacting creditors, so that Atticus, who set out from
Epirus as a conqueror, with flying banners, was reduced,
says Cicero, when he had arrived under the walls, to extract
from the Sicyonians a few poor crowns (*nummulorum
aliquid*) by means of prayers and flatteries.[2] We must,
however, suppose that Atticus was usually more lucky in the
investment of his funds, and by his well-known prudence we
are assured that he knew how to choose more solvent debtors.
All this business that he carried on would certainly soon
have made him very rich ; but he had no need to take so
much trouble, for while he was working so skilfully to make
his fortune it came to him ready made from another quarter.
He had an uncle, Q. Caecilius, who passed for the most
terrible usurer of Rome, where there were so many, and
who only consented to lend to his nearest relations, and as a
special favour, at the rate of one per cent. per month. He
was a hard, inflexible man, who had rendered himself so
hateful to everybody that the people could not be prevented
from outraging his corpse on the day of his funeral. Atticus
was the only person who had been able to get on with him.
Caecilius adopted him by will, and left him the greater
part of his property, ten million sesterces, a little more than
£80,000. Henceforth his fortune was made, he was
independent of everybody, and free to follow his own
inclinations.

[1] *Ad Att.* i. 13.   [2] *Ibid.* i. 19.

But was it not to be feared, that when he was back in Rome, the resolution that he took to shun all ties would have a bad look? He could not decently pretend indifference or fear as a reason for keeping aloof from parties; he had to find a more honourable motive and one that he might proclaim; a school of philosophy furnished him with it. The Épicureans, sacrificing everything to the conveniences of life, said that it was good to abstain from public employments to avoid the worry they brought. "Do not engage in politics," was their favourite maxim. Atticus professed to be an Epicurean; henceforth his abstention had a plausible pretext, fidelity to the opinions of his sect, and if he was blamed, the blame fell upon the whole school, which always makes the share of each individual very light. Was Atticus in reality a veritable and complete Epicurean? This is a question that the learned discuss, and that the character of this personage easily permits us to solve. To suppose that in anything whatever he attached himself scrupulously to a school, and pledged himself to be a faithful disciple of it, would be to know him ill. He had studied them all for the pleasure that this study gave to his inquisitive mind, but he was determined not to be a slave to their systems. He had found a principle in the Epicurean morals that suited him, and seized it in order to justify his political conduct. As to Epicurus himself and his doctrine, he cared very little about them, and was ready to abandon them on the first pretext. Cicero shows this very pleasantly in a passage of the *De Legibus*. He represents himself in this work chatting with Atticus on the banks of the Fibrenus, under the delightful shades of Arpinum. As he wishes to trace back the origin of laws to the gods, it is necessary for him first to lay down that the gods concern themselves with men, which the Epicureans denied. He turns then to his friend, and says: "Do you admit,

Pomponius, that the power of the immortal gods, their reason, their wisdom, or, if you like it better, their providence, rule the universe? If you do not admit it I must begin by demonstrating it.—Well then, replies Atticus, I admit it, if you like, for thanks to these birds that are singing, and to the murmuring of these brooks, I have no fear that any of my fellow-disciples may hear me." [1]   Here is a very accommodating philosopher, and the school will not get very much good from an adept who abandons it as soon as he is sure that it will not be known.   The character of Atticus is here well seen.   To embrace an opinion resolutely is to pledge oneself to defend it, and to expose oneself to the necessity of fighting for it.   Now, philosophical quarrels, although they be not bloody, are no less desperate than others ; this is war all the same, and Atticus wishes for peace in all things, at least for himself.   It is amusing to examine the part that Cicero gives him in the philosophical dialogues into which he introduces him.   In general he does not discuss, he incites to discussion.   Inquisitive and insatiable, he asks, he interrogates continually ; he compels a reply, he raises objections, he animates the combatants, and during this time he quietly enjoys the fight without ever taking part in it.   We shall see, by and by, that this was exactly the part he took in politics.

Atticus remained twenty-three years away from Rome, only visiting it at long intervals and usually remaining but a very short time.   When he thought that, by his long absence, he was quite free from the ties that attached him to the political parties, when he had gained independence with wealth, when he had secured himself against all the

[1] *De Leg.* i. 7.   He is still faithful to this part of an amateur in philosophy, when he says further on (i. 21), that Antiochus had made him take a few steps in the Academy, *deduxit in Academiam perpauculis passibus.*   He never penetrated further.

reproaches that might be made him on his conduct by giving
his prudence the appearance of a philosophical conviction,
he thought of returning definitively to Rome and there
resuming his interrupted course of life. He chose a
moment for returning when all was calm, and, as if to break
entirely with his past, he came back with a new surname,
by which people soon learnt to call him. This name of
Atticus, which he brought back from Athens, seemed to
indicate clearly that he would only live henceforth for the
study of letters and the enjoyment of the arts.

From this moment he divided his time between residence
in Rome and in his country houses. He quietly wound up
his banking affairs, some of which were still standing over,
and took measures to hide from the public the sources of
his wealth. He kept only his estates in Epirus and his
houses in Rome, which brought him in a good deal, and
the profits of which he could acknowledge. His property
continued to increase, thanks to the way in which he
managed it. Besides, he had none of those weaknesses
which might have endangered it; he did not care about
buying or building, he did not possess any of those splendid
villas at the gates of Rome or at the sea-side, the keeping
up of which ruined Cicero. He still sometimes lent money,
but, as it appears, rather to oblige than to enrich himself.
He was careful, besides, to choose safe persons, and showed
himself without pity when debts fell due. This he did,
he said, in the interest of his debtors, for, in tolerating their
negligence he would encourage them to ruin themselves.
But he did not stand upon ceremony in dismissing those
with whom his money would have run some risk, even if they
were his nearest relations. Cicero, relating to him one day
that their common nephew, the young Quintus, had come
to him and tried to move him by the picture of his poverty,
added : " I took then something of your eloquence; I

answered nothing." It was a good contrivance, and Atticus must have employed it more than once with regard to his brother-in-law and his nephew, who were always without money. He had learnt how to make for himself a high social position at small cost. He lived in his house on the Quirinal — which was more spacious and commodious within than handsome without, and which he repaired as little as possible—among the works of art that he had selected in Greece, and the lettered slaves whom he had carefully trained himself, and whom everybody envied him. He often assembled the cultivated people of Rome at feasts where there was a great display of learning. His hospitality did not cost much, if it is true, as Cornelius Nepos, who had seen his accounts, asserts, that he only spent 3000 asses (£6) a month on his table.[1] Cicero, always indiscreet, relates that Atticus often served to his guests very common vegetables on very costly dishes;[2] but what did it matter? every one considered himself fortunate in taking part in these select parties, where they heard Atticus talk and Cicero's finest works read before they were published, and it may be said that all the most distinguished persons of that great period held it an honour to frequent that house on the Quirinal.

II.

Of all the advantages of Atticus, one is most tempted to envy him his good fortune in attaching to himself so many friends. He took much trouble to do so. From his arrival at Rome we see him busied in putting himself on good terms with everybody, and using every means to please men

---

[1] *T. Pomp. Att.* 13. All the preceding details are taken from the life of Atticus by Cornelius Nepos.
[2] *Ad Att.* vi. 1.

of all parties. His birth, his wealth, and the manner in which he had acquired it, drew him towards the knights; these rich farmers of the taxes were his natural friends, and he soon enjoyed a great reputation among them; but he was not less connected with the patricians, usually so disdainful of all who were not of their caste. He had taken the surest means to conciliate them, which was to flatter their vanity. He took advantage of his historical knowledge to manufacture for them agreeable genealogies, in which he made himself partaker in a good many lies, and supported their most fanciful pretensions by his learning. This example shows at once his knowledge of the world, and the advantage he drew from it when he wished to gain the friendship of anybody. We can see what a close observer he must have been, and the talent that he had for seizing and profiting by the weak side of people, merely by considering the nature of the services that he rendered to each person. He had proposed to Cato to undertake the management of his affairs at Rome during his absence, and Cato hastened to accept this: a steward of such capacity was not to be despised by a man who cared so much for his wealth. He had gratified the vain Pompey, by busying himself in selecting in Greece some fine statues to ornament the theatre he was building.[1] As he well knew that Caesar was not accessible to the same kind of flattery, and that, to attract him, more real services were necessary, he lent him money.[2] Naturally, he attached himself by preference to the heads of parties; but he did not neglect others when he could serve them. He carefully cultivated Balbus and Theophanes, the confidants of Caesar and Pompey; he even went sometimes to visit Clodius and his sister Clodia, as well as other people of doubtful reputation. Having neither rigid scruples like Cato, nor violent aversions like

[1] *Ad Att.* iv. 9.   [2] *Ibid.* vi. I.

Cicero, he accommodated himself to everybody; his good-nature lent itself to everything; he suited all ages as well as all characters. Cornelius Nepos remarks with admiration, that while yet very young he charmed the old Sulla, and that when very old he could please the young Brutus. Atticus formed a common link between all these men who were so different in temper, rank, opinions, and age. He went continually from one to the other, as a sort of pacific ambassador, trying to bring them together and unite them, for it was his habit, says Cicero, to form friendships between others.[1] He removed the suspicions and prejudices which prevented them knowing one another; he inspired them with the desire to see each other and become intimate, and if, later, any differences arose between them, he became their intermediary, and brought about explanations which made them friends again. His masterpiece in this line is to have succeeded in reconciling Hortensius and Cicero, and making them live amicably together notwithstanding the violent jealousy that separated them. What trouble must he not have had to calm their irritable vanity, which was always ready to fly out, and which fate seemed to take pleasure in exciting still more, by putting them in constant rivalry!

All these acquaintanceships of Atticus were certainly not real friendships. He visited many of these personages only for the advantage that his safety or his wealth might draw from them; but there are a great number of others who were really his friends. To confine ourselves to the most important, Cicero loved no one so much as he did him; Brutus showed him an unreserved confidence to the last, and on the eve of Philippi wrote him his last confidences. There remain too many striking proofs of these two illustrious friendships for them to be called in question, and we must admit that he was able to inspire a lively affection in

[1] *Ad Att.* vii. 8 : *soles conglutinare amicitias.*

two of the noblest minds of that time. At first we are very much surprised at this. His prudent reserve, that openly avowed determination to keep clear of all entanglements in order to escape all danger, ought, as it seems, to have kept aloof from him men of conviction who sacrificed fortune and life for their opinions. By what merit was he nevertheless able to attach them to himself? How was a man so taken up with himself and so careful of his interests able to enjoy so fully the pleasures of friendship, which seem at first sight, to exact devotedness and self-forgetfulness? How did he succeed in making the moralists, who assert that egotism is the death of true affection, belie themselves?[1]

This is still one of those problems of which the life of Atticus is full, and it is the most difficult to solve. Seen from a distance, even through the praises of Cicero, Atticus does not seem attractive, and one would not be tempted to choose him for a friend. And yet it is certain that those who lived with him did not judge him as we do. They loved him, and felt themselves from the first inclined to love him. That general good-will that he inspired, that determination of every one to pardon or not to see his defects, those lively friendships that he called forth, are evidences that it is impossible to resist, whatever surprise they may cause us. There was, then, about this personage something else than we see; he must have possessed a kind of attraction that is inexplicable to us, which was personal to him, and which has disappeared with him. For this reason it is no longer possible for us to understand thoroughly that strange attraction that he exercised at first sight on all his contemporaries. We can, however, form some idea of it, and the writers who knew him, especially Cicero, give a glimpse of some of those brilliant or solid qualities by which

---

[1] It is the saying of Tacitus : *pessimum veri affectus venenum sua cuique utilitas.*

he gained over those who approached him. I shall enumerate them according to their testimony, and if they still do not seem sufficient to justify altogether the number of his friendships and their ardour, we must join to them in thought that personal charm that it is impossible now to define or recover because it vanished with himself.

Firstly, he had a good deal of cultivation, everybody agrees about that, and a sort of cultivation especially agreeable to the society that he frequented. He was not solely one of those pleasant triflers who charm for a moment on a passing acquaintance, but who have not the qualifications for a longer connection. He was a person of many attainments and solid knowledge ; not that he was a man of deep learning, this title is not a great recommendation in the intercourse of society ; Cicero thought that people like Varro, who are perfect mines of knowledge, are not always amusing, and relates that when the latter came to see him at Tusculum he did not tear his mantle in trying to retain him.[1] But, without being really a scholar, Atticus had touched on everything in his studies, the fine arts, poetry, grammar, philosophy, and history. Upon all these subjects he possessed just and sometimes original ideas ; he could discuss matters with learned men without too great disadvantage, and he always had some curious detail to tell those who were not so. Pascal would have called him a cultivated gentleman (*honnête homme*) ; in everything he was an intelligent and enlightened amateur. Now, for several reasons, the knowledge that an amateur acquires is of the kind most current in society. Firstly, as he does not study according to rule, he interests himself above all in curiosities ; he learns by preference racy and novel details, and it is precisely these that people of society want to know. Besides, the very multiplicity of the studies which tempt him, prevents him

[1] *Ad Att.* xiii. 33.

exhausting any; his caprice always carries him off elsewhere before he has thoroughly examined anything. The result is that he knows a great many things, and always within the limits in which it pleases men of the world to know them. In fact, the characteristic of the amateur is to do everything, even what he only does for a moment, with enthusiasm. As it is a personal taste that draws him to his studies, and as he only continues them as long as they interest him, his language is more lively when he speaks of them, his tone freer and more original, and consequently more agreeable, than that of scholars by profession. Such is the notion we must form of the learning of Atticus. It was too extensive for his conversation ever to become monotonous; it was not deep enough to run the risk of being tedious; it was, in fine, living, for when things are done with enthusiasm it is natural to speak of them with interest. This is what made his conversation so attractive, and this is how he charmed the most fastidious and least favourably disposed minds. He was still quite young when the aged Sulla, who had no reason to like him, met him at Athens. He took so much pleasure in hearing him read Greek and Latin verses and talk about literature, that he would not leave him, and wished by all means to take him back with him to Rome. Long after, Augustus felt the same charm; he was never tired of hearing Atticus talk, and when he could not go to see him, he wrote to him every day simply to receive his answers, and thus to continue, in some sort, those long conversations with which he was so delighted.

We can imagine, then, that the first time people met this accomplished man they felt themselves drawn towards him by the charm of his conversation. In proportion as he was better known, other and more solid qualities were discovered, which retained those whom his culture had attracted. In the first place there was a great security in his intercourse.

Although he was connected with people holding very diverse opinions, and though, through them, he had the secrets of all parties, he was never reproached with having betrayed these to anybody. We cannot see that he ever furnished a serious cause to any of his friends to keep aloof from him, or that any of his connections were broken otherwise than by death. This intercourse, so secure, was at the same time very easy. No one was ever more indulgent and accommodating. He took care not to weary by his demands or to repulse by bluntness. Those storms which so often troubled the friendship of Cicero and Brutus were not to be feared in his. It was rather one of those calm and uniform intimacies which grow stronger from day to day by their regular continuance. It was this especially that must have charmed those politicians who were oppressed and fatigued by that bustling activity which used up their lives. On coming out of this whirlwind of business, they were happy to find, at a few paces from the Forum, that peaceful house on the Quirinal into which outside quarrels did not enter, and to go and chat for a moment with that even-tempered and accomplished man who always received them with the same smile, and in whose good-will they had such a tranquil confidence.

But nothing, assuredly, could have won him so many friends as his readiness to oblige them. This was inexhaustible, and it could not be asserted that it was interested, since, contrary to custom, he gave much and demanded nothing. Here again is one of the reasons why his friendships were so lasting, for it is always this sort of interchange that we think we have a right to demand, and the comparisons that we make, in spite of ourselves, between good offices which we render and those which we receive, which in the end disturb the most firm friendships. Atticus, who knew this well, had so contrived as to have need of nobody. He was rich, he never had law-suits, he did not

seek public employments, so that a friend who was determined to recompense the services he had received could
never find the opportunity,[1] and remained always under
obligations to him, and his debt continued to increase, for
Atticus never wearied of being useful. We have an easy
means of appreciating the extent of this serviceableness, to
see it close, and, so to say at work, namely, to rapidly recall
the services of all sorts that he had rendered Cicero during
their long intimacy. Cicero had much need of a friend
like Atticus. He was one of those clever men who cannot
reckon; when his account-books were presented to him he
would gladly have said, like his pupil, Pliny the Younger,
that he was used to another sort of literature : *aliis sum
chartis, aliis litteris initiatus.* Atticus became his man of
business; we know his talent for this profession. He leased
Cicero's property very dear, saved as much as he could out
of the income and paid the most pressing debts. When
he discovered new ones, he dared to scold his friend, who
hastened to reply very humbly that he would be more careful for the future. Atticus, who did not much believe this,
set to work to make up the deficit. He went to see the
wealthy Balbus or the other great bankers of Rome with
whom he had business relations. If the calamities of the
times made it difficult to get credit, he did not hesitate to
dip into his own purse. Those who know him will not think
this generosity without merit. When Cicero wished to buy
some estate, Atticus at first would get angry ; but if his friend
did not give way, he quickly went to visit it and discuss the
price. If it was a question of building some elegant villa,
Atticus lent his architect, corrected the plans, and overlooked

---

[1] It must be remarked, however, that the last letter that we have from
Cicero to Atticus (xvi. 16) contains a proof of the very active steps that
Cicero took to save a part of the fortune of Atticus which was endangered
after the death of Caesar.

the work. When the house was built, it had to be adorned, and Atticus would send to Greece for statues. He excelled in selecting them, and Cicero was inexhaustible in his praises of the Hermathenae in Pentelican marble that he had procured for him. In a villa of Cicero, we can well understand that the library was not forgotten, and it was from Atticus again that the books came. He traded in them, and kept the handsomest for his friend. The books being bought, it was necessary to arrange them, so Atticus sent his librarian Tyrannion with his workmen, who painted the shelves, pasted together the detached leaves of papyrus, put the labels on the rolls, and arranged the whole in such good order that Cicero, enchanted, wrote: "Since Tyrannion has arranged my books one would say that the house has a soul."[1]

But Atticus did not stop at these services, which we might call external; he penetrated into the home, he knew all its secrets. Cicero kept nothing from him, and confided to him unreservedly all his domestic griefs. He tells him about the violent temper of his brother and the follies of his nephew; he consults him on the vexations that his wife and son cause him. When Tullia was of an age to marry, it was Atticus who sought her a husband. The one he proposed was the son of a rich and well-conducted knight. "Return," he said sagely to Cicero, "return to your old flock." Unfortunately he was not listened to. They preferred to the rich financier a broken-down nobleman, who squandered Tullia's dowry and forced her to leave him. When Tullia was dead, of grief perhaps, Atticus went to the nurse's to visit the little child she had left, and took care that it wanted for nothing. At the same time Cicero gave him plenty of occupation with his two divorces. After he had divorced his first wife, Terentia, it was Atticus whom he charged to get her to make a will in his favour. It was to him also

[1] *Ad Att.* iv. 8.

that he gave the disagreeable commission to remove the second, Publilia, when she was determined to forcibly re-enter the home of her husband, who would have nothing more to do with her.

These are doubtless great services; he rendered others still more delicate, still more appreciated. It was to him that Cicero entrusted what was most dear to him in the world, his literary glory. He communicated his works to him as soon as he had written them, he took his advice in making corrections, and waited for his decision to publish them. Thus he treated him as a friend with whom one feels at home, and to whom one unbosoms oneself completely. Although he was eager that his eloquence should be taken seriously, when he was sure of being heard by Atticus only, he made no scruple of joking about himself and his works. He introduced him without reserve to all the secrets of the craft, and showed him the receipts for his most popular effects. "This time, said he gaily, I employed the whole scent-box of Isocrates, and all the caskets of the disciples." [1] Nothing can be more curious than the way in which he related to him one day, one of his greatest oratorical successes. It was a question of celebrating the fame of the great consulship, a subject upon which, as we know, he was inexhaustible. That day he had a reason for speaking with more brilliancy than usual. Pompey was present; now Pompey had the weakness to be jealous of Cicero's glory. It was a good opportunity to enrage him, and Cicero took care not to neglect it. "When my turn came to speak, he writes to Atticus, immortal gods ! what rein I gave myself ! What pleasure I took in loading myself with praises in the presence of Pompey, who had never heard me extol my consulship ! If I ever called to my aid periods, enthymemes, metaphors, and all the other figures of rhetoric,

[1] *Ad Att.* ii. 1.

it was then. I did not speak, I shouted, for it was a question of my stock subjects, the wisdom of the senate, the good-will of the knights, the union of all Italy, the smothered remains of the conspiracy, peace and plenty re-established, etc. You know my thunders when I speak of these subjects. They were so fine that day that I have no need to tell you more about them; you may often have heard the like at Athens!"[1] It is impossible to quiz one-self with greater lightheartedness. Atticus repaid these confidences by the trouble he took for the success of his friend's works. As he had seen their birth, and had busied himself with them before they were known to the public, he almost regarded himself as their parent. It was he who took upon himself to start them in the world and make them succeed. Cicero says that he was admirably well skilled in this, and it does not surprise us. The means he most frequently employed to create a good opinion of them, was to have the finest passages read by his best readers to the clever men whom he assembled round his table. Cicero, who knew the usual frugality of his repasts, begged him to deviate from it a little on these occasions. "Have a care, he writes to him, to treat your guests well, for if they are in a bad humour with you, they will vent it on me."[2] It was natural that Cicero should be extremely grateful for all these services; but it would be judging him ill to suppose that he was only attached to him for the benefits he received from him. He really loved him, and all his letters are full of evidences of the most sincere affection. He was always happy with him; he was never tired of associating with him; he had scarcely left him than he ardently wished to see him again. "May I die, he wrote to him, if either my house at Tusculum, where I feel so comfortable, or the Isles of the Blest could please me without you!"[3] What-

[1] *Ad Att.* i. 14.   [2] *Ibid* xvi. 3.   [3] *Ibid.* xii. 3.

ever pleasure he experienced at being *fêted*, applauded, flattered, at having around him an obsequious and admiring multitude, in the midst of this crowd and noise he always turned with regret towards his absent friend. " With all these people, he tells him, I feel myself more alone than if I had only you." [1] All these people, in fact, are composed of political friends who change with circumstances, whom a common interest brings to you, and a rival ambition takes away again ; with them Cicero is obliged to be reserved and careful, which is a torture for such an open-hearted nature. On the other hand, he can tell Atticus everything, and confide in him without restraint. So he hastens to demand his presence when the least annoyance happens to him. " I want you, he writes to him, I have need of you, I am waiting for you. I have a thousand things that disturb and vex me, and a single walk with you will relieve me." [2] We should never end if we were to collect all those charming expressions of which the correspondence is full, and in which his heart plainly speaks. They leave no doubt about Cicero's feelings ; they prove that he regarded Atticus not only as one of those steadfast and serious friends on whose support he could count, but also, which is more surprising, as a sensitive and tender soul : " You take your share, he tells him, in all the troubles of others." [3]

Here is something far removed from the notion we usually have of him, and yet we cannot resist such clear testimony. How can we contend that he had only a doubtful affection for his friends when we see all his friends contented with it ? Are we to be more exacting than they, and would it not be wronging men like Brutus and Cicero to suppose that they had been dupes so long without perceiving it ? On the other hand, how can we explain the fact that posterity, which only judges by the documents

[1] *Ad Att.* xii. 51.   [2] *Ibid.* i. 18.   [3] *Ibid.* xii. 14.

L

that the friends of Atticus have furnished it, draws from these very documents an opinion quite the reverse of that held by them? Evidently it is because posterity and contemporaries do not judge men from the same stand-point. We have seen that Atticus, who had made a rule not to engage in public affairs, did not think himself obliged to partake the dangers that his friends might run, through having taken part in them. He left them both the honours and the perils. Sensitive, obliging, devoted to them in the ordinary business of life, when a great political crisis occurred that compromised them, he stood aside, and left them to expose themselves alone. Now, when we look at the facts from a distance, and are separated from them, as we are, by several centuries, we only perceive the most important events, and especially the political revolutions, that is to say, precisely those circumstances with which the friendship of Atticus had nothing to do. Hence the severe judgment we pronounce upon it. But his contemporaries judged otherwise. Those great crises are, after all, but rare and passing exceptions; without doubt contemporaries are much struck by them, but they are still more impressed by those numberless small incidents which make up everyday life, and which posterity does not perceive. They judge of a man's friendship by those services which are rendered every moment, and which are important by their mere number, much more than by any exceptional service which may be given on one of these great and rare occasions. This accounts for the fact that they had an opinion of Atticus so different from ours.

It is, beyond doubt, one of the characteristic traits of this person, that it was a necessity to him to have many friends, and that he took trouble to attract and retain them. We may refuse to admit, if we will, that this need was, with him, the effect of a generous and sympathetic nature, that it came from what Cicero admirably calls "the impulse of the soul that desires to love;" but, even supposing that he only thought of occupying and filling up his life, we must acknowledge that to fill it up in this manner is not a mark of a vulgar nature. This refined Epicurean, this master in the art of living at ease, knew "that life is no longer life if we cannot repose on the affection of a friend." [1] He had given up the excitement of political strife, the triumphs of eloquence, the joys of satisfied ambition, but, as a compensation, he was determined to enjoy all the pleasures of private life. The more he confined and limited himself to it, the more particular and refined he became with regard to the pleasures it could give; as he had only left himself these, he wished to enjoy them fully, to relish them, to live on them. He needed friends, and among them the greatest minds, the noblest souls of his time. He expended all that energy which he did not employ in anything else, in procuring for himself those pleasures of society that Bossuet calls the greatest good of human life. Atticus enjoyed this good even beyond his desires, and friendship generously repaid him for all the trouble he had taken for it. It was his single passion; he was able to satisfy it completely, and friendship, after having adorned his life, has shed a lustre on his name.

III.

Atticus appears in a favourable light in private life. He is less fortunate when we study the course he followed in public affairs. On this point he has not been spared blame, and it is not easy to defend him.

We should not however be very unfavourable to him if

---

[1] *Cui potest esse vita vitalis, ut ait Ennius, qui non in amici mutua benevolentia conquiescat?* (Cicero, *De Amicit.* 6.)

we judged his conduct entirely according to the ideas of
our days. Opinion has become less severe now on those
who openly make profession of living apart from politics.
So many men aspire to govern their country, and it has
become so difficult to make choice among this multitude,
that we are tempted to look kindly upon those who have
not this ambition. Far from being blamed, they are called
moderate and wise ; they form an exception which is encouraged in order to lessen the number of aspirants. At
Rome they thought otherwise, and it is not difficult to find
reasons for this difference. There, what we may call the
political body was in reality very circumscribed. Besides
the slaves, who did not count, and the common people, who
contented themselves with giving or rather selling their
votes in the elections, and whose greatest privilege it was
to be entertained at the expense of the candidates, and fed
at the expense of the public treasury, there remained only
a few families of ancient lineage or more recent celebrity
who divided all public employments among themselves.
The aristocracy of birth and of fortune was not very
numerous, and scarcely sufficed to furnish the required
number of officials of all sorts to govern the world. It was
necessary therefore that no one should refuse to take his
part, and to live in retirement was considered a desertion.
It is not the same in our democracy. As all offices are
open to everybody, and as, thanks to the diffusion of
education, men worthy to occupy them may arise in all
ranks, we need no longer fear lest the absence of a few
quiet people, friends of peace and repose, will make a
sensible and regrettable gap in the serried ranks of those
who struggle from all quarters for power. Moreover, we
think now that there are many other ways of serving one's
country besides public life. Romans of high birth knew
no other; they looked upon commerce as a not very

honourable means[1] that a private man might employ to
make his fortune, and did not see what the state might
gain by it ; literature seemed an agreeable but trivial
pastime, and they did not understand its social importance.
It follows that among them, a man of a certain rank could
only find one honourable mode of employing his activity
and being useful to his country, namely, to fill political
offices.[2] To do anything else was, according to their ideas,
to do nothing ; they gave the name of idlers to the most
laborious scholars, and it did not come into their heads
that there was anything worth the trouble of occupying a
citizen's time beyond the service of the state. All the ancient
Romans thought thus, and they would have experienced a
strange surprise if they had seen any one claim the
right, as Atticus did, not to serve his country within the
limits of his powers and talents. Assuredly Cato, who
never rested, and who, at ninety years of age, bravely
quitted his villa at Tusculum to go and accuse Servius
Galba, the butcher of the Lusitanians, would have thought
that to remain in his house on the Quirinal, or on his estate
in Epirus in the midst of his books and statues, while the
fate of Rome was being decided in the Forum or at
Pharsalia, was to commit the same crime as to remain in
his tent on the day of battle.

This systematic abstention of Atticus was not, then, a
Roman custom ; he had it from the Greeks. In those
small ungovernable republics of Greece, where they knew
no repose, and which passed constantly and without warning
from the sternest tyranny to the most unbridled licence, we
can understand that quiet and studious men should have

[1] *T. Liv.* xxi. 63 : *Quaestus omnibus patribus indecorus visus.*
[2] Scipio says so in the *Republic* (i. 22) : *Quum mihi sit unum opus
hoc a parentibus majoribusque meis relictum, atque administratio rei
publicae,* etc.

grown weary of all this sterile agitation, and ceased to desire public employments which were only obtained by flattering the capricious multitude, and only kept on condition of obeying it. Moreover, what value could this power, so hardly acquired, so seldom preserved, have, when it was necessary to share it with the most obscure demagogues? was it really worth while to take so much trouble in order to become the successor or the colleague of Cleon? At the same time that weariness and disgust kept honourable men aloof from these paltry struggles, philosophy, more studied every day, communicated to its disciples a sort of pride which led them to the same result. Men who passed their time in meditating upon God and the world, and who endeavoured to understand the laws that govern the universe, did not deign to descend from these heights to govern states a few leagues square. Thus they constantly discussed in the schools, whether a man should occupy himself with public affairs, whether the sage ought to seek public office, and whether the active or the contemplative life was the better. A few philosophers hesitatingly gave the preference to active life, the greater number sustained the opposite opinion, and under cover of these discussions many men thought themselves authorized to create a sort of elegant indolence in voluptuous retreats embellished by letters and the arts, where they lived happily while Greece was perishing.

Atticus followed their example. Importing this custom from Greece into Rome, he openly announced his resolution not to take part in political discussions. He began by adroitly keeping aloof during all those quarrels that continually agitated Rome from the time of Cicero's consulship to the civil wars. At the very moment when these struggles were most active he frequented all parties, he had friends on all sides, and found in these widespread friendships a new pretext for remaining neutral. Atticus was more than sixty years old when Caesar passed the Rubicon, an age when the obligation of military service ceased among the Romans. This was another reason for remaining quiet, and he did not fail to use it. "I have taken my discharge,"[1] he replied to those who wished to enrol him. He held the same course, and with the same success, after the death of Caesar; but he then disappointed public opinion still more. He was so well known to be the friend of Brutus that it was thought he would not hesitate to take his side this time. Cicero himself, who ought to have known him, reckoned upon it; but Atticus was not inconsistent with himself, and took advantage of an important occasion to let the public know that he would not be drawn in against his will. While Brutus was raising an army in Greece, some knights, his friends, started the idea of raising a subscription among the richest men of Rome to give him the means of maintaining his soldiers. They applied at first to Atticus, whose name they wished to put at the head of the list. Atticus bluntly refused to subscribe. He answered that his fortune was at the service of Brutus, if he had need of it, and asked him as a friend, but he declared at the same time that he would take no part in a political manifestation, and his refusal caused the failure of the subscription. At the same time, true to his habit of flattering all parties, he welcomed Fulvia, Antony's wife, as well as Volumnius the superintendent of his workmen, and, sure of having friends everywhere, he waited for the result of the struggle without much fear.

The strangest thing is that this man, while so persistent in remaining neutral, was not indifferent. His biographer gives him this praise, that he always belonged to the best party,[2] and that is true; only he made it a rule not

[1] Corn. Nep. *Attic.* 7 : *Usus es aetatis vacatione.*   [2] Nep. *Attic.* 6.

to serve his party; he was contented with giving it his
good wishes. But these good wishes were the warmest
imaginable. He had, though we should scarcely believe
it, political passions which he dared to express in private
with incredible vigour. He hated Caesar so much that he
went as far as to blame Brutus for having permitted his
interment.[1] He would have wished, no doubt, as the most
furious demanded, that his corpse should be thrown into the
Tiber. Thus he did not abstain from having preferences,
and showing them to his most intimate friends. His reserve
only began when it was necessary to act. He never consented to take part in the struggle; but if he did not share
its danger he felt at least all its excitement. We smile at
seeing him become animated and excited as if he were a
real combatant; he takes his share in all successes and
all reverses, he congratulates the energetic, he entreats
the lukewarm, and even scolds the faltering, and permits
himself to advise and reprimand those who seem to him, who
did not act at all, to act too languidly. It is amusing to
hear the reproaches he addresses to Cicero when he sees
him hesitating to go and join Pompey; he adopts the most
pathetic tone, he reminds him of his actions and his words,
he entreats him in the name of his glory, he quotes his
own words to him to persuade him.[2] This excess of
audacity into which he allows himself to be drawn for
others, sometimes produces rather comic incidents. At
the moment when Pompey had just shut himself up in
Brundusium, Atticus, moved by the most lively grief, wished
for some attempts to be made to save him, and went so
far as to ask Cicero to do some striking action before
leaving. "It only requires a banner, said he, every one
will flock to it."[3] The worthy Cicero felt himself quite
excited by these lively exhortations of his friend, and there

[1] *Ad Att.* xiv. 10.   [2] *Ibid.* viii. 2.   [3] *Ibid.* x. 15.

were times when he was tempted to be bold, and when he
only demanded the opportunity to strike a heavy blow.
The opportunity came, and he relates in the following
words how he took advantage of it. "As I arrived at my
house at Pompeii, your friend Ninnius came to tell me that
the centurions of three cohorts who were there, asked to see
me the next day, as they wished to deliver up the place to
me. Do you know what I did? I went away before daylight in order not to see them. What are, in fact, three
cohorts? And if there had been more, what should I have
done with them?"[1] This was speaking like a prudent
man and one who knows himself well. As for Atticus we
ask whether he were really sincere in the ardour that he
showed for his cause when we see him obstinately refuse to
serve it. Those grand passions that confine themselves
so prudently in the breast, and never show themselves outwardly, are with good reason suspected. Perhaps he only
wished to enliven a little that part of spectator that he
had reserved for himself by taking part, up to a certain
point, in the excitement of the struggle. The wise man of
Epicurus always remains on the serene heights whence he
tranquilly enjoys the view of shipwrecks and the spectacle
of human conflicts; but he enjoys them from too far off,
and the pleasure that he feels is diminished by the distance.
Atticus is more skilful and understands his pleasure better;
he goes into the midst of the fight itself, he sees it close, and
takes part in it, while always sure that he will retire in time.

The only difficulty he found was to make everybody
accept his neutrality. This difficulty was so much the
greater for him as his conduct especially offended those
whose esteem he was the most anxious to preserve. The
republican party, which he preferred, and in which he
reckoned most friends, was much less inclined to pardon

[1] *Ad Att.* x. 16.

him than that of Caesar. In antiquity itself, and still more in our days, great praise has been bestowed on that saying of Caesar at the beginning of the civil war : " He who is not against me is for me," and the contrary saying of Pompey has been much blamed : " He who is not for me is against me." However, looking at things fairly, this praise and this blame appear equally unreasonable. Each of the two rivals, when he expressed himself thus, speaks in character, and their words were suggested by their position. Caesar, however we may judge him, came to overturn the established order, and he naturally was grateful to those who gave him a free hand. What more could he reasonably ask of them? In reality, those who did not hinder him served him. But lawful order, established order, considers it has the right to call upon every one to defend it, and to regard as enemies all who do not respond to its appeal, for it is a generally recognized principle that he who does not bring help to the law when openly attacked before him, makes himself the accomplice of those who violate it. It was, then, natural that Caesar, on arriving at Rome, should welcome Atticus and those who had not gone to Pharsalia, as it was also that those in Pompey's camp should be very much irritated against them. Atticus was not much moved by this anger : he let them talk, those thoughtless and fiery young men who could not console themselves for having left Rome, and who threatened to avenge themselves on those who had remained. What did these menaces matter to him? He was sure that he had preserved the esteem of the two most important and most respected men of the party, and he could oppose their testimony to all the indignation of the rest. Cicero and Brutus, notwithstanding the strength of their convictions, never blamed him for his conduct, and they appear to have approved of his not taking part in public affairs. " I know the honourable and

noble character of your sentiments, said Cicero to him
one day when Atticus thought it necessary to defend himself ; there is only one difference between us, and that is, that
we have arranged our lives differently. I know not what
ambition made me desire public office, while motives in
no way blameworthy have made you seek an honourable
leisure ! " [1]   Again, Brutus wrote to him towards the end of
his life : " I am far from blaming you, Atticus; your age, your
character, your family, everything makes you love repose." [2]

This good-will on the part of Brutus and Cicero is so
much the more surprising, as they knew very well the
mischief such an example might do to the cause that they
defended. The republic did not perish by the audacity of
its enemies alone, but also by the apathy of its partisans.
The sad spectacle it offered for fifty years, the public sale of
dignities, the scandalous violence that took place on the
Forum every time a new law was discussed, the battles that
at each new election stained the Campus Martius with
blood, those armies of gladiators needed for self-defence, all
those shameful disorders, all those base intrigues in which
the last strength of Rome was used up, had completely discouraged honest men. They held aloof from public life ;
they had no more relish for power since they were forced
to dispute it with men ready for every violence. It required
Cato's courage to return to the Forum after having been
received with showers of stones, and having come out with
torn robe and bleeding head. Thus, the more the audacious
attempted, the more the timid let them alone, and from the
time of the first triumvirate and the consulship of Bibulus,
it was evident that the apathy of honest men would deliver
the republic over to the ambitious nobles who desired to

[1] *Ad Att.* i. 17.   See also *de Offic.* i. 21, and especially i. 26.
This last passage evidently contains an allusion to Atticus.
[2] *Epist. Brut.* i. 17.

dominate it. Cicero saw this clearly, and in his letters
never ceases his bitter railleries against those indolent rich
men, doting on their fish-ponds, who consoled themselves
for the ruin that they foresaw by thinking that they
would save at least their lampreys. In the introduction to
the *De Republica* he attacks with admirable energy those
who, being discouraged themselves, try to discourage others,
who maintain that a man has the right to withhold his services
from his country, and to consult his own welfare while
neglecting that of his country. " Let us not listen, says he
in finishing, to that signal for retreat that sounds in our
ears, and would recall those who have already gone to the
front."[1] Brutus also knew the evil of which the republic
was dying, and complained more than once of the weakness
and discouragement of the Romans. "Believe me, he
wrote, we are too much afraid of exile, death, and
poverty."[2] It was Atticus to whom he wrote these noble
words, and yet he does not dream of applying them to
him ! What strange charm then did this man possess, what
influence did his friendship exercise, that these two great
patriots have thus belied themselves in his favour, and have
so freely pardoned in him what they condemned in others ?

The more we think of it, the less can we imagine the
reasons he could give them to justify his conduct. If he
had been one of those scholars who, wedded to their researches in history or philosophy, only dwell in the past
or the future, and are not really the contemporaries of the
people with whom they live, we might have understood his
not taking part in their struggles since he held himself aloof
from their passions ; but we know that, on the contrary, he
had the most lively relish for all the small agitations and
obscure intrigues of the politics of his time. He was anxious
to know them, he excelled in unravelling them, this was the

[1] *De Rep.* i. 2.   [2] *Epist. Brut.* i. 17.

regular food of his inquisitive mind, and Cicero applied to him by choice when he wished to know about such matters. He was not one of those gentle and timid souls, made for reflection and solitude, who have not the energy necessary for active life. This man of business, of clear and decided judgment, would, on the contrary, have made an excellent statesman. To be useful to his country he would only have needed to employ in its service a little of that activity and intelligence he had used to enrich himself, and Cicero was right in thinking that he had the political temperament. And, finally, he had not even left himself the poor resource of pretending that he sided with no party because all parties were indifferent to him, and that, having no settled opinions, he did not know which side to take. He had said the contrary a hundred times in his letters to Cicero and Brutus; he had charmed them a hundred times by the ardour of his republican zeal, and yet he remained quiet when the opportunity came of serving this government to which he said he was so much attached. Instead of making a single effort to retard its fall, he was only careful not to be crushed under its ruins. But if he did not try to defend it, did he, at least, pay it that last respect of appearing to regret it? Did he show in any way that, although he had not appeared in the combat, he felt that he shared in the defeat? Did he know, while he grew old under a power to which he was forced to submit, how to retire in a dignified sadness which forces respect even from a conqueror? No, and it is assuredly this that is most repugnant to us in his life; he showed an unpleasant eagerness to accommodate himself to the new order of things. The day after he had himself been proscribed, we see him become the friend of the proscribers. He lavishes all the charms of his mind on them, assiduously frequents their houses, attends all their *fêtes.* However habituated we may be to see him welcome all triumphant governments, we cannot get used to the notion that the friend of Brutus and the confidant of Cicero should become so quickly the familiar of Antony and Octavius. Those most disposed to indulgence will certainly think that those illustrious friendships created duties which he did not fulfil, and that it was a treason to the memory of these men who had honoured him with their friendship, to choose just their executioners as their successors.

If we are not disposed to show ourselves as indulgent towards him as Cicero and Brutus, with still more reason shall we not partake in the naïve enthusiasm that he inspires in Cornelius Nepos. This indulgent biographer is only struck, in the whole life of his hero, with the happy chance by which he escaped such great dangers. He cannot get over his surprise when he sees him, from the time of Sulla to that of Augustus, withdraw himself from so many civil wars, survive so many proscriptions, and preserve himself so skilfully where so many others perished. "If we overwhelm with praises, says he, the pilot who saves his vessel from the rocks and tempests, ought we not to consider admirable the prudence of a man who in the midst of those violent political storms succeeded in saving himself?"[1] Admiration is here too strong a word. We keep that for those courageous men who made their actions agree with their principles, and who knew how to die to defend their opinions. Their ill success does not injure them in our esteem, and, whatever the friend of Atticus may say, there are fortunate voyages from which less honour is drawn than from some shipwrecks. The sole praise that he thoroughly deserves is that which his biographer gives him with so much complacency, namely, that he was the most adroit man of that time; but we know that there are other forms of praise which are of more value than this.

[1] *Attic.* 10.

CAELIUS

THE ROMAN YOUTH IN THE TIME OF CAESAR

THERE is perhaps no more curious figure than that of
Caelius in the history we are studying. His life has a
special interest for us. He was not, like Brutus, a brilliant
exception among his contemporaries; on the contrary, he
quite belongs to his time; he lived as others lived around
him. All the young men of that time, the Curios, the Dola-
bellas, resemble him. They are all, like him, corrupted
early, little concerned about their dignity, prodigal of their
wealth, friends of facile pleasures; they all throw themselves
into public life as soon as they can, with a restless ambition
and great needs to satisfy, and with few scruples and no
beliefs. His history, then, is that of all the rest, and the
advantage we find in studying it is that we know at once
the whole generation of which he formed part. Now, thanks
to Cicero, this study is easy for us. Notwithstanding so
many differences in conduct and principles, Cicero always
felt a singular inclination for Caelius; he liked the conversation of this clever man who laughed at everything, and
was more at ease with him than with people like Cato or
Brutus, whose severity somewhat alarmed him. He defended
him in the law courts when a woman whom he had loved
tried to ruin him, and this speech of his is certainly one of
the most interesting that remain to us. Later, when he
was obliged to go to Cilicia, he chose him for his political

correspondent. By a happy chance Caelius' letters have come down to us with those of Cicero, and there are none in all this collection that are more witty and more racy. Let us collect all the details scattered through them; let us try, in collecting them, to reproduce an account of Caelius, and by it to gain an idea of what the Roman youth of that time was. It is not without interest to know them, for they played an important part, and Caesar made use of them more especially for the revolution that he wished to accomplish.

I.

Caelius did not come of an illustrious family. He was the son of a Roman knight of Puteoli, who had been in trade and acquired great wealth in Africa. His father, who had all his life no other concern than that of enriching himself, showed, as often happens, more ambition for his son than for himself: he wished him to become a politician, and as he saw that dignities were reached only through eloquence, he took him betimes to Cicero, that he might make him a great orator, if it were possible.

It was not yet the custom to confine young men to the schools of the rhetoricians, and to be contented with exercising them in imaginary cases. As soon as they had assumed the *toga virilis*, that is, when they were about sixteen years old, no time was lost in taking them to some statesman of reputation, whom they did not leave. Admitted to his most intimate society, they listened to his conversations with his friends, his disputations with his adversaries; they saw him prepare himself in silence for the great battles of eloquence, they followed him into the basilicas and the Forum, they heard him pleading causes or speaking to the assembled people, and when they had become capable of speaking themselves, they made their first appearance at his side

and under his patronage. Tacitus much regrets this manly
education, which, placing a young man under the conditions
of reality instead of retaining him among the fictions of
rhetoric, gave him a taste for real and natural eloquence
which strengthened him, by throwing him from the first into
the midst of real contests, and, according to his expression,
taught him war on the field of battle, *pugnare in praelio
discebant.*[1] This education, however, had its dangers. It
taught him things that it is better to be ignorant of for a
long time, it familiarized him with the scandalous and
corrupt sights that public life usually offers, it gave him
a too rapid maturity and inflamed him with precocious ambition. Must not a young man of sixteen, who thus lived
in intimacy with old and unscrupulous statesmen, and to
whom were laid bare without precaution the basest manœuvres of parties, must he not have lost something of the
generosity and sensitiveness of his age? Was it not to be
feared that this corrupting intercourse might end by giving
him a taste for intrigue, for the worship of success, an unbridled love of power, the desire to attain a high position
quickly and by any means, and as, generally, the worst means
are also the quickest, the temptation to employ them by
preference? This is what happened to Caelius. For three
entire years, three honest and laborious years, he did not
leave Cicero; but he perceived at length, that a young man
like himself, who had his political fortune to make, would
gain more with those who wished to destroy the government
than with him who wished to preserve it, and he abandoned
Cicero to attach himself to Catiline. The change was
sudden, but Caelius never took the trouble to delay about
these transitions. Henceforth, we can easily understand, his
life took another turn; he became a seditious and turbulent
man, whose biting speech in the Forum and violence in the

[1] *De Orat.* 34.

M

Campus Martius were dreaded. At the election of a pontif he struck a senator. When he was appointed quaestor, every one accused him of having bought his votes. Not content with disturbing the comitia at Rome, we see him stirring up a popular tumult at Naples, we do not know why. At the same time, he did not neglect his pleasures. The debaucheries of those noisy young men of whom he was one, continually disturbed the public peace. It is said that the streets of Rome were unsafe when they returned at night from their suppers, and that, after the manner of those giddy fellows that Plautus and Terence depict, they molested honest women whom they met on their road. All these follies did not go on without great expense, and the father of Caelius, although he was rich, was not of a temper to be always paying. No doubt at this time the honest merchant of Puteoli must have regretted his ambition for his son, and thought it cost him dear to have wished to make him a politician. Caelius, on his side, was not of a temper to put up with reprimands easily; he left the paternal house, and, under pretext of being nearer the Forum and business, rented a lodging on the Palatine, in the house of the famous tribune Appius Clodius, for ten thousand sesterces (£80). This was an important event in his life, for it was there that he became acquainted with Clodia.

If we relied on the evidence of Cicero we should have a very bad opinion of Clodia; but Cicero is a too partial witness to be altogether just, and the furious hatred he bore the brother renders him very much suspected when he speaks of the sister. Moreover, he partly contradicts himself when he tells us she had kept up relations with very honourable people, which would be very surprising if it were true that she had committed all the crimes that he lays to her charge. It is very difficult to believe that persons of consideration in the republic, and persons who were careful of their reputation, would have continued to see her if they had thought that she had poisoned her husband, and was the mistress of her brothers. Cicero, however, did not invent this; it was public rumour that he complacently repeated. Many people in Rome believed it, Clodia's enemies liked to repeat it, and mischievous verses were made about it which were written upon every wall. Clodia's reputation was, then, very bad, and it must be admitted that, notwithstanding some exaggerations, she partly deserved it. There is nothing to show that she killed her husband, as she was accused of doing; these accusations of poisoning were then widespread, and were accepted with incredible levity, but she had made him very unhappy during his life, and did not appear very much grieved at his death. It is doubtful, also, whatever Cicero may assert, that her brothers were her lovers, but it is unfortunately too certain that she had a good many others. The sole excuse that can be pleaded for her is that this way of living was then very general. Scandals of this kind had never been more common among the great ladies of Rome. Roman society was passing through a crisis whose causes, which go back a long way, deserve to be considered. We must say a few words about them, in order to account for the grave injury that public morals had received.

In a country where the family was respected as it was at Rome, women could not fail to have much importance. It was impossible that their influence, which was already so great within the house, should not attempt to show itself outside, and the honourable place they held in private life must one day tempt them to invade public life also. The ancient Romans, so jealous of their authority, had the consciousness of this danger, and neglected nothing in order to defend themselves against it. We know how they affected to treat women; there was no sort of unkind remarks they did

not make about them; they got them attacked on the stage
and mocked them even in their political speeches: [1] but we
must not mistake the sense of these railleries and pity the
objects of them too much. They are only attacked thus
because they are feared, and all these pleasantries are not so
much insults as precautions.   These rough soldiers, these
rude peasants, have learnt, in living with them, how subtle
and enterprising their minds are, and in how many ways they
are more capable than themselves; consequently they take
a good deal of trouble to confine them to their households,
and even that does not suffice to reassure them; in the
household itself they must be subjugated and bridled. They
affect to think and to say that they are weak and untamed
beings (*indomita animalia*), incapable of governing themselves alone, and they hasten to provide for their management.   They are kept, under this pretext, in a continual
state of tutelage; they are always " under the hand " of their
father, brother, or husband; they cannot sell, buy, trade, or
do anything without a council to assist them : in acting thus
the men pretend they are protecting them, in reality it is
themselves they are protecting against them.   Cato, their
great enemy, ingenuously admits it in a moment of frankness.   " Remember," Livy makes him say *à propos* of the
lex Oppia, " all those regulations our ancestors made to
subject wives to their husbands.   Shackled as they are, you

---

[1] In the time of the Gracchi, the Censor Metellus thus expressed
himself in a speech in which he vigorously attacked bachelors : " Citizens, if we could live without wives we should all dispense with that
encumbrance (*omnes ea molestia careremus*) ; but, as nature has willed
it to be as impossible to do without them as it is disagreeable to live
with them, let us sacrifice the charms of so short a life to the interests
of the republic, which must always endure." This way of encouraging
men to marry seemed apparently very efficacious, since, at the time
when men married less than ever, Augustus thought he ought to have
the speech of old Metellus read to the people.

have trouble to manage them. What will happen if you give them their liberty, if you allow them to enjoy the same rights as yourselves? Do you think you will then be their masters? The day they become your equals they will be your superiors."[1] This day arrived just about the time of which we are treating. In the midst of the weakening of ancient usages, the laws against women were not more respected than others. Cicero says that the gallant lawyers furnished them with ingenious means to free themselves from these laws without appearing to violate them.[2] At the same time, men were accustomed to see them take a more important place in society, and to recognize their influence in the government of the republic. Almost all the politicians of that time are governed by their wives or by their mistresses, thus the innumerable gallantries of Caesar must have passed in the eyes of many people, as later those of Augustus did, for profound policy, as it might be supposed that he only sought to please the women in order to lead their husbands.

Thus, by the abolition of the old laws, and by the alteration of ancient maxims, women had become free. Now, it is to be remarked that, in general, the first use made of regained liberty is to abuse it. We cannot enjoy quietly the rights of which we have been long deprived, and the first moments of liberty bring a sort of intoxication that it is difficult to check. This is what happened to the Roman society of that time, and all these irregularities that we notice in the conduct of women then are partly explained by the allurements and intoxication of their new liberty. Those who love money, like Terentia, Cicero's wife, hasten to take advantage of the right of disposing of their fortune, that has been restored to them, they associate themselves with freedmen and agents for doubtful gains,

[1] Liv. xxxiv. 3.   [2] *Pro Muraen.* 12.

rob their husbands without scruple, and throw themselves
into speculations and trade, to which they bring, together
with an almost incredible rapacity, that taste for small
savings and economies which is natural to them.   Those
who prefer pleasure to wealth give themselves up to all
pleasures with a passionate eagerness.   The less bold
take advantage of the facilities of divorce to pass from one
amour to another under cover of the law.   Others do not
even take this trouble, and impudently flaunt their scandalous
behaviour.

Clodia was one of the latter; but among all her vices,
which she took no care to hide, we are forced to recognize
in her some good qualities.   She was not grasping; her
purse was open to her friends, and Caelius was not ashamed
to dip into it.   She liked clever men, and attracted them
to her house.   At one time she wished to persuade Cicero,
whose talents she much admired, to give up his foolish
Terentia for her and to marry her; but Terentia, who
suspected it, succeeded in mortally embroiling them.   An
old scholiast says that she danced better than it was proper
for an honest woman to do.[1]   This was not the only art
for which she had a taste, and it has been thought possible
to infer from a passage of Cicero that she also wrote verses.[2]
To cultivate letters, to seek out clever men, to like refined
and elegant pleasures, does not seem at first sight to be
blameworthy; on the contrary, these are among us the
qualities that a woman of society is obliged to possess or
to feign.   They thought otherwise at Rome, and, as the
courtesans alone had then the privilege of following this
free and accomplished life, every woman who sought this
ran the risk of being confounded with them, and of being
treated with the same rigour by public opinion; but Clodia

---

[1] Schol. Bob. *p. Sext.* ed. Or. p. 304.
[2] Schwab. *Quaest. Catull.* p. 77.

did not care for public opinion. She brought into her private conduct, into her affections, the same passionateness and the same ardour that her brother did into public life. Ready for all excesses, and not blushing to avow them, loving and hating furiously, incapable of self-control, and hating all restraint, she did not belie that great and haughty family from which she was descended, and even in her vices her blood was recognized. In a country where so much respect was shown for ancient customs, in that classic land of *decorum* (the thing and the word are Roman), Clodia took pleasure in shocking the established customs; she went out publicly with her male friends; she was accompanied by them in the public gardens or on the Appian road, constructed by her great ancestor. She boldly accosted people whom she knew; instead of timidly lowering her eyes as a well-brought-up matron should have done, she dared to speak to them (Cicero says that she even kissed them sometimes), and invited them to her repasts. Grave, staid, and rigid people were indignant; but the young, whom this freedom did not displease, were charmed, and went to dine with Clodia.[1]

Caelius was at that time one of the fashionable young men of Rome. Already he had a great reputation as an orator. He was dreaded for the satirical sharpness of his speech. He was bold to temerity, always ready to throw himself into the most perilous enterprises. He spent his money freely, and drew after him a train of friends and clients. Few men danced as well as he,[2] no one surpassed him in the art of dressing with taste, and the beauty and breadth of the purple band that bordered his toga were spoken of on all hands in Rome. All these qualities, the

[1] All these details, and those that follow, are taken from the *Pro Caelio* of Cicero.
[2] Macr. *Sat.* ii. 10.

serious as well as the trivial, were of a nature to attract
Clodia. Neighbourhood made their acquaintance more
easy, and she soon became the mistress of Caelius.

Cicero, notwithstanding his reserve, permits us to guess
the life they then led. He speaks in hints of those
brilliant *fêtes* that Clodia gave to her lover and to the
youth of Rome in her gardens on the banks of the Tiber;
but it seems that Baiae was the chief theatre of these
amours. Baiae had been for some time already the
regular rendezvous of the fashionable people of Rome
and Italy. The hot-springs that are found there in abund-
ance served as the occasion or pretext for these gatherings.
Some invalids went there for their health, and their presence
provided an excuse for a crowd of healthy people who
went there to amuse themselves. People flocked there
from the month of April, and during the fine season a
thousand light intrigues were carried on, the report of
which reached Rome. Grave folks took great care not to
be seen in this whirl of pleasure, and later Clodius accused
Cicero, as if it were a crime, simply of having passed through
it; but Caelius and Clodia were not anxious to hide themselves; consequently they gave themselves up without
restraint to all the pleasures that were to be found in that
country that Horace calls the most beautiful in the world.
All Rome talked of their races on the shore, the brilliancy
of their feasts and water-parties in boats carrying singers
and musicians. This is all that Cicero tells us, or rather
only gives us a glimpse of, for, contrary to his habit, and to
our great loss, he has for once in a way been discreet, in
order not to compromise his friend Caelius. Fortunately
we can learn more about this society and satisfy our
curiosity; to do so we have only to turn ourselves to
him who was, with Lucretius, the greatest poet of that time,
Catullus. Catullus lived among these persons who were so

well worthy of study, and had relations with them which
permitted him to depict them well. Everybody knows that
Lesbia whom his verses have immortalized ; but it is not
so well known that Lesbia was not one of those fictitious
persons that the elegiac poets often create. Ovid tells us that
this name covered that of a Roman lady, probably a great
lady, since he will not name her, and by his way of speaking
we see clearly that everybody then knew her.[1] Apuleius,
who lived much later, is less reticent, and he tells us that
Lesbia was Clodia.[2] Catullus, then, was the lover of Clodia,
and the rival of Caelius : he also frequented that house on
the Palatine, and those fine gardens on the Tiber, and his
verses complete our knowledge of that society of which he
was one of the heroes.

I said just now that Clodia did not love money with the
avidity of the women of gallantry of that time and of all
times. The history of Catullus proves this well. This
young provincial of Verona, although he belonged to an
honourable family, was not very rich, and after he had
lived a life of dissipation and pleasure for some time at
Rome, he had nothing left. His poor little estate was soon
deeply mortgaged. "It is not exposed, he says gaily,
either to the impetuous north wind, or to the fury of the
auster : it is a hurricane of debts that blows on it from all
sides. Oh! the horrible and pestilent wind!"[3] By the
picture that he draws of some of his friends, still poorer and
more indebted than himself, we see clearly that he could not
reckon upon them, and that his purse which was "full of
spiders" had no great help to expect from them. It was not,

[1] Ovid, *Trist.* ii. 427.
[2] Apul. *de Mag.* 10. A learned German, M. Schwab, in a book
that he has just published on Catullus (*Quaest. Catull.* 1862), seems to
me to have put the truth of this assertion of Apuleius beyond doubt.
[3] *Catull. Carm.* 26.

then, fortune or birth that Clodia loved in Catullus, but wit and talent. What attracted him in her, what he so passionately loved, was distinction and grace. These are not usually the qualities of women who live like Clodia; but, however low she might have descended, she was still a great lady. Catullus says so in an epigram in which he compares Lesbia to a celebrated beauty of that time—" Quintia is considered beautiful by many men. I think her tall, fair, erect: these are her attractions; I recognize them all. But that their union forms beauty, that I deny. There is nothing graceful in her, and in all that vast body there is not a spark of wit or charm. It is Lesbia who is beautiful, more beautiful than all, and she has so much grace that there is none left for the rest."[1]

A woman like Clodia, who had such a decided taste for clever people, must have been pleased to frequent the society in which Catullus lived. We see plainly, by what he relates to us of it, that there was none more witty and agreeable in Rome. It united writers and politicians, poets and noblemen, differing in position and fortune, but all friends of letters and pleasure. There were Cornificius, Quintilius Varus, Helvius Cinna, whose verses had then much reputation, Asinius Pollio, who was as yet only a youth of great promise; there was above all Licinius Calvus, at once statesman and poet, one of the most striking figures of that time, who, at twenty-one, had attacked Vatinius with so much vigour, that Vatinius, terrified, had turned towards his judges, saying: " If my opponent is a great orator, it does not follow that I am guilty!" In the same group we must place Caelius, who, by his wit and tastes, was worthy to belong to it, and over it Cicero the protector of all this brilliant youth, which was proud of his

---

[1] *Catull. Carm.* 86.

genius and renown, and which saluted in him, according to the expression of Catullus, the most eloquent of the sons of Romulus.

In these assemblies of clever men, of whom many were political personages, politics were not excluded; they were very republican, and from them issued the most violent epigrams against Caesar. We know the tone in which those of Catullus are written; Calvus had composed others which are lost, and which were, it is said, still more cutting. Literature, however, we can well understand, held in them at least as high a place as politics. They did not fail to laugh at bad writers from time to time, and in order to make an example, ceremoniously burnt the poems of Volusius. Sometimes, at the end of the repast, when wine and laughter had heated their brains, they sent each other poetic challenges; the tablets passed from hand to hand, and each wrote the most incisive verses he could make. But it was pleasure more than anything else that occupied them. All these poets and politicians were young and amorous, and whatever pleasure they may have found in rallying Volusius, or tearing Caesar to pieces, they preferred to sing their loves. It is this which has made them famous. The lyrical poetry of the Latins has nothing to compare with those short and charming pieces that Catullus wrote for Lesbia. Propertius mingles too much mythology with his sighs; Ovid is only an inspired debauchee, Catullus alone has tones that touch the heart, because he alone was mastered by a deep and sincere love. Till then he had led a gay and dissipated life, and his heart was wearied with passing connections; but the day that he met Lesbia he learnt the meaning of passion. Whatever we may think of Clodia, the love of Catullus elevates her, and we never see her in a more favourable light than in this exquisite poetry. The verses of Catullus seem to make real and living those *fêtes* that she gave to the youth of Rome, and of which we regretted just now the absence of sufficient details ; for was it not for these charming parties, for these free and sumptuous repasts, that he composed his finest works ? It was there, no doubt, under the groves on the banks of the Tiber, that he sang that fine imitation of Sappho's most fervid ode that he made for Lesbia. It was, perhaps, on the shore of Baiae, fronting Naples and Capreae, under that voluptuous sky, in the midst of the attractions of that enchanted land, that for the first time were read those verses in which so much grace is mingled with so much passion, and which are so worthy of the exquisite landscape in the midst of which I take pleasure in placing them :

"Let us live, let us love, my Lesbia, and laugh together at all the reproaches of stern old age. The sun dies to be born again ; but we, when our short-lived light is once extinguished, must sleep an eternal night without awakening. Give me a thousand kisses, a hundred, a thousand, a hundred once more, then a thousand and a hundred again. Afterwards, when we have embraced thousands of times, we will confuse the reckoning to know it no longer, and leave the jealous no pretext to envy us by letting them know how many kisses we have given each other." [1]

That is a remarkable moment in Roman society, when we meet with these polished assemblies, in which everything is talked of and all ranks are mingled, where the writers have their place beside the politicians, where they dare openly express their love for the arts and treat imagination as a power. We may say, to use a quite modern expression, that it is here that the life of society begins. There was nothing like it among the old Romans. They lived on the Forum or in their houses. Between the multitude and the family they knew little of that middle point that

---

[1] *Cat. Carm.* 5.

we call society, that is to say, those elegant and select assemblies, numerous without confusion, where we are at once more at liberty than among unknown persons in public places, and yet less at home than in the family circle. Before reaching this point it was necessary to wait until Rome was civilized and literature had won her place, which scarcely happened until the last age of the republic. And yet we must not exaggerate. That *society* which then had its beginning, seems to us at times very coarse. Catullus tells us that at those luxurious entertainments where such fine poems were read, there were guests who would even steal the napkins.[1] The conversations they held were often risky, to judge by certain epigrams of the great poet. Clodia who assembled at her house these clever men, had singular eccentricities of conduct. The elegant pleasures sought by a woman of society were far from satisfying her, and she fell at last into excesses that made her former friends blush. They themselves, those heroes of fashion, whose good taste was vaunted on all sides, who talked with so much charm and made such tender verses, did not behave much better than she, and were not much more delicate. They had much to reproach themselves with while their connection with Clodia lasted ; when it ended, they committed the unpardonable fault of not respecting the past, and of failing in that consideration that is always due to a woman whom one has once loved. Catullus stung with coarse epigrams her who had inspired his finest verses. Caelius, alluding to the price paid to the vilest courtesans, called her, in open court, the quarter of an as (*quadrantaria*) woman, and this cruel epithet stuck to her. We see that this society had still much progress to make ; but it will do it quickly, thanks to the monarchy which was about to commence. Everything changed with Augustus. Under

[1] *Cat. Carm.* 12.

the new government, these remains of coarseness which savoured of the old republic, disappeared ; men made such progress, and became so fastidious, that the refined were not slow in laughing at Calvus and Catullus, and that Plautus passed for a barbarian. They polish and refine themselves, and at the same time become insipid. A courtly tone is spread over gallant literature, and the change is so sudden, that little more than a quarter of a century was needed for the descent from Catullus to Ovid. The amours of Clodia and Catullus ended very sadly. Clodia did not pride herself on being faithful, and justified her lover only too well when he wrote to her : " A woman's promises must be confided to the wind, or written on running water." [1] Catullus, who knew he was deceived, was angry with himself for submitting to it. He reasoned with himself, he chid himself, but he did not cure himself. Notwithstanding all the trouble he took to gain courage, love was the stronger. After painful struggles which rent his heart, he returned sad and submissive to the feet of her whom he could not help despising, and whom he yet continued to love. " I love and I hate, said he ; you ask me how that can be, I cannot tell ; but I feel that it is so, and my soul is in tortures." [2] So much suffering and resignation touched Clodia very slightly. She plunged deeper and deeper in obscure amours, and the poor poet, who had no more hope, was compelled to separate from her for ever. The rupture between Clodia and Caelius was much more tragic. It was by a criminal trial that their amour was ended. This time Caelius wearied first. Clodia, who, as we have seen, usually took the first step, was not used to such an end to her amours. Enraged at being abandoned, she concerted with the enemies of Caelius, who were not few, and had him accused of several crimes, and particularly of having tried

[1] *Cat. Carm.* 70.   [2] *Ibid.* 85.

to poison her. This, it must be admitted, was a very sad morrow to the charming *fêtes* of Baiae! The trial must have been very amusing, and we may believe that the Forum that day did not lack curious hearers. Caelius appeared accompanied by those who had been his protectors, his friends, and his teachers, the wealthy Crassus and Cicero. They had divided his defence between them, and Cicero specially undertook the part regarding Clodia. Although he declared, in the opening of his speech, " that he was not the enemy of women, and still less of a woman who was the friend of all men," we may well believe that he did not miss such a good opportunity of avenging himself for all the ill this family had done him. That day Clodia suffered for her whole family. Never had Cicero been so sharp and stinging ; the judges must have laughed much, and Caelius was acquitted.

Cicero had solemnly promised in his speech that his client would alter his conduct. In fact, it was quite time for him to reform, his youth had lasted only too long. He was then twenty-eight, and it was really time for him to think of becoming aedile or tribune, if he wished to play that political part that had been his father's ambition for him. We do not know whether, in the sequel, he rigorously carried out all the undertakings Cicero had made in his name ; perhaps he avoided henceforth compromising himself by too open scandals, and perhaps the ill-success of his amours with Clodia had cured him of these noisy adventures ; but it is very difficult to suppose that he became austere and lived after the mann of the old Romans. We see that, several years later when he was aedile and taking part in the most serious business, he found time to learn and repeat all the scandalous tales of Rome. This is what he wrote to Cicero, then proconsul of Cilicia :—

" Nothing new has happened except a few little adventures

that, I am sure, you will be glad to hear about. Paula Valeria, the sister of Triarius, has divorced herself, without any reason, from her husband, the very day he was to arrive from his province; she is going to marry Decimus Brutus. Have you never suspected it? Since your absence incredible things of this kind have happened. No one would have believed that Servius Ocella was a man of intrigue, if he had not been caught in the act twice in the space of three days. You will ask me where? In truth it was where I should not wish it to be,[1] but I leave you something to learn from others. I should be glad to think that a victorious proconsul will go and ask everybody with what woman a man has been caught."[2]

Evidently he who wrote this entertaining letter was never so thoroughly converted as Cicero made believe, and it seems to me that we still find the harebrained young fellow who made so much racket in the streets of Rome, and the lover of Clodia, in the man of wit who recounts so pleasantly these trifling intrigues. We may affirm, then, without temerity that, although from this moment his private life is unknown to us, he never entirely renounced the dissipations of his youth, and that, magistrate and politician as he was, he continued to the end to mix pleasure with business.

II.

But Caelius was not only a hero of amorous adventures, and did not content himself with the empty honour of giving the tone for elegance of manners to the youth of Rome. He had more solid qualities. Thanks to Cicero's

---

[1] Probably with some woman that Caelius loved. Cicero, in replying to this letter, tells him that the rumour of his exploits has reached Mount Taurus. Many suppose he means amorous exploits.

[2] *Ad fam.* viii. 7.

lessons he speedily became a great orator. A short time after he had escaped from this honourable tutelage, he made a brilliant commencement in a case in which he was opposed to Cicero himself, and this time the disciple beat the master. Since this success his reputation had continued to increase. There were orators in the Forum that men of taste admired more, and whose gifts they considered more perfect; there were none more dreaded than he, such was the violence of his attack and the bitterness of his raillery. He excelled in seizing the ridiculous side of his opponents, and in making, in a very few words, those ironical and cutting observations on them which are never forgotten. Quintilian quotes one as a model of its kind, which well exemplifies the talent of this terrible wit. He is speaking, in this passage, of that Antony who had been the colleague of Cicero in his consulship, and who, in spite of all the eulogies that the Orations against Catiline lavish on him, was but an inferior intriguer and a coarse debauchee. After having, according to custom, pillaged Macedonia, which he governed, he had attacked some neighbouring tribes in order to obtain a pretext for a triumph. He counted upon an easy victory, but as he was more taken up with his pleasures than with the war, he was ignominiously beaten. Caelius, who attacked him on his return, described, or rather imagined, in his speech, one of those orgies during which the general, while dead drunk, allowed himself to be surprised by the enemy.

"Women, his ordinary officers, fill the banqueting-hall, stretched on all the couches, or lying about on the ground. When they learn that the enemy is come, half-dead with fright, they try to awaken Antony; they shout his name, they raise him up by the neck. Some whisper soft words in his ear, others treat him more roughly and even strike him; but he, who recognizes their voices and touch,

N

stretches out his arms by habit, seizes and wishes to embrace the first he meets with. He can neither sleep, so much they shout to awaken him, nor wake, so drunk is he. At last, powerless to shake off this drowsiness, he is carried off in the arms of his centurions and his mistresses." [1]

When a man possesses such a biting and incisive talent it is natural for him to have an aggressive temper ; nothing therefore suited Caelius better than personal struggles. He liked and sought disputation because he was sure to succeed in it, and because he could make use of those violent modes of attack that could not be resisted. He wished to be con tradicted, for contradiction excited him and gave him energy. Seneca relates that one day one of the clients of Caelius, a man of pacific temper, and who, no doubt, had suffered from his rudeness, confined himself during a meal to agreeing with him. Caelius at last grew enraged because the man gave him no opportunity for getting angry, and exclaimed : " Do contradict me that there may be two of us." [2] The talents of Caelius, such as I have just depicted them, marvellously suited the time in which he lived. This thoroughly explains the reputation that he enjoyed, and the important position he took among his contemporaries. This fiery debater, this pitiless wit, this vehement accuser would not have been altogether in his place in quiet times ; but in the midst of a revolution he became a valuable auxiliary whom all parties contended for. Caelius was moreover a statesman as well as an orator, and it is for this that Cicero most frequently praises him. " I know no one, he told him, who is a better politician than you." [3] He knew men thoroughly, he had a clear insight into situations ; he decided quickly, a quality that Cicero much appreciated in others, for it was just that which he most lacked, and when once he had decided, he set to work with a vigour

[1] Quint. *Inst. or.* iv. 2.   [2] *De Ira.* iii. 8.   [3] *Ad fam.* ii. 8.

and force that gained him the sympathies of the multitude. At a time when power belonged to those who were
bold enough to seize it, the audacity of Caelius seemed to
promise him a brilliant political future.

Nevertheless, he had also great defects, which sometimes
arose from his very good qualities. He knew men well, a
great advantage no doubt, but in studying them it was
their bad side that struck him most. By dint of trying
them in every way, his startling penetration succeeded in
laying bare some weakness. He did not reserve his severity
for his adversaries only; his best friends did not escape his
clear-sighted analysis. We see in his private correspondence
that he knew all their defects, and did not stand on
ceremony in speaking of them. Dolabella, his companion
in pleasure, is a poor babbler, "incapable of keeping a
secret, even though his imprudence should ruin him."[1]
Curio, his usual associate in political intrigues, "is only an
unstable busybody, changing with every breath of wind,
who can do nothing sensible,"[2] nevertheless, at the time
when he is treating them thus, Curio and Dolabella had
sufficient influence over him to draw him into Caesar's
party. As to Caesar himself, he speaks no better of him,
although he is preparing to embrace his cause. This son of
Venus, as he calls him, appears to him "but an egotist who
scoffs at the interests of the republic and only cares for his
own,"[3] and he has no scruple in confessing that in his
camp, where, nevertheless, he is going, there are only dishonourable men, "all of whom have causes for apprehension
in the past and criminal hopes for the future."[4] With such
a disposition of mind, and so decided a leaning to judge
every one harshly, it was natural that Caelius should not

[1] *Ad fam.* viii. 6.   [2] *Ibid.* viii. 4.
[3] *Ibid.* viii. 5. The sense of this phrase is altered in Orelli.
[4] *Ibid.* viii. 14.

trust any one entirely, and that no one dared to count upon him with confidence. To serve a cause usefully you must give yourself up to it completely ; now, how can you do so if you cannot shut your eyes a little and not see too clearly its bad sides ? Those cautious and clear-sighted persons, who are entirely taken up with the fear of being dupes, and who always see the faults of others so plainly, are never anything but lukewarm friends and useless allies. While they inspire no confidence in the party that they wish to serve, because they always make reservations in serving it, they are not sufficiently enthusiastic to form a party themselves, and always fall short of that degree of passion that leads a man to undertake great things. Therefore it happens that, as they can neither be chiefs nor privates, and cannot attach themselves to others or attach others to themselves, they end by finding themselves alone.

Let us add that Caelius, who had no illusions about persons, seemed also to have no preference for parties. He never sought the reputation of being a man of principle, nor to put order and consistency into his political life. In that, as in his private affairs, he lived from hand to mouth. The circumstances of the moment, interest, or friendship, gave him an accidental conviction to which he did not pretend to be long faithful. He went over from Cicero to Catiline when Catiline seemed to him the stronger ; he returned to Cicero when Cicero was victorious. He was the friend of Clodius as long as he remained Clodia's lover ; he abandoned the brother at the same time that he left the sister, and suddenly embraced Milo's party. He passed several times from the people to the senate, and from the senate to the people without scruple or embarrassment. At bottom, the cause that he served was of little consequence to him, and he had not to make much effort to disengage himself from it. At the time that he seemed to be taking the most trouble for it, he spoke of it in a tone that left people to imagine it was quite foreign to him. Even in the gravest affairs, and when it was a question of the fate of the republic, he did not appear to suppose that it had anything to do with him, and that he was interested in its safety or ruin. "It is your business, rich old men," [1] he said. But what did it matter to him? As he is always ruined he never has anything to lose. Therefore all forms of government are indifferent to him, and curiosity alone makes him take an interest in these struggles, in which, nevertheless, he plays such an active part. If he plunges with so much ardour into the tumult of public life, it is because events and men are seen closer, and one can make piquant reflections on it, or find amusing scenes in it. When he announces to Cicero, with remarkable perspicacity, the approaching civil war and the misfortunes that are coming, he adds : "If you were not running some risk, I should say that fortune was preparing a great and curious spectacle for you ! " [2] A cruel speech that Caelius paid for dearly in the sequel, for one does not play at these deadly games without peril, and often becomes a victim while thinking to be only a spectator.

When this war, which he thus announced to Cicero, was on the point of breaking out, Caelius had just been appointed aedile, and his great anxiety was to have some Cilician panthers for the games that he wished to give to the people. At this time, after having belonged more or less to all parties, he made profession of defending the cause of the senate, that is to say, that in speaking of the senators, he said, " our friends," and that he affected to call them "good citizens " ; which did not prevent him, according to his custom, having his eyes open to the faults that the " good citizens " might commit, and scoffing at his

---

[1] *Ad fam.* viii. 13.　　　　[2] *Ibid.* viii. 14.

"friends" bitterly when the opportunity presented itself. Cicero thought him cold and undecided; he would have wished to see him pledge himself deeper. At the time of his departure for Cilicia, he did not cease to extol the great qualities of Pompey to him : "Believe me, he said, trust yourself to this great man, he will gladly welcome you."[1] But Caelius took good care not to do anything of the kind. He knew Pompey, of whom he has drawn satirical portraits on different occasions ; he did not much admire him, and did not like him at all. If he kept aloof from him at the time of his greatest power, he certainly would not, we can well understand, throw himself into his arms when this power was threatened. In proportion as the crisis that he had foreseen advanced, he took more care to hold himself in reserve, and waited for the turn of events.

It was, moreover, a time when the most honourable hesitated. This irresolution, which does not seem to have been very surprising then, has been much blamed in our days. It is easy, however, to understand this. Questions do not present themselves to the eyes of contemporaries with the same clearness as to those of posterity. When they are looked at from a distance, and with a mind free from all prejudice ; when, besides, the results and the causes are taken in at the same time, and when we can judge the causes by the results, nothing is easier than to come to a decision ; but it is not so when one lives in the midst of the events, and too near them to take in the whole, when one's mind is influenced by previous ties or personal preferences, and when the decision one is about to take may endanger one's safety and fortune. It is not possible, then, to see things so clearly. The state of anarchy in which the old parties of the Roman republic were added to the confusion at that time. To speak the truth, there were no

[1] *Ad fam.* ii. 8.

longer parties, but coalitions. For fifty years they had struggled, not for questions of principle, but for personal questions. Parties being no longer organized as formerly, it followed that timid minds which have need to attach themselves to ancient traditions to guide them, drifted about, and often changed. These striking changes of opinion in honourable and respected persons disturbed the less settled minds, and rendered it difficult to make out the right. Caesar, who knew of these vacillations, and hoped to profit by them, did what he could to increase their causes. At the very moment when he was preparing to destroy the constitution of his country, he had the art to appear to respect it more than anybody. An expert judge in these matters, and one who knows the Roman laws thoroughly, has declared, after mature examination, that the law was on the side of Caesar, and that the grievances he complained of were well founded.[1] He took good care not to disclose all his projects then, or to speak with so much freedom as he did afterwards, when he was master. Sometimes he presented himself as the successor of the Gracchi, and the defender of popular rights ; sometimes he affected to say, in order to re-assure everybody, that the republic was not interested in the dispute, and reduced the quarrel to a struggle for influence between two powerful competitors. While he was gathering his legions in the cities of Upper Italy, he only spoke of his desire to preserve the public peace ; in proportion as his enemies became more violent he became more moderate, and he never proposed conditions so acceptable as when he was sure that the senate would not listen to them. On the other side, on the contrary, in the camp where moderate and wise men ought to be found, there was nothing but rashness and stupidity.

[1] See the excellent memoir of M. Th. Mommsen, entitled *Die Rechtsfrage zwischen Caesar und dem Senat.* Breslau, 1857.

Those who showed some repugnance to civil war were treated as public enemies ; they talked only of proscribing and confiscating, and the example of Sulla was in every one's mouth. It happened then, by a strange contradiction, that it was in the camp where profession was made of defending liberty, that exceptional measures were most persistently demanded ; and while the man who expected everything from the war, and whose army was ready, offered peace, those who had not a soldier under arms were eager to refuse it. Thus the two sides exchanged characters, and each appeared to speak and act contrary to its interests, or its principles. Is it surprising that in the midst of such obscurity, and among so many reasons for hesitation, honourable men like Sulpicius and Cicero, devoted to their country, but fitter to serve it in quiet times than in these violent crises, should not have decided at once ?

Caelius also hesitated ; but not altogether for the same reasons as Cicero and Sulpicius. While they anxiously asked themselves where the right lay, Caelius only sought where the superior force lay. He admitted this himself with singular candour : " In intestine quarrels," he writes to Cicero, " as long as one struggles by legal means, and without having recourse to arms, one ought to attach oneself to the most honourable party ; but when one comes to war it is necessary to turn towards the stronger, and regard the safest party as the best." [1] From the moment that he was satisfied with simply comparing the strength of the two rivals, his choice became easier ; in order to decide it was enough to open his eyes. On one side there were eleven legions, supported by tried auxiliaries, and commanded by the greatest general of the republic, ranged on the frontiers, and ready to open the campaign at the first signal ; [2] on the

[1] *Ad fam.* viii. 14.

[2] We see at the end of the eighth book *De Bello Gallico*, that Caesar

other, few or no trained troops, but a great number of young men of illustrious families as incapable of commanding as they were little disposed to obey, and many of those great names that honour a party more than they help it ; on one side, military rule and the discipline of a camp ; on the other, quarrels, disputes, resentments, rival authorities, differences of opinion, in short, all the inconvenient habits of civil life transported into a camp. These are the ordinary difficulties of a party that claims to defend liberty, for it is difficult to impose silence on people who fight to preserve the right of free speech, and all authority quickly becomes suspected when men have taken up arms to oppose an abuse of authority. But it was the character of the two chiefs, more than anything else, that made the difference between the two parties. Caesar appeared to all the world, even to his greatest enemies, a prodigy of activity and foresight. As to Pompey it was clearly seen that he committed only faults, and it was not any easier then than it is now to explain his conduct. The war had not taken him unawares; he told Cicero that he had foreseen it for a long time.[1] There was no great difficulty in foreseeing it, he had appeared to wish for it ; Caesar's proposals had been rejected by his advice, and the majority of the senate did nothing without consulting him. He had, then, seen the crisis approaching from afar, and during all that long diplomatic war which preceded actual hostilities he had had the time necessary to prepare himself. Every one, therefore, believed that he was ready, although nothing showed it. When he said, with his usual boastfulness, that he had only to stamp his foot to bring up legions, it was supposed he meant to speak of secret levies,

---

had eight legions in Gaul, one in Cisalpine Gaul, and two that he gave to Pompey. At the first threat of war he ordered those that were in Gaul to approach the frontier. After the capture of Corfinium he had three of his old legions with him.

[1] *Ad Att.* vii. 4.

or of alliances not generally known, that at the last moment would bring him troops. His confidence restored courage to the most terror-stricken. In truth, such a strange self-confidence in the midst of such real danger, in a man who had conquered kingdoms, and conducted great affairs, passes our comprehension.

Whence then could this confidence come to Pompey? Had he no exact information of the strength of his enemy? did he really believe, as he said, that his troops were discontented, his generals unfaithful, and that no one would follow him in the war he was going to wage against his country? or did he reckon on the good fortune of his earlier years, on the prestige of his name, on the happy chances that had given him so many victories? It is certain that, at the moment when the veterans of Alesia and Gergovia were assembling at Ravenna, and approaching the Rubicon, Pompey imprudently exhibited a great disdain for the general and for his troops, *vehementer contemnebat hunc hominem !* [1] But this foolish boasting did not last long; on the news that Caesar was marching resolutely on Rome, it ceased at once, and this same man whom Cicero showed us just now disdaining his rival and predicting his defeat, he shows us a few days later, terrified and flying into the depths of Apulia without daring to halt or make a stand anywhere. We have the letter that Pompey then wrote to the consuls, and to Domitius, who attempted at least to hold out in Corfinium : " Know, he tells them, that I am in great uneasiness (*scitote me esse in summa sollicitudine*).[2] What a contrast to the over-confident words of just now ! This is just the tone of a man who, waking up with a start from exaggerated hopes, passes suddenly from one extreme to another. He had prepared nothing because he had been too well assured of success ; he

[1] *Ad Att.* vii. 8.	[2] *Ibid.* viii. 12.

dared undertake nothing because he was too certain of failure. He has no confidence or hope in any one; all resistance seems to him useless; he does not even count upon the awakening of a patriotic spirit, and it does not occur to him to make an appeal to the republican youth of the Italian municipia. At each step that his enemy takes in advance, he retreats still farther. Brundusium itself, with its strong walls, does not give him confidence; he thinks of quitting Italy, and does not believe that he is safe until he has put the sea between himself and Caesar.

Caelius had not waited so long to take a side. Even before the struggle commenced it was easy for him to see where the superior strength lay and on which side victory would be. He had then boldly faced about and put himself in the front rank among Caesar's friends. He took his side openly when he supported with his usual vigour the proposition of Calidius, who demanded that Pompey should be sent back to his province of Spain. When the hope of peace was completely lost, he left Rome with his friends Curio and Dolabella, and went to join Caesar at Ravenna. He followed him in his triumphal march through Italy; he saw him pardon Domitius, who had been taken in Corfinium, pursue Pompey, and shut him up closely in Brundusium. In the intoxication of these rapid successes he wrote to Cicero: " Have you ever seen a man more foolish than your Pompey, who brings us into such great troubles, and whose conduct is so childish? On the other hand, have you ever read or heard of anything that surpasses the ardour of Caesar in action and his moderation in victory? What do you think of our soldiers, who, in the depth of winter, notwithstanding the difficulties of a wild and frozen country, have finished the war in an unopposed march?"[1]

---

[1] *Ad fam.* viii. 15.

When Caelius had once decided, his only thought was to draw Cicero after him. He knew that he could do nothing more agreeable to Caesar. Victorious though he was, Caesar, who did not delude himself about those who served him, felt that he wanted a few honest men to give his party a better appearance. The great name of Cicero would have sufficed to correct the bad impression that the character of those about him produced. Unfortunately it was very difficult to get Cicero to decide. From the day when the Rubicon was passed till the capture of Brundusium he wavered and changed his mind every day. Both sides were equally anxious to secure him, and the two chiefs themselves approached him, but in a very different manner. Pompey, always bungling, wrote him short and imperious letters: "Take the Appian road as soon as possible, come and join me at Luceria, at Brundusium, there you will be safe." [1] Strange language in the vanquished who persists in speaking as a superior! Caesar was much more judicious: "Come, he says to him, come and aid me with your counsel, your name, and your glory!" [2] This consideration, these advances from a victorious general, who humbly solicited when he had the right to command, could not fail to influence Cicero. At the same time, to be more sure of gaining him over, Caesar got his dearest friends to write to him, Oppius, Balbus, Trebatius, and especially Caelius, who knew so well how to approach him. They attacked him on all his weak sides at once; they revived his old grudges against Pompey; they moved him by the picture of the misfortunes that threatened his family; they excited his vanity by pointing out to him the honour of reconciling parties and pacifying the republic.

So many assaults were bound to end by shaking a mind so undecided. At the last moment, he resolved to remain

---

[1] *Ad Att.* viii. 11.   [2] *Ibid.* ix. 6.

in Italy, in some isolated country-house or in some neutral town, living apart from public affairs, not siding with any one, but preaching moderation and peace to all. Already he had begun an eloquent treatise on peace among citizens ; he wished to finish it at leisure, and, as he had a good opinion of his eloquence, he hoped it would cause the most stubborn to lay down their arms. It was an idle fancy, no doubt; but we must not forget that Cato, who is beyond suspicion, regretted that Cicero had given up his plan so soon. He blamed him for going to Pharsalia, where his presence was not a great assistance to the combatants, while, by remaining neutral, he could preserve his influence over the two rivals and serve as intermediary between them. But one single day overturned all these fine projects. When Pompey quitted Brundusium, where he did not think he was safe, and embarked for Greece, Caesar, who counted upon this news to retain Cicero, hastened to transmit it to him. It was precisely this that made him change his mind. He was not one of those men who, like Caelius, turn with fortune and decide for success. On the contrary, he felt himself drawn to Pompey as soon as he saw him unfortunate. "I have never desired to share in his prosperity, said he ; I could wish to share his misfortune !"[1] When he knew that the republican army had departed, and with it almost all his old political friends ; when he felt that on that Italian soil there were no longer magistrates, consuls or senate, he was seized with profound grief ; it seemed that there was a blank around him, and that the sun itself, according to his expression, had disappeared from the world. Many people came to congratulate him on his prudence, but he reproached himself with it as a crime. He bitterly accused his weakness, his age, his love of repose and of peace. He had but one thought, to

[1] *Ad Att.* ix. 12.

leave as quickly as possible. "I cannot support my regret, he said; my books, my studies, my philosophy are of no use to me. I am like a bird that wishes to fly away, and I always look seawards." [1]

From that time his resolution was taken. Caelius tried in vain to retain him at the last moment, by a touching letter, in which he spoke to him of the probable loss of his fortune, and of the danger of jeopardizing the future of his son. Cicero, although he was much moved, was content to reply with a firmness unusual with him: "I am glad to see that you are so anxious for my son; but, if the republic continues, he will always be rich enough with his father's name; if it must perish, he will suffer the common fate of all the citizens." [2] And, soon after, he crossed the sea to repair to Pompey's camp. Not that he counted upon success; in joining a party whose weaknesses he was acquainted with, he well knew that he was going voluntarily to take his share in a disaster. "I come, said he, like Amphiaraüs to cast myself alive into the abyss." [3] It was a sacrifice that he thought he ought to make for his country, and it is proper to give him so much the more credit for it as he did it without illusions and without hope.

While Cicero thus went to rejoin Pompey, Caelius accompanied Caesar to Spain. All relations became henceforth impossible between them; consequently their correspondence, which had until then been very active, stops from this moment. There remains, however, one letter, the last that passed between them, and which forms a strange contrast to those that precede. Caelius addressed it to Cicero a few months only after the events that I have just spoken of, but under very different circumstances. Although it has only come down to us very mutilated, and it is not easy to restore the sense of all the phrases, we see

---

[1] *Ad Att*. ix. 10.   [2] *Ad fam*. ii. 16.   [3] *Ibid*. vi. 6.

clearly that the writer was a prey to violent irritation. This zealous partisan of Caesar, who sought to convert others to his opinion, has suddenly become a furious enemy ; that cause that he lately defended with so much warmth, he now only calls a detestable cause, and thinks "it is better to die than remain on that side."[1] What had happened, then, in the interval? What motives had led Caelius to this last change, and what was the result of it? It is well to relate it, for the narrative may throw some light on the policy of the dictator, and above all make us acquainted with those about him.

III.

In his treatise, *De Amicitia*, Cicero affirms that a tyrant cannot have friends.[2] In speaking thus he was thinking of Caesar, and it must be admitted that this example seems to justify him. Courtiers are not wanting when a man is master, and Caesar, who paid them well, had more than any other, but we know of scarcely any sincere and devoted friends. Perhaps he had some among those obscure servants whose memory history has not preserved,[3] but none of those whom he placed in the first rank, and whom he invited to share in his good fortune, remained faithful to him. His liberalities only brought him ingratitude, his clemency disarmed no one, and he was betrayed by those on whom he had lavished most favours. His soldiers alone

---

[1] *Ad fam.* viii. 17. [2] *De amic.* 15.

[3] It would be wrong to pass over the name of Matius in silence. A very fine letter of his on the death of Caesar remains (*Ad fam.* xi. 28). He was a true friend of Caesar ; but it is to be remarked that he was not one of those whom he made praetors and consuls, and whose debts he had often paid. Matius never filled any important political office, and his name would not have come down to us if it had not been for Cicero's correspondence.

can really be called his friends, those veterans who remained from the great Gallic wars; his centurions, all of whom he knew by name, and who let themselves bravely be killed for him under his eyes : that Scaeva, who at Dyrrhachium had his shield pierced with two hundred and thirty arrows ; [1] that Crastinus, who said to him on the morning of Pharsalia, " This evening you shall thank me dead or alive." [2] These men served him faithfully, he knew them and relied upon them ; but he well knew that he could not trust his generals. Although he had heaped money and honours upon them after his victories, they were discontented. A few, and those the most honourable, were grieved to think that they had destroyed the republic and shed their blood to establish absolute power. The greater number had not these scruples, but all thought their services ill rewarded. Caesar's liberality, great as it was, had not sufficed to satisfy them. The republic was delivered up to them, they were praetors and consuls, they governed the richest provinces, and yet they ceased not to complain. Everything served them as a pretext for murmuring. Antony had got Pompey's house awarded to him at a low price ; when they came for the money he got in a passion and only paid with insults. No doubt he thought that day that they were wanting in respect for him, and called Caesar ungrateful. It is not uncommon to see those warriors, so brave before the enemy, and so admirable on the day of battle, become again in private life vulgarly ambitious, full of base jealousy and insatiable greed. They began by murmuring and complaining ; they almost all ended by betraying him. Among those who killed Caesar were found perhaps his best generals, Sulpicius Galba, the conqueror of the Nantuates, Basilus, one of his most brilliant cavalry officers, Decimus Brutus and Trebonius, the heroes of the

---

[1] *De bell. civ.* iii. 53.   [2] *Ibid.* iii. 91.

siege of Marseilles. Those who were not in the plot did not conduct themselves any better that day. When we read in Plutarch the narrative of the death of Caesar, our heart bleeds at seeing that no one tried to defend him. The conspirators were only about sixty in number, and there were more than eight hundred senators. The greater number among them had served in his army; all owed to him the honour of sitting in the curia, of which they were not worthy, and these wretches, who held their fortune and their dignity from him, who begged for his protection and lived on his favours, saw him killed without saying a word. All the time this horrible struggle lasted, while, "like a beast attacked by the hunters, he strove among the swords drawn against him," they remained motionless on their seats, and all their courage consisted in flying when Brutus, beside the bleeding corpse, essayed to speak. Cicero recalled this scene, of which he had been a witness, when he said later, "It is on the day when the oppressors of their country fall that we see clearly that they have no friends." [1]

When Caesar's generals, who had so many motives for remaining faithful to him, betrayed him, could he reckon more on those doubtful allies that he had recruited on the Forum, and who before serving him had served all parties? To accomplish his designs he had need of politicians; in order that the new government should not appear to be a wholly military rule he had need of the greatest number possible. Therefore he was not squeamish, he took them without selection. It was the dishonest men of all parties that came to him by preference. He received them well, although he esteemed them little, and carried them everywhere in his train. Cicero had been very much afraid of them when Caesar came with them to see him at Formiae: "There is not a rascal in all Italy," said he, "who is not

[1] *De amic.* 15.

O

with him," [1] and Atticus, usually so reserved, could not help calling this retinue an infernal troop.[2] However habituated we may be to see the initiative in such revolutions taken by men who have not much to lose, there is reason, nevertheless, to be surprised that Caesar did not find a few more honourable allies. Even those who are most opposed to him are compelled to recognize that much which he wished to destroy did not deserve preservation. The revolution that he contemplated had profound causes, it was natural that it should have also sincere partisans. How does it happen then that, among those who aided him to change a government of which many complained, and from which every one had suffered, there are so few who seem to act from conviction, and that almost all, on the contrary, are only paid conspirators working without sincerity for a man whom they do not love, and for a purpose that they consider bad?

Perhaps we must explain the composition of Caesar's party by the means that he usually took to recruit it. We do not see that when he wished to gain any one over to his cause he lost his time in demonstrating to him the defects of the old government and the merits of that by which he wished to replace it. He employed more simple and sure arguments : he paid. This showed that he knew well the men of his time, and he was not deceived in thinking that, in a society altogether given up to luxury and pleasure, weakened beliefs only left room for self-interest. He organized then without scruple a vast system of corruption. Gaul furnished the means. He pillaged it as vigorously as he had conquered it, "seizing," says Suetonius, "all that he found in the temples of the gods, and taking towns by assault, less to punish them than to have a pretext for plundering them." [3] With this money he made himself

---

[1] *Ad Att.* ix. 19.   [2] *Ibid.* ix. 18.   [3] Suet. *Caes.* 54.

partisans. Those who came to see him never went away empty-handed. He did not even neglect to make presents to the slaves and freedmen who had any influence over their masters. While he was absent from Rome, the clever Spaniard Balbus and the banker Oppius, who were his agents, distributed bounties in his name; they discreetly helped embarrassed senators; they became the treasurers of young men of high family who had exhausted the paternal resources. They lent money without interest, but the services by which they would have to repay the loans were well known to every one. It was thus they bought Curio, who set a high price on himself; he was in debt for more than 60,000,000 sesterces (£480,000). Caelius and Dolabella, whose affairs were in a not much better state, were probably gained by the same means. Never was corruption practised on a greater scale and displayed with more impudence. Almost every year, during the winter, Caesar returned to Cisalpine Gaul with the treasures of the Gauls. Then the market was opened, and the great personages arrived one after another. One day, at Lucca, so many came at once that two hundred senators were counted in the apartments, and one hundred and twenty lictors at the door.

In general, the fidelity of people who are bought does not last much longer than the money they receive; now, in their hands, money does not last long, and the day one tires of providing for their prodigality, one is obliged to begin to distrust them. There was besides, in the case of all these political friends of Caesar, a special reason why, one day or other, they should become discontented. They had grown up amidst the storms of the republic; they had thrown themselves early into that active and bustling life, and they had acquired the taste for it. No men more than they, had used and abused liberty of speech;

to it they owed their influence, their power, and their renown. By a strange inconsistency, these men, who worked with all their might to establish an absolute government, were those who could least do without the struggles of public life, the turmoil of business, and the excitement of the rostrum, that is to say just those things which exist only under free governments. There were no men who would sooner find despotic power burdensome than those who had not been able to support even the light and equitable yoke of the law. Accordingly they were not long in perceiving the error they had committed. They soon found out that in aiding a master to destroy the liberty of others, they had delivered up their own. At the same time it was easy for them to see that the new government that they had established with their own hands could not give them what the old one had given them. What, in fact, were those dignities and those honours with which it was pretended to reward them, when one man alone possessed real power? There were, no doubt, still praetors and consuls; but what comparison could be made between these magistrates, dependent on one man, subject to his caprices, dominated by his authority, overshadowed, and, as it were, obliterated by his glory, and those of the old republic? So then must inevitably arise mistakes, regrets, and often also treasons. This is why those allies whom Caesar had recruited in the different political parties, after having been very useful to him, all finished by causing him great trouble. None of those restless and intractable minds, undisciplined by nature and habit, had willingly consented to submit to discipline, or heartily resigned himself to obey. As soon as they were no longer under the eye of the master and restrained by his powerful hand, the old instincts in them gained the upper hand; they became again, on the first opportunity, seditious as before, and though Rome had been pacified by absolute power, troubles recommenced every time Caesar was absent. It is thus that Caelius, Dolabella, and Antony compromised the public tranquillity they had been charged to maintain. Curio, the head of that youth that rallied round the new government, died too soon to have had the time to be discontented ; but we may conjecture, from the light and flippant manner in which he already spoke of Caesar in his private conversation, from the small degree of illusion he seemed to have about him, that he would have acted like the rest.[1]

It is easy now to understand what reasons Caelius had to complain, and how that ambition which the dignities of the old republic had not satisfied at last found itself ill at ease under the new government. The strange letter that he wrote to Cicero, and that declaration of war which he made to Caesar and his party are now explained. He had early become discontented. From the very beginning of the civil war, when he was congratulated on the success of his party, he answered gloomily : " What do I care about that glory which never reaches to me ? "[2] The truth is that he was beginning to understand that there was only room for one man in the new government, and that he alone for the future would have glory as well as power. Caesar took him on his expedition to Spain without giving him, it appears, an opportunity of distinguishing himself. On his return to Rome he was appointed praetor, but he did not have the urban praetorship which was the most honourable, and Trebonius was preferred to him. This preference, which he regarded as an insult, caused him great vexation. He resolved to revenge himself, and only waited for an opportunity. He thought it had come when he saw Caesar set out with all his troops for Thessaly, in pursuit of Pompey. He thought that in the absence of the

---

[1] *Ad Att.* x. 4. [2] *Ad fam.* viii. 15.

dictator and his soldiers, in the midst of the excitement of Italy, where a thousand contradictory rumours on the result of the struggle were circulating, he might attempt a decisive stroke. The moment was well chosen; but what was still better chosen was the question on which Caelius resolved to begin the fight. Nothing does more credit to his political ability than to have so clearly discerned the weak sides of the victorious party, and to have seen at a glance the best position he could take up for a successful attack upon it.

Although Caesar was master of Rome and of Italy, and it was seen that the republican army would not check him, he still had great difficulties to surmount. Caelius knew this well; he knew well that in political struggles success is often an ordeal full of danger. After the enemy has been vanquished one's own friends have to be provided for, a task which is often troublesome. That greed must be resisted which has hitherto been tolerated, or even encouraged, when the time to satisfy it seemed distant; it is necessary above all to defend oneself against the exaggerated hopes that victory produces in those who have gained it, and which yet cannot be realized. Usually, when one belongs to the weaker party and wishes to gain adherents, promises are not spared; but when one reaches power it is very difficult to keep all the engagements that have been made, and those fine programmes that have been accepted and scattered abroad become then a source of great embarrassment. Caesar was the recognized chief of the democratic party; thence came his strength. We remember that he had said, on entering Italy, that he came to restore liberty to the republic which was enslaved by a handful of aristocrats. Now, the democratic party of which he thus proclaimed himself the representative had its programme ready prepared. It was not exactly that of the Gracchi. After a century of often bloody struggles, hatred had become envenomed, and the senseless resistance of the aristocracy had made the people more exacting. Each of the chiefs who, since Caius Gracchus, had come forward to lead them, had formulated for them some fresh demand the more surely to draw them after him. Clodius had aimed at establishing the unlimited right of association and of governing the republic by secret societies. Catiline promised confiscation and pillage; accordingly his memory had remained very popular. Cicero speaks of the funeral banquets which were celebrated in his honour, and of the flowers that his tomb was covered with.[1] Caesar, who presented himself as their successor, could not altogether repudiate their heritage; he must promise that he would finish their work and satisfy the wishes of the democracy. At this moment the democracy did not appear to care much about political reforms; what it wanted was a social revolution. To be fed in idleness at the expense of the state, by means of gratuitous distributions very frequently repeated; to appropriate the best lands of the allies by sending colonies into the richest Italian cities; to arrive at a sort of division of property, under pretext of recovering from the aristocracy the public domain which it had appropriated, such was the ordinary idea of the plebeians; but what they most urgently demanded, what had become the watchword of all this party, was the abolition of debts, or, as they said, the destruction of the registers of the creditors (*tabulae novae*), that is to say, the authorized violation of public faith, and a general bankruptcy decreed by the law. This programme, violent as it was, Caesar had prepared to accept in proclaiming himself the head of the democracy. As long as the struggle was doubtful, he took care to make no reservations, for fear of weakening his party by divisions. Therefore it was thought that as soon

[1] *Pro Flacco*, 38.

as he was victorious he would set himself to work to realize it.

But Caesar had not only come to destroy a government, he wished to found another, and he knew very well that nothing solid can be established on spoliation and bank-ruptcy.   After having used, without compunction, the programme of the democracy to overturn the republic, he understood that he would have to take up a new part.   On the day that he became master of Rome, his statesman's instinct, and his interest as a sovereign made him a con-servative.   While he extended his hand to the moderate men of the old parties, he had no scruple in often returning to the traditions of the old government.

It is certain that the work of Caesar, taking it altogether, is far from being that of a revolutionary ; some of his laws were praised by Cicero after the Ides of March ; which is as much as to say that they were not conformable to the wishes and hopes of the democracy.   He sent eighty thousand poor citizens into the colonies, but over sea, to Africa and to Greece.   He could not think of altogether abolishing the donations made by the State to the citizens of Rome, but he diminished them.   In the place of the three hundred and twenty thousand citizens who shared in these under the republic, he only admitted a hundred and fifty thousand ; he ordered that this number should not be exceeded, and that every year the praetor should fill up the place of those persons, thus privileged by poverty, who had died within the year.   Far from changing anything in the prohibitive regulations that were in force under the republic, he established import duties on foreign merchan-dise.   He promulgated a sumptuary law, much more severe than the preceding, which regulated in detail the manner in which people should dress and live, and had it executed with tyrannical rigour.   The markets were guarded by soldiers lest anything should be sold that the law forbade, and the soldiers were authorized to enter houses and seize prohibited food even on the tables. Caesar had taken these measures, which hampered commerce and industry, and consequently were hurtful to the interests of the people, from the traditions of the aristocratic governments. They could not therefore be popular ; but the restriction he put upon the right of meeting was still less so. This right, to which the democracy clung more than to any other, had been respected even to the last days of the republic, and the tribune Clodius had skilfully used it to frighten the senate and to terrorize the Forum. Under pretext of honouring the tutelar deities of each cross-way, associations of the districts (*collegia compitalicia*), comprising the poor citizens and the slaves, had been formed. Beginning by being religious, these societies soon became political. In the time of Clodius they formed a sort of regular army of the democracy, and played the same part in the riots of Rome as the " sections " in '93 did among us. By the side of these permanent associations, and on the same model, temporary associations were formed, every time a great election took place. The people were enrolled by districts, they were divided into decuries and centuries ; chiefs, who led them to vote in military order, were appointed ; and as in general the people did not give their votes for nothing, an important person named *sequester* was appointed beforehand, in whose hands the sum promised by the candidate was deposited, and distributors (*divisores*) charged, after the voting, to divide it among each tribe. This is how universal suffrage was exercised in Rome towards the close of the republic, and thus this race, naturally inclined to discipline, had succeeded in giving an organization to disorder. Caesar, who had often made use of these secret associations, who by them had managed elections and dominated the deliberations of the Forum, would no longer suffer them when he had no longer need of them. He thought that a regular government would not last long if he allowed this underground government to work by its side. He did not shrink then from severe measures to rid himself of this organized disorder. To the great scandal of his friends, he suppressed, at a single stroke, all the political societies, only allowing the most ancient, which presented no danger, to continue in existence.

These were vigorous measures, and such as must have offended many people; accordingly he did not venture to take them till late, after Munda and Thapsus, when his authority was no longer disputed and he felt himself strong enough to resist the democracy, his ancient ally. When he set out for Pharsalia he had still to observe much caution; prudence commanded him not to displease his friends, while so many enemies remained. Moreover, there were certain questions which could not be deferred, so important were they in the eyes of the democracy which demanded their immediate settlement. One of the chief of these was the abolition of debts. Caesar turned his attention to it immediately on his return from Spain; but here again, notwithstanding the difficulties of his position, he was not so radical as he was expected to be. Placed between his conservative instincts and the demands of his friends, he adopted a middle course: instead of abolishing the debts completely, he contented himself with reducing them. Firstly, he ordered that all sums paid up to that time as interest should be deducted from the capital sums; then, to make payment of the amount thus reduced easier, he ruled that the property of the debtors should be valued by arbitrators; that they should assess it, not at its present value, but at that which it had before the civil war, and that the creditors should be obliged to take it at that rate. Suetonius says that, in this manner, debts were reduced by more than one-fourth. These measures certainly still appear to us sufficiently revolutionary. We cannot approve this intervention of authority, to despoil without reason private persons of a part of their wealth, and nothing can seem to us more unjust than that the law itself should annul contracts which have been placed under its protection ; but at that time the effect produced on men's minds was very different. The creditors, who had feared that nothing would be left them, thought themselves very fortunate not to lose all, and the debtors, who had reckoned upon being altogether freed, bitterly complained because they were still required to pay part. Hence disappointment and murmuring. "At this moment," wrote Caelius, "with the exception of a few usurers, everybody here is Pompeian." [1]

This was a good opportunity for a secret enemy like Caelius. He hastened to seize it, and to take advantage of the disaffection which he clearly perceived. His tactics were bold. The plan which he devised was to take upon himself this character of advanced democrat, or, as we should say now, of socialist, which Caesar rejected, to form a more radical party of all these malcontents, and to declare himself their head. While the arbitrators appointed to value the property of the debtors performed their delicate functions to the best of their ability, and the praetor of the city, Trebonius, settled the disputes which arose upon their decisions, Caelius had his curule chair placed beside the tribunal of Trebonius, and setting himself up, by his own authority, as judge of the sentences of his colleague, he declared that he would support the demands of those who had any complaints ; but whether it was that Trebonius satisfied everybody, or rather, that they were

[1] *Ad fam.* viii. 17.

afraid of Caesar, no one dared to come forward. This first check did not discourage Caelius : he thought, on the contrary, that the more difficult his position became, the more necessary it was to put a bold face on the matter, and therefore, notwithstanding the opposition of the consul Servilius, and of all the other magistrates, he published two very daring laws, one remitting a year's rent to all tenants, the other abolishing entirely all debts. This time the people seemed disposed to come to the aid of him who took their part so resolutely ; disturbances took place ; blood was shed as in former times in the Forum ; Trebonius, attacked by a furious multitude, was thrown down from his tribunal and only escaped by a miracle. Caelius triumphed, and no doubt thought that a new revolution was about to commence ; but, by a singular coincidence, he soon found himself the victim of the same error that later ruined Brutus. In causes quite opposed, these two men so unlike each other deceived themselves in the same manner : both had reckoned too much on the people of Rome. One restored them liberty, and thought them capable of desiring and defending it, the other called them to arms, promising to share among them the wealth of the rich ; but the people listened neither to the one nor the other, for they were no more powerfully stirred by evil passions than by noble senti-ments ; they had played their part and they were aware of it. On the day that they had surrendered themselves to absolute power they seem to have lost entirely all memory of the past. From that time we see that they have re-nounced all political activity, and nothing can rouse them from their apathy. Those rights, which they had desired with such ardour, and gained with so much trouble, that greed so carefully encouraged by the popular leaders, even the tribunate and the agrarian laws, all become indifferent to them. They are already that populace of the empire which is so admirably painted by Tacitus, the most worthless of all peoples, cringing to the successful, cruel to the defeated, welcoming all who triumph with the same applause, whose sole part in all revolutions consists in joining the train of the conqueror, when the struggle is over.

Such a people could not be a real support to anybody, and Caelius was wrong to reckon upon them. If, by force of habit, they appeared one day to be moved by those great promises which had stirred them so often, when they were free, the feeling was but a passing one, and a small body of cavalry which chanced to be marching through Rome was sufficient to reduce them to order. The consul Servilius was armed by the senate with the famous formula which suspended all legal powers, and concentrated authority in a single hand. Aided by these passing troops, he forbade Caelius to exercise the functions of his office, and when Caelius resisted, he had his curule chair broken,[1] and dragged him from the tribune from which he would not descend. This time the people remained quiet, not a voice answered when he tried to awaken the old passions in these dead souls. Caelius went home with rage in his heart. After such a public disgrace it was not possible to remain longer in Rome. Accordingly he hastened to quit it, telling everybody that he was going to have an explanation with Caesar; but he had quite other projects. Since Rome abandoned him, Caelius was going to attempt to rouse Italy and recommence the social war. It was a bold enterprise, and yet with the help of an intrepid man whose support he had procured he did not despair of success. There was at

[1] A very curious detail preserved by Quintilian, shows us that Caelius retained his levity of character and bantering humour in the midst of these grave affairs in which he staked his life. After his curule chair had been broken he had another made entirely of leather thongs, and took it to the consul. All the spectators burst out laughing. The story ran that Servilius had had a strapping in his youth.

that time in Italy an old conspirator, Milo, who had made himself dreaded by his violence during the anarchy which followed Cicero's consulship, and when condemned later for assassination, he had taken refuge at Marseilles. Caesar, in recalling all the exiles, had excepted this man whose incorrigible audacity he feared; but, on the invitation of Caelius, he had secretly returned and awaited the turn of events. Caelius went to see him, and both wrote pressing letters to the free towns of Italy, making them great promises, and exciting them to take up arms. The free towns remained quiet. Caelius and Milo were forced to make use of the last resource that remained to them. Abandoned by the free citizens of Rome, and of Italy, they appealed to the servile population, opening the prisons of the slaves, and calling upon the shepherds of Apulia and the gladiators of the public games. When they had by these means got together some partisans, they parted to tempt fortune separately, but neither succeeded. Milo, who had dared to attack an important town defended by a praetor with a legion, was killed by a stone. Caelius, after having vainly essayed to induce Naples and Campania to declare in his favour, was obliged to retreat to Thurium. There he met some Spanish and Gallic cavalry who had been sent from Rome, and as he advanced to speak with them and promised them money if they would follow him, they killed him.

Thus perished at the age of thirty-four years this intrepid young man who had hoped to equal the fortunes of Caesar. Never had such vast designs so miserable an end. After having shown an incredible audacity, and formed projects which grew more and more bold as the first attempts failed; after having in a few months successively tried to raise the people of Rome, Italy, and the slaves, he died obscurely by the hand of some barbarians whom he wished to induce to betray their duty; and his death, happening at the moment when all eyes were fixed on Pharsalia, passed almost unobserved. Who would dare to say, however, that this end, sad as it may be, was not deserved? Was it not just, after all, that a man who had lived by adventures should perish as an adventurer? He was not a consummate politician, whatever Cicero may assert; he failed to be that, because he lacked conviction and a genuine devotion. The instability of his feelings, the inconsistency of his conduct, that sort of scepticism that he affected for all convictions were not less hurtful to his talents than to his character. If he had known how to put greater unity into his life, if he had early attached himself to some honourable party, his capacities, finding employment worthy of them, would have attained their perfection. He might have no doubt failed, but to die at Pharsalia or Philippi is still considered an honour by posterity. On the contrary, as he changed his opinions as often as his interests or caprices, as he served by turns the most opposite parties without belief in the justice of any, he was never anything but an immature orator and a hap-hazard politician, and he died on the high-road like a common malefactor. However, notwithstanding his faults, history has some difficulty in judging him harshly. The ancient writers never speak of him without a secret liking. The brilliancy that surrounded his youth, the charms of his mind, the elegance which he knew how to preserve in his worst disorders, a sort of daring frankness which prevented him seeking honourable pretexts for dishonourable actions, his clear judgment of political situations, his knowledge of men, his fertility of resource, his strength of resolution, his boldness in daring all and in constantly risking his life; these many brilliant qualities though mingled with so many great defects have disarmed the most severe judges. The sage Quintilian himself, little fitted as he was to understand that passionate nature, dared not be severe upon him.   After having praised the graces of his mind and his incisive eloquence, he contented himself with saying, by way of moral : " He was a man who deserved to have had a juster sense of conduct and a longer life, *dignus vir cui mens melior et vita longior contigisset !* " [1]

At the time that Caelius died, that elegant youth of which he was the model, and which the verses of Catullus and the letters of Cicero have helped us to know, had already partly disappeared.   There remained scarcely any of those young men who had shone in the *fêtes* of Baiae and who had been applauded in the Forum.   Catullus died first, at the very moment when his talents were being ripened by age, and were becoming more serious and more elevated.   His friend Calvus was soon to follow him, carried off at thirty-five, no doubt by the fatigues of public life.   Curio had been killed by Pompey's soldiers, as Caelius was by Caesar's.   Dolabella survived, but only for a short time, and he also was to perish in a tragic manner.   It was a revolutionary generation which the revolution mowed down, for it is true, according to the celebrated saying, that in all times as in all countries revolution devours her own children.

[1] *Inst. orat.* x. 1.

CAESAR AND CICERO

I

CICERO AND THE CAMP OF CAESAR IN GAUL

CICERO was not wrong when he said one day to Caesar: "After our time, there will be great debates about you, as there have been among ourselves."[1] It is certain that he is that historical personage whom men still discuss with most heat. None has excited more sympathy or roused more animosity, and it must be admitted that there seems to be something in him to justify both the one and the other. He cannot be admired or blamed without some reservations, and he always attracts on some side those whom he repels on another. The very people who hate him the most, and who cannot pardon him the political revolution that he accomplished, are forced into a secret admiration for him when they think of his victories, or read his writings.

The more complex and disputable his character, the more necessary it is, in order to form a just idea of him, to interrogate those who were in a position to know him. Although Cicero was almost all his life separated from Caesar by grave disagreements, twice he had occasion to maintain a close intercourse with him: during the Gallic war he was his political ally and his assiduous correspondent; after Pharsalia he became his friend again, and acted as intermediary between the conqueror and those he had con-

[1] *Pro Marcello*, 9.

demned to exile.   Let us inquire what he says of him at
these two periods of his life when he saw him most closely,
and let us collect from his correspondence, through which
we become so well acquainted with the eminent men of that
time, the information it contains about him who was the
greatest of all.

I.

I must first recall the events which led Cicero to desert
the aristocratic party to which he had been attached since
his consulship, in order to serve the triumvirs, and how the
courageous friend of Hortensius and of Cato became so
subservient to Pompey and Caesar.   It is not an honourable
period in his life, and his most convinced admirers say as
little about it as possible.   However, there is some interest,
perhaps even some profit, in pausing upon it for a moment.

Cicero's return from the exile to which he had been condemned after his consulship by the efforts of Clodius, was
a veritable triumph.   Brundusium, where he disembarked,
celebrated his arrival by public rejoicings.   All the citizens
of the free towns that bordered the Appian Way, waited for
him on the road, and the heads of families with their
wives and children came from all the neighbouring farms
to see him pass.   At Rome, he was received by an
immense multitude crowded on the public squares, or
ranged on the steps of the temples.   "It seemed," said
he, "that all the city was drawn from its foundations to
come and salute its liberator." [1]   At his brother's house,
where he was going to live, he found the most eminent
members of the senate awaiting him, and at the same time
congratulatory addresses from all the popular societies of
the city.   It is probable that some who had signed these,

[1] *In Pis.* 22.

had voted with the same eagerness the preceding year for
the law that exiled him, and that many clapped their hands
on his return who had applauded his departure ; but the
people have occasionally these strange and generous impulses. It sometimes happens that they break away by a
sudden bound from the malice, distrust, and narrowness of
party spirit, and, at the very moment when passions seem
most inflamed and divisions most clearly marked, they
unite all at once to render homage to some great genius or
to some great character, which, we know not how, has compelled their recognition. Usually, this gratitude and admiration last but a short time ; but, should they endure only
a day, they do eternal honour to him who has been their
object, and the glory they leave behind is sufficient to
illumine a whole life. Therefore we must pardon Cicero
for having spoken so often and with so much effusiveness
of this glorious day. A little pride was here both legitimate
and natural. How could a soul so sensitive to popular
applause have resisted the intoxication of a triumphal return ?
" I do not feel as though I were simply returning from exile,"
said he, " I appear to myself to be mounting to heaven." [1]

But he was not long in descending again to earth. Whatever he may have thought at first, he soon recognized that
this city which welcomed him with so much rejoicing was
not changed, and that he found it much the same as when
he left it. Anarchy had reigned there for three years, an
anarchy such as we have difficulty in imagining, notwithstanding all the examples that our own revolutions have
given us. Since the triumvirs had let loose the rabble in
order to seize upon the government of the republic, it had
become entirely master. A daring tribune, a deserter from
the aristocracy, and one who bore the most illustrious name
in Rome, Clodius, had taken upon himself to lead it, and as

[1] *Pro Dom.* 28.

far as possible, to discipline it. He had displayed in this difficult work many talents and much audacity, and had succeeded well enough to deserve to become the terror of honest people. When we speak of the Roman mob, we must not forget that it was much more frightful than our own, and was recruited from more formidable elements. Whatever just dismay the populace that emerges all at once from the lowest quarters of our manufacturing cities, on a day of riot, may cause us, let us remember that at Rome, this inferior social stratum descended still lower. Below the vagabond strangers and the starving workmen, the ordinary tools of revolutions, there was all that crowd of freedmen demoralized by slavery, to whom liberty had given but one more means for evil-doing; there were those gladiators, trained to fight beast or man, who made light of the death of others or themselves; there were, still lower, those fugitive slaves, who were indeed the worst of all classes, who, after having robbed or murdered at home, and lived by pillage on the road, came from all Italy to take refuge and disappear in the obscurity of the slums of Rome, an unclean and terrible multitude of men without family, without country, who, outlawed by the general sentiment of society, had nothing to respect as they had nothing to lose. It was among these that Clodius recruited his bands. Enlistments were made in open day, in one of the most frequented spots in Rome, near the Aurelian steps. The new soldiers were then organized in decuries and centuries, under energetic leaders. They assembled by districts in secret societies, where they went to receive the password, and had their centre and arsenal at the temple of Castor. When the day arrived, and a popular manifestation was wanted, the tribunes ordered the shops to be closed; then, the artisans were thrown on the public streets, and all the army of the secret societies marched together towards the Forum. There

they met, not the honest folks, who, feeling themselves the
weaker party, stayed at home, but the gladiators and herds-
men whom the senate had fetched to defend them from the
wilds of Picenum or Gaul, and then the battle commenced.
"Imagine London," says M. Mommsen, "with the slave
population of New Orleans, the police of Constantinople,
and the industrial condition of modern Rome, and think of
the political state of Paris in 1848 : you will have some idea
of republican Rome in its last days."

No law was any longer respected, no citizen, no magistrate
was secure from violence. One day the fasces of a consul
were broken, the next a tribune was left for dead. The
senate itself, led away by these examples, had at last lost
that quality which Romans lost the last, its dignity. In
that assembly of kings, as a Greek had called it, they
debated with revolting coarseness. Cicero surprised no
one when he gave his adversaries the names of swine, filth,
rotten flesh. Sometimes the discussions became so heated
that the noise reached that excited crowd that filled the
porticoes near the curia, which then took part in them, with
so much violence that the terrified senators hastened to
fly.[1] We can easily understand that it was much worse in
the Forum. Cicero relates that, when they were tired of
insulting, they spat in each other's faces.[2] When a man
wished to address the people, he had to take the rostrum
by storm, and he risked his life in trying to keep his place
there. The tribunes had found a new way of obtaining
unanimity of votes for the laws that they proposed: namely,
to beat and drive away all who took it into their heads not
to agree with them. But contests were nowhere more
violent than on the Campus Martius on election days.
Men were driven to regret the time when they trafficked
publicly in the votes of the electors. Now, they did not

[1] *Ad Quint.* ii. 1.   [2] *Ibid.* ii. 3.

even take the trouble to buy public offices; they found it more convenient to seize them by force. Each party went before daylight to the Campus Martius. Collisions took place on the roads leading to it. Each party hastened to arrive before its adversaries, or, if these were already established there, attacked them in order to dislodge them: naturally the appointments belonged to those who remained masters of the place. In the midst of all these armed bands there was no security for any one. Men were obliged to fortify themselves in their houses for fear of being surprised. They could only go out with a train of gladiators and slaves. To go from one quarter of the city to another, they took as many precautions as if they had to traverse a desert country, and they met at the turning of a street with the same fear they would have had at the corner of a wood. In the midst of Rome there were real battles and regular sieges. It was an ordinary manœuvre to set fire to the houses of their enemies at the risk of burning down a whole quarter, and, towards the end, no election or popular assembly took place without bloodshed. "The Tiber," says Cicero, speaking of one of these combats, "was full of the corpses of the citizens, the public sewers were choked with them, and they were obliged to mop up with sponges the blood that streamed from the Forum." [1]

Such were the obscure convulsions in which the Roman republic perished, and the shameful disorders that sapped its remaining strength. Cicero well knew that bloody anarchy and the dangers he was about to run, and had therefore resolved, before re-entering Rome, to be prudent, so as not to run the risk of having to leave it again. His was not one of those minds that misfortune strengthens, and that feel a kind of pleasure in struggling against ill-fortune. Exile had discouraged him. During the long weariness of his sojourn

[1] *Pro Sext.* 35.

in Thessaly, he had made a sad review of the past. He had reproached himself for his occasional courage and independence, for his boldness in combating the powerful, and for the mistake he had made in joining himself too closely to the party which he had judged the best, but which was evidently the weakest, as though to act thus had been a crime. He came back thoroughly resolved to entangle himself as little as possible with any one, to disarm his enemies by concession, and to keep on good terms with everybody. This was the course he followed on his arrival, and his first speeches are masterpieces of policy. It is plain that he still leans towards the aristocracy which had taken an active part in his restoration, and to praise it he has noble expressions of patriotism and gratitude ; but already he commences to flatter Caesar, and he calls Pompey " the most virtuous, the wisest, the greatest of the men of his age or of any age." [1] At the same time, he tells us himself, he took good heed not to appear in the senate when irritating questions were to be discussed, and was very careful to escape from the Forum as soon as the debate became too heated. " No more violent remedies," he replied to those who tried to urge him to some brilliant action ; " I must put myself on diet." [2]

However, he soon perceived that this adroit reserve was not sufficient to ward off all danger. While he was rebuilding his house on the Palatine, which had been destroyed after his departure, the bands of Clodius threw themselves on the workmen and dispersed them, and, emboldened by this success, set fire to the house of his brother Quintus, which was close by. A few days later, as he was walking on the Via Sacra, he heard all at once a great noise, and on turning round saw sticks raised and naked swords. It was the same

---

[1] *Ad pop. pro red.* 7.
[2] *Ad Att.* iv. 3. *Ego diaeta curari incipio, chirurgiae taedet.*

men who came to attack him. He had great difficulty in escaping into the vestibule of a friendly house while his slaves fought bravely before the door to give him time to escape. Cato would not have been moved by this violence; Cicero must have been very much frightened; above all it taught him that his system of prudent reserve did not sufficiently assure his safety. It was, in fact, probable that no party would expose itself to defend him as long as he had only compliments to give it, and as he could not stand alone and without support in the midst of all these armed factions, it was really necessary that, in order to find the support he needed, he should consent to attach himself more closely to one of them.

But which should he choose? This was a grave question in which his interests were at variance with his sympathies. All his inclinations were evidently for the aristocracy. He had closely attached himself to it about the time of his consulship, and since that time he had professed to serve it, and it was for it that he had just braved the anger of the people and exposed himself to exile. But this very exile had taught him how the most honourable course was also the least safe. At the last moment, the senate had not found better means of saving him than to make useless decrees, to put on mourning, and go and throw themselves at the feet of the consuls. Cicero thought that this was not enough. Seeing himself so ill-defended, he had suspected that people who did not take his interests in hand more resolutely were not very sorry for his misfortunes; and perhaps he was not wrong. The Roman aristocracy, whatever he had done for it, could not forget he was a "new" man. The Claudii, the Cornelii, the Manlii, always looked with a certain displeasure on this insignificant townsman of Arpinum, whom the popular vote had made their equal. Still they might have pardoned his good fortune if he had borne it with more modesty ; but we know his vanity ; though it was only ridiculous, the aristocracy, whom it offended, thought it criminal. They could not tolerate the legitimate pride with which he constantly recalled that he was only a *parvenu*. They thought it strange that, when attacked by insolence, he dared to reply by raillery ; and quite recently they had shown themselves scandalized that he had forgotten himself so far as to buy the villa of Catulus at Tusculum, and to go and live on the Palatine in the house of Crassus. Cicero, with his usual shrewdness, very clearly discerned all these sentiments of the aristocracy, and even exaggerated them. Since his return from exile he had yet other grievances against them. They had taken much trouble to get him recalled ; but had not foreseen the splendour of his return, and it did not seem that they were very well pleased with it. "Those who have clipped my wings," said Cicero, "are sorry to see them grow again."[1] From this moment his good friends in the senate would do nothing more for him. He had found his finances much embarrassed, his house on the Palatine burnt, his villas at Tusculum and Formiae plundered and destroyed, and they decided with reluctance to indemnify him for these losses. What irritated him still more, was that he saw clearly that they did not share in his anger against Clodius. They showed themselves cool or remained silent during his violent fits of anger. A few even, the most adroit, affected to speak only with esteem of this factious tribune, and did not blush to give him their hand in public. Whence came their regard for a man who had so little for them ? It was that they hoped to make use of him, and that they secretly nourished the thought of calling in the mob to the help of the endangered aristocracy. This alliance, although less usual than that of the mob with despotism, was not impossible,

[1] *Ad Att.* iv. 2.

and the bands of Clodius, if they could be enlisted, would have permitted the senate to hold the triumvirs in check. Cicero, who perceived this policy, feared to become its victim; he bitterly regretted then the services he had tried to render to the senate, and which had cost him so dear. In recalling the dangers to which he had exposed himself in order to defend it, the obstinate and unsuccessful struggles that he had maintained for four years, the ruin of his political position and the disasters of his private fortune, he said with sorrow: "I see clearly now that I have been only a fool (*scio me asinum germanum fuisse*").[1]

It only remained for him then to turn to the triumvirs. This was the advice given to him by his friend the prudent Atticus, and his brother Quintus, whom the burning of his house had rendered cautious contrary to his habit; this was the resolution he was himself tempted to take every time he ran some fresh danger. Nevertheless, he had some trouble in making up his mind. The triumvirs had been heretofore his most cruel enemies. Without speaking of Crassus, in whom he detected an accomplice of Catiline, he well knew that it was Caesar who had let Clodius loose against him, and he could not forget that Pompey, who had sworn to defend him, had lately abandoned him to the vengeance of his two friends; but he had no choice of alliances, and since he dared no longer trust the aristocratic party, he was forced to put himself under the protection of others. He had then to resign himself to his fate. He authorized his brother to pledge him to Caesar and Pompey, and prepared himself to serve their ambition. His first act, after his return, had been to demand for Pompey one of those extraordinary powers of which he was so greedy: by his exertions Pompey had been entrusted for six years with the victualling of Rome, and on this occasion he had been

[1] *Ad Att.* iv. 5.

invested with an almost unlimited authority. A short time after, although the public treasury was exhausted, he had a sum of money granted to Caesar for the payment of his legions, and permission to have ten lieutenants under his orders. When the aristocracy, who understood with what design Caesar was carrying out the conquest of Gaul, wished to prevent him continuing it, it was again Cicero who demanded and obtained for him permission to finish his work. It was thus that the old enemy of the triumvirs became their usual defender before the senate. The support that he consented to give was not useless to them. His great name and his eloquence drew towards him the moderate men of all parties, those whose opinion was wavering and their convictions undecided; those, above all, who, wearied with a too tempestuous liberty, sought everywhere a firm hand that might give them repose; and these, joined to the personal friends of Caesar and Pompey, to the tools that the rich Crassus had made by bribery, and to the ambitious men of all sorts who foresaw the advent of the monarchy and wished to be the first to salute it, formed in the senate a majority of which Cicero was the head and the orator, and which rendered to the triumvirs the important service of giving a legal sanction to that power which they had gained by violence and exercised illegally.

Cicero had at length obtained repose. His enemies feared him, Clodius dared no longer risk attacking him, his familiarity with the new masters was envied, and yet this skilful conduct, which gained for him the thanks of the triumvirs and the congratulations of Atticus, did not fail at times to disturb him. It was in vain for him to say to himself that "his life had regained its splendour," he did not feel less remorse in serving men whose ambition he knew, and whom he knew to be dangerous to the liberty of his country. In the midst of the efforts that he made to satisfy them, he had sudden awakenings of patriotism which made him blush. His private correspondence bears everywhere the trace of the alternations of mood through which he passed. One day he wrote to Atticus in a light and resolute tone : " Let us give up honour, justice, and fine sentiments. . . . Since those who can do nothing will not love me, let us try to make ourselves loved by those who can do everything." [1] But shame seized him the next day, and he could not avoid saying to his friend : " Is anything sadder than our life, mine above all ? If I speak according to my convictions I pass for a madman ; if I listen to my interests, I am accused of being a slave ; if I am silent, they say I am afraid." [2] Even in his public speeches, notwithstanding the restraint he puts on himself, we can feel his secret dissatisfaction. It seems to me that we discover it above all in that extraordinary tone of bitterness and violence which was then habitual to him. Never, perhaps, did he pronounce more passionate invectives. Now this excess of violence towards others often comes from a mind ill at ease. What made his eloquence so bitter at this time was that uneasy feeling which a man has who is in the wrong path and has not the courage to leave it. He did not forgive his old friends their raillery and his new ones their demands ; he reproached himself secretly for his base concessions ; he had a spite against others and against himself, and Vatinius or Piso suffered for all the rest. In this condition of mind he could not be a safe friend for anybody. It happened sometimes that he suddenly turned on his new friends, and gave blows so much the more disagreeable that they were not expected. Sometimes he diverted himself by attacking their best friends, to show others and prove to himself that he had not entirely lost his liberty. People had been very much surprised to hear him, in a speech in which he defended Caesar's interests,

[1] *Ad Att.* iv. 5.   [2] *Ibid.* iv. 6.

praise to excess Bibulus, whom Caesar detested. One day even he seemed quite ready to return to those whom he had called honest men before he abandoned them. It seemed to him a good opportunity to break with his new party in a formal manner. The friendship of the triumvirs had become very cool. Pompey was not pleased with the success of that Gallic war which threatened to make his own victories forgotten. Cicero, who heard him speak without restraint against his rival, thought he might without danger give some satisfaction to his irritated conscience, and wished by a brilliant stroke to deserve the pardon of his old friends. Taking advantage of some difficulty that was raised in regard to the carrying out of Caesar's agrarian law, he formally announced that on the Ides of May he would speak on the sale of the Campanian lands which by this law were distributed among the people. The effect of his declaration was very great. The allies of the triumvirs were as much offended as they were surprised, and the aristocratic party hastened to welcome with transports of joy the return of the eloquent deserter, but in a few days everything turned against him. At the very moment when he decided on this brilliant stroke, the alliance between the triumvirs that was thought to be broken, was renewed at Lucca, and, amid a concourse of their flatterers, they once more divided the world between them. Cicero, then, was about to find himself again alone and without support in the presence of an angry and all-powerful enemy who threatened to deliver him up again to the vengeance of Clodius. Atticus scolded; Quintus, who had pledged himself for his brother, complained roughly that his promises were being broken. Pompey, although he had secretly encouraged the defection, affected to be more angry than anybody. The unhappy Cicero, attacked on all sides, and trembling at the passions which he had raised, hastened to submit, and promised everything that was required. Thus this attempt at independence only made his slavery heavier.

From this moment he seems to have resolutely accepted his new position, from a feeling that he could not change it. He resigned himself to heap more and more exaggerated praises on the vain Pompey, who never had enough. He consented to become the agent of Caesar with Oppius and Balbus, and to supervise the public buildings he was constructing. He went further, and was willing at the request of his powerful protectors to give his hand to men whom he regarded as his greatest enemies. This was not a small sacrifice for a man who had such strong aversions; but from the time that he joined their party so decidedly, he was obliged to accept their friendship as he defended their plans. They began to take steps to reconcile him to Crassus. This was a great matter which was not done in a day, for when it was thought that their old enmity was appeased, it broke out all at once in a discussion in the senate, and Cicero abused his new ally with a violence that surprised himself. " I thought my hatred exhausted," said he naïvely, "and did not imagine any remained in my heart." [1] He was then asked to undertake the defence of Vatinius; he consented with a pretty good grace, although he had pronounced a furious invective against him the year before. The advocates in Rome were accustomed to these sudden changes, and Cicero had done the same thing more than once. When Gabinius returned from Egypt, after having restored King Ptolemy against the formal command of the senate, Cicero, who could not abide him, thinking it a good opportunity to ruin him, prepared to attack him; but Pompey came to beg him urgently to defend him. He dared not refuse, changed his part, and submitted to speak in favour of a man whom he detested and a cause which he

[1] *Ad fam.* i. 9.

considered bad. He had at least the consolation of losing his case, and although he was always anxious for success, it is probable that this failure did not give him much pain.

But he well understood that so much deference and submission, all these notorious self-contradictions to which he was forced, would end by rousing public opinion against him. Therefore, about this time, he decided to write an important letter to his friend Lentulus, one of the chiefs of the aristocracy, which he probably intended to be circulated, and in which he explains his conduct.[1] In this letter, after having related the facts in his own way and sufficiently abused those whom he had abandoned, a convenient and common mode of anticipating their complaints and making them responsible for the mischief he was about to do them, he ventures to present, with singular candour, a sort of apology for his political instability. The reasons he gives to justify it are not always very good; but we must believe that better cannot be found, since they have not ceased to be used. Under the pretence that Plato has somewhere said, "one must not do violence to one's country any more than to one's father," Cicero lays it down as a principle, that a politician ought not to persist in wishing for what his fellow-citizens do not wish, nor lose his pains in attempting useless opposition. Circumstances change, one must change with them, and suit oneself to the wind that blows, so as not to go to pieces on the rocks. Besides, is that really to change? Cannot one in the main wish for the same thing and serve one's country under different banners? A man is not fickle for defending, according to circumstances, opinions that seem contradictory if by opposite routes he marches to the same goal, and do we not know "that we must often shift the sails when we wish to arrive in port"?

[1] *Ad fam.* i. 9.

These are only the general maxims which an inventive politician can make up to hide his weaknesses, and there is no need to discuss them. The best way to defend Cicero is to remember in what a time he lived, and how little fitted he was for that time. This elegant literary man, this skilful artist, this friend of the arts of peace, had been placed, by a caprice of fate, in one of the most stormy and troubled periods of history. What could a man of leisure and study do among those deadly struggles where force was master, a man who had no arms but his words, and who always dreamed of the pleasures of peaceful times and the pacific laurels of eloquence? A more manly soul than his would have been needed to make head against these assaults. Events stronger than himself confounded his designs every instant and played with his hesitating will. On his entry into public life he had taken for his motto, leisure and honour, *otium cum dignitate;* but these two things are not easy to unite in revolutionary times, and almost always one of the two is lost when we are too anxious to preserve the other. Resolute characters, who know this well, make their choice between them at once, and, according as one is a Cato or an Atticus, one decides from the very first day either for leisure or for honour. The undecided, like Cicero, pass from one to the other, according to circumstances, and thus jeopardize both. We have arrived at one of those painful moments in his life when he sacrifices honour to leisure ; let us not be too severe upon him, and let us remember that, later, he sacrificed not only his leisure, but even his life, to save his honour.

II.

One of the results of the new policy of Cicero was to give him an opportunity of becoming well acquainted with

Caesar. Not that they had been hitherto strangers to one another. The taste of both for letters and the similar nature of their studies, had united them in their youth, and from these early relations, which men never forget, there had remained some natural sympathy and good-will. But as in later life they had attached themselves to opposite parties, circumstances had separated them. In the Forum, and in the senate, they had acquired the habit of always being of opposite opinions, and naturally their friendship had suffered from the vivacity of their dissensions. Yet Cicero tells us that, even when they were most excited against each other, Caesar could never hate him.[1]

Politics had separated them, politics reunited them. When Cicero turned towards the party of the triumvirs their intimate relations recommenced ; but this time their position was different, and their connection could no longer have the same character. The old school-fellow of Cicero had become his protector. It was no longer a mutual inclination or common studies, it was interest and necessity that united them, and their new ties were formed by a sort of reciprocal agreement in which one of the two gave his talents and a little of his honour, that the other might guarantee him repose. These are not very favourable circumstances, it must be admitted, to produce a sincere friendship. However, when we read Cicero's private correspondence, in which he speaks unreservedly, we cannot doubt but that he found many charms in these relations with Caesar which seemed to him at first to be so difficult. Probably this was because he compared them with those which he had at the same time to keep up with Pompey. Caesar at least was affable and polite. Although he had the gravest affairs on his hands, he found time to think of his friends and to joke with them. Victorious as he was,

[1] *In Pis.* 32.

he allowed them to write to him "familiarly and without subserviency." [1]   He answered with amiable letters, "full of politeness, kind attentions and charm," [2] which delighted Cicero. Pompey, on the contrary, seemed to take a pleasure in wounding him by his lofty airs.   This pompous and vain man, whom the adoration of the Orientals had spoilt, and who could not avoid assuming the deportment of a conqueror merely in going from his house at Alba to Rome, affected an imperious and haughty tone which alienated everybody.   His dissimulation was still more displeasing than his insolence.   He had a sort of dislike of communicating his projects to others ; he hid them even from his most devoted friends, who wished to know them in order to support them.   Cicero complains more than once that he could never discover what he wanted ; it even happened that he was completely deceived as to his real intentions and made him angry, thinking he was doing him a service. This obstinate dissimulation passed, no doubt, for profound policy in the eyes of the multitude ; but the more skilful had no difficulty in discerning its motive.   If he did not express his opinion to anybody, it was because most frequently he had no opinion, and, as it very commonly happens, silence with him only served to cover the fact. He went at random, without fixed principles or settled system, and never looked beyond present circumstances. Events always took him by surprise, and he showed clearly that he was no more capable of directing them than of foreseeing them.   His ambition itself, which was his dominant passion, had no precise views or decided aims. Whatever dignities were offered to satisfy it, it was plainly seen that he always desired something else ; this was perceived without his saying it, for he tried very awkwardly to hide it.   His ordinary stratagem was to pretend indifference,

[1] *Ad Quint.* ii. 12.   [2] *Ibid.* ii. 15.

and he wished to be forced to accept what he most ardently desired. We can well understand that this pretence when too often repeated deceived nobody. Upon the whole, as he had successively attacked and defended all parties, and after having often appeared to desire an almost royal authority, had not endeavoured to destroy the republic when he had the power to do so, it is impossible for us to discover now what plan he had conceived, or even if he had conceived any distinct plan at all.

It is not so with Caesar. He knew the object of his ambition, and saw distinctly what he wished to do. His plans were settled even before he entered public life ;[1] in his youth he had formed the design to become master. The spectacle of the revolutions on which he had looked had given rise to the thought ; the confidence that he had in his own capacity, and in the inferiority of his enemies, gave him strength to undertake it, and a sort of superstitious belief in his destiny, not uncommon in men who attempt these great adventures, assured him in advance of success. Therefore he marched resolutely towards his end, without showing undue haste to attain it, but without ever losing sight of it. To know exactly what one wants is not a common quality, above all in those troubled times in which good and evil are mingled, and yet success only comes to those who possess it. What, above all, gave Caesar his superiority was, that in the midst of those irresolute politicians who had only uncertain projects, hesitating convictions, and occasional ambitions, he alone had a deliberate ambition and a settled design. One could not approach him without coming under the influence of that tranquil

---

[1] This at least was the opinion of all the historians of antiquity. We read in a fragment of a letter from Cicero to Q. Axius quoted by Suetonius (*Caes.* 9): *Caesar in consulatu confirmavit regnum de quo aedilis cogitaret.*

and powerful will, which had a clear idea of its projects,
the consciousness of its own strength, and the confidence of
victory. Cicero felt it like the rest, notwithstanding his
prejudices. In presence of such consistency and firmness
he could not avoid making unfavourable comparisons with
the perturbation and inconsistency of his old friend. " I
am of your opinion about Pompey, he hinted to his brother,
or rather you are of mine, for I have sung the praises of
Caesar for a long time." [1] In fact, it was sufficient to
approach a man of real genius to recognize the emptiness
of this semblance of a great man, whose easy successes
and air of inflated majesty had imposed so long upon the
admiration of fools.

We must not, however, suppose that Caesar was one of
those stubborn men who will not give way to circumstances,
and never consent to alter anything in the plans they have
once conceived. No one, on the contrary, knew how to
bend to necessity better than he. His aim remained the
same, but he did not hesitate to take the most diverse
means to attain it, when it was necessary. One of these
important modifications took place in his policy, precisely at
the period with which we are occupied. What distinguishes
Caesar from the men with whom he is usually compared,
Alexander and Napoleon, has been well stated by M.
Mommsen, namely, that originally he was a statesman
rather than a general. He did not, like them, come from
the camp, and he had as yet merely passed through it
when, by force of circumstances and almost in spite of himself, he became a conqueror. All his youth was passed in
Rome in the turmoil of public life, and he only set out for
Gaul at an age at which Alexander was dead and Napoleon
vanquished. He had evidently formed the plan of making
himself master without employing arms ; he reckoned upon

[1] *Ad Quint.* ii. 13.

destroying the republic by a slow and internal revolution, and by preserving as much as possible, in so illegal an attempt, the outward form of legality. He saw that the popular party had more taste for social reforms than for political liberties, and he thought, with reason, that a democratic monarchy would not be repugnant to it. By multiplying dissensions, by becoming the secret accomplice of Catiline and Clodius, he wearied timid republicans of a too troubled liberty and prepared them to sacrifice it willingly to repose. He hoped in this way that the republic, shaken by these daily attacks, which exhausted and tired out its most intrepid defenders, would at last fall without violence and without noise. But, to our great surprise, at the moment when this skilfully-planned design seemed on the point of succeeding, we see Caesar suddenly give it up. After that consulship in which he had governed alone, reducing his colleague to inaction and the senate to silence, he withdraws from Rome for ten years, and goes to attempt the conquest of an unknown country. What reasons decided him to this unexpected change ? We should like to believe that he felt some disgust for that life of base intrigues that he led at Rome, and wished to invigorate himself in labours more worthy of him ; but it is much more likely that, after having seen clearly that the republic would fall of itself, he understood that he would require an army and military renown to gain the mastery over Pompey. It was, then, without enthusiasm, without passion, designedly and on calculation, that he decided to set out for Gaul. When he took this important resolution, which has contributed so much to his greatness, he was forty-four.[1] Pascal thinks it was very late to begin, and that he was too old to

[1] Or only forty-two, if we place his birth in 654. See, on this point, an interesting note in the *Life of Caesar*, by Napoleon III., Bk. II. ch. i.

interest himself in the conquest of the world. It is, on the contrary, as it seems, one of the most admirable efforts of that energetic will that, at an age when habits are irrevocably fixed, and when a man has definitely entered on the road he must follow to the end, Caesar suddenly commenced a new life, and, leaving in a moment the business of popular agitator that he had followed for twenty-five years, set himself to govern provinces and lead armies. This spectacle, indeed, is more surprising now than it was then. It is no longer the custom to turn oneself into an administrator or a general at fifty, and these things seem to us to demand a special vocation and a long apprenticeship ; history shows us that it was otherwise at Rome. Had they not just seen the voluptuous Lucullus, on his way to command the army of Asia, learn the art of war during the voyage, and conquer Mithridates on his arrival? As to administration, a rich Roman learnt it in his own home. Those vast domains, those legions of slaves that he possessed, the management of an immense fortune which often surpassed the wealth of several kingdoms of our days, familiarized him early with the art of government. It was thus that Caesar, who had as yet only had occasion to practise himself in the government of provinces and the command of armies during the year of his praetorship in Spain, had no need of further study to be able to conquer the Helvetii and to organize the conquered countries, and that he found himself at the very first attempt an admirable general and an administrator of genius.

It was at this epoch that his intimate relations with Cicero recommenced, and they lasted as long as the Gallic war. Cicero often had occasion to write to him to recommend people who wished to serve under his command. The ambition of the young men at that time was to set out for Caesar's camp. Besides the desire of taking part in great deeds under such a general, they had also the secret hope of enriching themselves in those distant countries. We know with what charms the unknown is usually adorned, and how easy it is to lend it all the attractions we wish. Gaul was for the imagination of that time what America was to the sixteenth century. It was supposed that in those countries that no one had visited there lay immense treasures, and all who had their fortune to make hastened to Caesar to have their share of the booty. This eagerness was not displeasing to him; it bore witness to the fascination his conquests exercised, and helped his designs, and accordingly he readily invited men to come to him. He wrote gaily to Cicero, who had begged a commission for some unknown Roman : " You have recommended M. Offius to me; if you like I will make him King of Gaul, unless he prefers to be lieutenant of Lepta. Send me whom you will that I may make him rich." [1] Cicero had with him at that moment two persons whom he loved very much and who had great need of being enriched, the lawyer Trebatius Testa and his own brother Quintus. It was a good opportunity, and he sent them both to Caesar.

Trebatius was a young man of much talent and great zeal for study, who had attached himself to Cicero and did not leave him. He had early left his poor little town of Ulubrae, situated in the midst of the Pontine marshes, for Rome,—Ulubrae the deserted, *vacuae Ulubrae*, whose inhabitants were called Ulubran frogs. He had studied law, and, as he had become very learned in it, no doubt he rendered many services to Cicero, who does not appear ever to have known much of law, and who found it more convenient to laugh at it than to learn it. Unfortunately, consultations being gratuitous, lawyers did not make their fortune at Rome. Accordingly Trebatius was poor, in

[1] *Ad fam.* vii. 5.

spite of his knowledge. Cicero, who liked him unselfishly, consented to deprive himself of the pleasure and use that he found in his society, and sent him to Caesar with one of those charming letters of recommendation that he knew so well how to write, and in which he displayed so much grace and wit. " I do not ask of you," he says, " the com-- mand of a legion, or a government for him. I ask for nothing definite. Give him your friendship, and if after- wards you care to do something for his fortune and his glory I shall not be displeased. In fact, I abandon him to you entirely; I give him to you from hand to hand as they say, and I hope he will find himself well off in those faithful and victorious hands." [1] Caesar thanked Cicero for the present that he had made him, which could not fail to be very valuable to him, " for," he wittily remarked, " among the multitude of men who surround me, there is not one who knows how to prepare a suit." [2]

Trebatius left Rome reluctantly; Cicero said that he had to turn him out of doors.[3] The first sight of Gaul, which resembled very little the France of to-day, was not cheering. He passed wild countries, among half-subdued and threaten- ing people, and in the midst of these barbarian surroundings which oppressed his heart, he always thought of the plea- sures of that cultivated city that he had just left. The letters that he wrote were so disconsolate, that Cicero, forgetting that he had felt the same regrets during his own exile, reproached him gently for what he called his foolish- ness. When he arrived at the camp his ill-humour was redoubled. Trebatius was not a warrior, and it is very likely that the Nervii and the Atrebates frightened him very much. He arrived just at the moment when Caesar was setting out on the expedition to Britain, and refused, one

---

[1] *Ad fam.* vii. 5.   [2] *Ad Quint.* ii. 15.
[3] *Ad fam.* vii, 6 : *nisi te extrusissemus.*

knows not on what pretext, to accompany him : perhaps he alleged, like Dumnorix, that he feared the sea ; but, even in remaining in Gaul there was no want of danger and tedium. Their winter quarters were not comfortable ; they suffered from cold and rain under that inclement sky. In summer they had to take the field, and his terror recommenced. Trebatius was always complaining. What added to his discontent was that he had not found all at once the advantages he had expected. He had set out unwillingly, and wished to return as quickly as possible. Cicero said that he had looked on the letter of recommendation that he had given him to Caesar as a bill of exchange payable to bearer.[1] He thought he had only to present himself in order to take the money, and return. It was not only money he went to look for in Gaul; he expected to find there a post of distinction and importance. He wished to approach Caesar and make himself appreciated. Cicero writes to him : "You would much rather be consulted than covered with gold."[2] Now, Caesar was so busy that he was difficult to approach, and he did not at first pay any great attention to this learned lawyer who came to him from Rome. He contented himself with offering him the title and emoluments of a military tribune, without the duties, of course. Trebatius did not think this a sufficient reward for the length of his journey and the dangers of the country, and thought of returning. Cicero had much trouble to prevent this rash conduct. I do not think there is any part of his correspondence more amusing and more lively than the letters he wrote to Trebatius to induce him to remain. Cicero is at his ease with this obscure young man, for whom he had such a lively affection. He dares to laugh freely, which he does not do with everybody, and he laughs all the more readily as he knows Trebatius was

[1] *Ad fam.* vii. 17. [2] *Ibid.* vii. 13.

low-spirited, and he wishes to console him. It seems to
me that this trouble that he takes to cheer up an unhappy
friend makes his pleasantries almost touching, and that his
good heart here lends one more charm to his wit. He
quizzes him good-naturedly in order to make him laugh,
and jokes about things that he knows the good Trebatius
does not mind being bantered on. For instance, one day
he asks him to send him all the details of the campaign :
" For an account of a battle," he says, " I trust above all
the most timorous ; "[1] probably because, having held themselves aloof from the fight, they will have been better able
to see the whole. Another time, after having expressed
some fear at seeing him exposed to so many dangers, he
adds : " Happily I know your prudence ; you are much
bolder in presenting writs than in harassing the enemy,
and I remember that, although you are a good swimmer,
you would not cross over into Britain for fear of taking a
bath in the ocean."[2]

To soothe his impatience he threatens him with the
wags. Was it not to be feared that if he returned, Laberius
would put him in one of his farces? A frightened lawyer
travelling in the train of an army, and exercising his profession among the barbarians, would make a funny figure
in a comedy ; but, to silence the wags he had only to make
his fortune. Let him return later, he would certainly return
richer ; Balbus had said so. Now, Balbus was a banker ;
he did not speak in the sense of the Stoics, who affirm that
one is always rich enough when one can enjoy the spectacle
of the sky and the earth ; he spoke as a Roman and meant
that he would return well furnished with crown-pieces,
more romano bene nummatum. Trebatius remained, and
he did well to do so. Caesar was not long in noticing him,
and was pleased with his friendship. He got accustomed

---

[1] *Ad fam.* vii. 18.   [2] *Ibid.* vii. 10.

to camp life, and in time became a little less timid than he was on his arrival. It is probable that he returned rich, as Balbus had predicted, for if they did not find all the treasures they went to seek in Gaul, Caesar's liberality was an inexhaustible mine that enriched all his friends. At a later period Trebatius passed through trying times, and yet preserved the reputation of an honest man; this was an act of justice that all parties did him, although they were not much in the habit of doing justice. He had the rare good fortune to escape all the perils of the civil wars, and was still living in the time of Horace, who addressed one of his most agreeable satires to him. We see in it that he was then an amiable and indulgent old man who readily laughed and amused himself with the young. He talked to them, no doubt, about that grand epoch of which he was one of the last survivors, of the Gallic war in which he had taken part, of Caesar and his captains whom he had known. By the privilege of his age he could speak of Lucretius to Virgil, of Cicero to Livy, of Catullus to Propertius, and formed a sort of link between the two most illustrious periods of Latin literature.

The other person whom Cicero sent to Caesar was his brother Quintus. As he holds a large place in Cicero's life, and played a rather important part in the Gallic war, it will be proper, I think, to say a few words about him. Although he listened to the same lectures and learned from the same masters as his brother, he never had any taste for eloquence, and always refused to speak in public. "One orator," he said, "is enough in a family, and even in a city." [1] He was of a hard and yet changeable disposition, and gave way to violent fits of anger without reason. In spite of an appearance of great energy he was soon discouraged, and although he always affected to be

[1] *De orat.* ii. 3.

the master, he was led by those about him. These faults, that Cicero bewailed to himself although he tried to excuse them, prevented Quintus succeeding in his public career, and troubled his private life.

He had been early married to Pomponia, the sister of Atticus. This marriage that the two friends had hoped would draw closer their connection very nearly broke it. The couple found that their characters matched too well: both were hasty and passionate, and they could never agree, and the unbounded ascendency that Statius, a slave, had over his master's mind completed the disunion of the household. In connection with this, it would be easy to show, from Cicero's letters, what influence the slave often exercised in ancient families; a much greater one than is commonly supposed. Now that the servant is free, it would seem natural that he should take a more important place in our houses than before. But the contrary has happened; he has lost in influence what he has gained in dignity. When he became independent his master ceased to have any obligations towards him. They now live together bound by a temporary contract, which, by imposing reciprocal obligations, appears irksome to both sides. As this fragile bond may be broken at any moment, and as these allies of one day may become indifferent to each other or enemies on the next, there is no longer any ease or confidence between them, and they pass all the time during which chance brings them together in surrounding themselves with defences, and in watching one another. It was quite otherwise in antiquity when slavery was flourishing. Then, it was not for a short time only, it was for a whole life-time that they were united; accordingly, they set themselves to know each other, and to adapt themselves one to the other. To gain the master's favour was the important thing for the future of the slave, and he took trouble to gain it. As he had no position to defend, or dignity to preserve, he gave himself up to him entirely. He flattered and served his worst passions without scruple, and at last made himself necessary to him. Once confirmed in this intimacy, by his constant subserviency, by private and secret services which his master was not afraid to demand, and which he never refused to give, he ruled the family, so that, however strange it may appear at first sight, it is true to say that the servant was never nearer being master than when he was a slave. This is what happened to Statius. Through the knowledge that he had of the defects of Quintus, he had insinuated himself so well into his confidence that the whole family gave way to him. Pomponia alone resisted, and the annoyance she suffered for this reason made her still more insupportable. She constantly worried her husband with unfriendly remarks; she refused to appear at the dinners that he gave on the pretext that she was only a stranger at home, or if she consented to be present, it was only to make the guests the witnesses of the most unpleasant scenes. It was, no doubt, one day when she was more peevish and cross-grained than usual that Quintus composed these two epigrams, the only examples that remain of his poetic talent.

"Trust your ship to the winds, but do not give up your soul to a woman. There is less safety in a woman's words than in the caprices of the waves."

"No woman is good; or if by chance you find a good woman, I know not by what strange fate a bad thing has become good in a moment."

These two epigrams are not very gallant, but we must excuse them in the unfortunate husband of the shrewish Pomponia.

The political career of Quintus was not brilliant any more than his private life was happy. He owed the offices which

he obtained more to the illustrious name of his brother than
to his own merit, and did nothing to make himself worthy
of them. After he had been aedile and praetor, he was
appointed governor of Asia. To be invested with an
unlimited authority was a severe test for a character like
his. Absolute power turned his head; his violence, which
nothing now restrained, knew no bounds; like an oriental
despot he only talked of burning and hanging. He wished
above all to obtain the glory of being a great lover of justice.
Having had occasion to order two parricides to be sewn up
in a sack and thrown into the water in the lower part of his
province, he wished to give the same spectacle to the other
part on his visit to it, that there might be no jealousy between
them. He sought therefore to seize a certain Zeuxis, an
important person, who had been accused of killing his
mother, and who had been acquitted by the tribunals. On
the arrival of the governor, Zeuxis, who guessed his intentions, fled, and Quintus, vexed at losing his parricide, wrote
him most friendly letters to induce him to return. Usually,
however, he dissembled less and spoke more openly. He
sent word to one of his lieutenants to seize and burn alive
a certain Licinius and his son who had embezzled. He
wrote to a Roman knight named Catienus "that he hoped
to have him suffocated one day in the smoke, with the
applause of the province."[1] It is true that when he was
reproached with having written these furious letters, he
replied that they were simple jokes, and that he had wished
to laugh for a moment, but it was a strange way of joking,
and shows his barbarous nature. Quintus had none the
less an enlightened mind, he had read Plato and Xenophon,
he spoke Greek admirably well, he even wrote tragedies in
his leisure hours. He had all the appearance of a polished
and civilized man, but it was only the appearance. Even

[1] *Ad Quint.* i. 2.

among the most well-bred Romans, civilization was often only on the surface, and under their polished exterior we often find the rough and savage soul of a pitiless race of soldiers.

Quintus came back from his province with a rather bad reputation, but, what is more surprising, he did not come back rich. Apparently he had embezzled less than his colleagues, and was not able to bring back enough money to restore his fortune, which was very much embarrassed by his extravagance; for he liked to buy and to build, like his brother; he had a taste for rare books, and probably also could refuse nothing to his favourite slaves. The exile of Cicero completed the confusion of his affairs, and at the time of his brother's return Quintus was quite ruined. This did not prevent him, at the time of his greatest financial distress, rebuilding his house at Rome, and buying a country house at Arpinum and another in the suburbs, constructing in his villa at Arcae, baths, porticoes, fish-ponds, and such a fine road that it was taken for a work of the state. It is true that the poverty of a Roman of that time would make the fortune of many of our nobles. However, a day came when Quintus was altogether in the hands of his creditors, and when he could borrow no more. Then it was that he bethought him of the last resource of embarrassed debtors : he went to Caesar.

It was not, then, only the love of glory that attracted Quintus to Gaul; he went there, like so many others, to get rich. Up to that time, the results had not answered to men's expectations, and they had not found among people like the Belgae and Germani all the treasures that they looked for; but they were not yet discouraged; rather than give up their brilliant fancies, after each disappointment, they put farther off that enchanted country where they thought they must find riches. As at this moment they were going to attack Britain, it was in Britain that they placed it. Every one expected to make a fortune there, and Caesar himself, by what Suetonius says, hoped to bring back many pearls.[1] These expectations were deceived once more ; in Britain were neither pearls nor gold mines. They had a great deal of trouble to take a few slaves who were not of much value, for it was no use thinking of making them men of letters and musicians. For all wealth, these men only possessed heavy chariots, from which they fought with courage. Accordingly Cicero wrote humorously to Trebatius, who sent him news of this ill-luck of the army : "Since you find there neither gold nor silver, my opinion is that you should carry off one of those British chariots, and should come to us at Rome without stopping." [2] Quintus was very much of the same opinion. Although he had been well received by Caesar, who had appointed him his lieutenant, when he saw that wealth did not come as quickly as he expected, he lost courage, and, like Trebatius, he had for a moment the idea of returning ; but Cicero, who did not joke this time, prevented him.

He did him a very great service, for it was precisely during the winter that followed the war in Britain that Quintus had the opportunity of performing the heroic action that commended his name to the respect of military men. Although he read Sophocles with ardour and had written tragedies, he was at bottom only a soldier. In the presence of the enemy, he became himself again, and displayed an energy that had not been suspected in him. In the midst of populations which were in revolt, in entrenchments hastily raised in one night, and with a single legion only, he was able to defend the camp Caesar had entrusted to him, and to make head against innumerable enemies, who had just destroyed a Roman army. He replied in firm language

[1] *Caes.* 47. [2] *Ad fam.* vii. 7.

to their insolent boasts. Although he was ill, he displayed incredible activity, and it was only after a sedition among his soldiers that he could be induced to take care of himself. I have no need to relate the details of this affair that Caesar has told so well in his *Commentaries*, and which is one of the most glorious incidents of the Gallic war. This grand feat of arms raises Quintus in our esteem; it effaces the meannesses of his character, and helps him to play with a little more credit the ungrateful and difficult part of younger brother of a great man.

III.

Cicero had clearly foreseen that, although Caesar in writing his *Commentaries* professed only to prepare materials for history, the perfection of his work would prevent sensible men from attempting to re-write it. Accordingly Plutarch and Dio have taken care not to re-write it; they are contented to epitomize it, and now we only know the Gallic war by the narrative of him who was the hero of it. However perfect the narrative may be, or rather because of its very perfection, we have much difficulty in contenting ourselves with it. It is the characteristic of these great works, which, as we might think, ought to exhaust public curiosity, on the contrary, to make it more active. By interesting us in the facts which they relate, they excite in us the desire to know them better, and one of the surest marks of their success is that they do not suffice for the readers, and make them wish to know more than they tell. This desire, for fresh details on the most important events of history, it is which renders Cicero's letters to Trebatius and to his brother so valuable for us. Although they are fewer in number and shorter than we could wish, they have the merit of adding some information to that which Caesar

R

gives on his campaigns. As they are more familiar than a narrative composed for the public, they introduce us farther into the private life of the conqueror of Gaul, and they permit us to see him in his tent, at those times of leisure and repose, of which he has not thought of speaking to us himself. This is certainly an interesting spectacle, it is the true complement of the *Commentaries*, and we cannot do better than carefully collect the scattered details they contain, in order to become well acquainted with Caesar and his surroundings.

I imagine that Caesar's army did not resemble those old Roman armies that are depicted to us in such grave and temperate guise, always trembling under the rod of the lictors, and submissive at all times to an inflexible discipline. It was, doubtless, sternly controlled in time of danger, and never complained of this. No other army has ever undergone greater fatigues and executed greater deeds; but when the danger was over discipline relaxed. Caesar allowed his soldiers rest, and sometimes diversion. He let them decorate themselves with splendid arms, and even adorn themselves with studied elegance. "What does it matter if they use perfumes?" he said, "they will know very well how to fight." [1] And in fact these soldiers, whom the Pompeians called effeminate, are the same who, though dying of hunger at Dyrrhachium, declared that they would eat the bark of the trees rather than let Pompey escape. They were recruited for the most part among those Cisalpine Gauls from whom Roman civilization had not taken the good qualities of their race, an amiable and brilliant people who loved war and carried it on gaily. The chiefs very much resembled the common soldiers; they were lively and ardent, full of resources in critical moments, and trusted more to inspiration than to routine. It is to be remarked

[1] Suet. *Caes.* 67.

that no one of them had gained his reputation in earlier
wars. Caesar seems to have wished that their military glory
should come from him only. A few, and among these
Labienus, perhaps the greatest of them, were his political
friends, old conspirators like himself, who, after his example,
and without any more preparation, from popular agitators
had become excellent generals. Others, on the contrary, like
Fabius Maximus and Servius Galba, bore illustrious names ;
they were partisans whom he secured in the aristocracy, or
hostages that he took from it. The greater number, Crassus, Plancus, Volcatius Tullus, Decimus Brutus, and later
Pollio, were young men whom he treated with marked
preference, and whom he readily trusted in perilous enterprises. He liked the young by personal preference, and
also by policy : as they did not yet belong to any party,
and had not had time to attach themselves to the republic
by serving it, he hoped they would have less difficulty in
accustoming themselves to the new *régime* that he wished
to establish.

These lieutenants, whose number varied, did not alone
form the ordinary retinue of a proconsul. We must remember to add that crowd of young Romans, sons of
illustrious houses, destined by their birth for public office,
who came to serve their apprenticeship in war under him.
They were called his tent-comrades, *contubernales*. Soldiers
like the rest, and exposing themselves on the day of battle,
they became after the fight the friends, the companions of
the chief whom they followed in all his expeditions, as the
clients accompanied their patron in the city. They were
present at his receptions, took part in all his recreations
and diversions, sat at his table, surrounded him when he sat
on the judgment-seat ; they formed, in sum, what was called
the cohort, we should almost say the court, of the praetor
(*praetoria cohors*). Scipio Africanus, it is said, invented

this means of adding splendour to the public display of
the supreme power in the eyes of the conquered nations,
and after him governors had taken great care to preserve
all this pomp which added to their prestige.   These were
not all; by the side of these military men there was room
for men of very various abilities and positions.   Able
financiers, intelligent secretaries, and even learned lawyers
might be necessary for the administration of those vast
countries that a proconsul governed.   Thus Trebatius himself, the pacific Trebatius, was not out of place in the train
of an army, and he had opportunities of exercising his profession even among the Nervii and the Belgae.   If we add
to these men, to whom their high offices gave a certain
importance, a crowd of inferior officers or subaltern servants,
such as lictors, ushers, scribes, interpreters, apparitors,
doctors, men-servants, and even soothsayers, we shall have
some idea of that truly royal retinue which a proconsul
always carried about with him.

Caesar's train must have been even more magnificent
than that of others.   The ten legions that he commanded,
the extent of country that he had to conquer and govern,
explain the great number of officers and persons of all sorts
by whom he was surrounded.   Moreover, he naturally loved
magnificence.   He readily welcomed all who came to see
him, and always found some office to give them in order to
retain them.   Even in those wild countries he took pleasure
in astonishing them by his reception.   Suetonius relates
that he took with him everywhere marquetry or mosaic
floors, and that he had always two tables laid at which rich
Romans who visited him and provincials of distinction took
their places.[1]   His lieutenants imitated him, and Pinarius
wrote to Cicero that he was delighted with the dinners his
brother gave him.[2]   Caesar did not care much for these

---

[1] Suet. *Caes.* 46, 48.   [2] *Ad Quint.* iii. 1.

sumptuous repasts, and these rich dwellings, on his own account. We know that he was temperate, that in case of need he could sleep well in the open air, and eat rancid oil without blinking; but he had a taste for display and luxury. Although the republic still existed, he was almost a king; even in his camps in Britain and Germany he had assiduous followers and courtiers. He could only be approached with difficulty; Trebatius made the attempt, and we know that it was a long time before he could reach him. No doubt Caesar did not receive men with that stiff and solemn majesty that repelled them in Pompey; but, however gracious he might wish to be, there was always something in him that inspired respect, and it was felt that that ease of manner that he affected with everybody proceeded from a superiority which was sure of itself. This defender of the democracy was none the less an aristocrat who never forgot his birth, and willingly spoke of his ancestors. Had they not heard him, at the commencement of his political life, at the very time when he attacked with most vivacity the institutions of Sulla, and tried to get back their ancient powers for the tribunes, had they not heard him pronounce over his aunt a funeral oration full of genealogical fictions, in which he complacently related that his family was descended at once from the kings and the gods? But in this he only followed the traditions of the Gracchi, his illustrious predecessors. They also defended public interests with ardour, but they called to mind the aristocracy from which they had sprung by the haughty elegance of their manners. We know that they had a court of clients at their rising, and that they were the first who thought of making distinctions between them which resembled the public and private admissions to the court of Louis XIV.

The most remarkable thing in those around Caesar was

their love of letters. Assuredly they belonged no longer to
the times when Roman generals burnt master-pieces of art,
or took a pride in being ignorant. Since Mummius and
Marius, letters had succeeded in penetrating even the
camps, which, as we know, are not their usual abode.
Nevertheless, I do not think that so many enlightened men
of letters, so many men of culture and men of fashion have
ever been seen united in any other army. Almost all
Caesar's lieutenants were private friends of Cicero, and
they took pleasure in maintaining a constant intercourse
with him who was regarded as the official patron of literature
at Rome. Crassus and Plancus had learnt eloquence in
pleading at his side, and in what remains to us of the letters
of Plancus, we recognize, by a certain oratorical exuberance,
that he had profited by his lessons. Trebonius, the conqueror of Marseilles, professed to relish his witticisms very
much, and even published a collection of them. Cicero,
however, to whom this admiration was not displeasing,
thought that his editor had put too much of himself into
the introduction under pretence of preparing the effect of
the jokes and making them easier to understand. "They
have exhausted their laughter," he said, "when they get to
me." Hirtius was a distinguished historian, who undertook
later to finish the *Commentaries* of his chief. Matius, a
devoted friend of Caesar, who showed himself worthy of
this friendship by remaining faithful to him, translated the
Iliad into Latin verse. Quintus was a poet also, but a
tragic poet. During the winter that he had to fight the
Nervii, he was seized with such an ardour for poetry, that
he composed four pieces in sixteen days : but this was to
treat tragedy in a somewhat military fashion. He sent the
one he thought the best, the *Erigone*, to his brother ; but
it was lost on the road. " Since Caesar has commanded
in Gaul," said Cicero, " the *Erigone* alone has not been able

to travel in safety." [1]   It is surprising no doubt to meet all at one time with so many generals who are also men of letters ; but what is still more astonishing is that all those Roman knights who followed the army, and whom Caesar made his commissaries and purveyors, collectors of stores, and farmers of the taxes, seem to have loved literature more than their habits and occupations usually admit.   We find one of those he employed in offices of this kind, Lepta, thanking Cicero for sending him a treatise on rhetoric as though he were a man capable of appreciating the present. The Spaniard Balbus, that intelligent banker, that skilful administrator, who was able to put the finances of Rome into such good order, and what was still more difficult, those of Caesar, loved philosophy with more enthusiasm than one would expect in a banker.   He hastened to have Cicero's works copied before they were known to the public, and although he was by character the most discreet of men, he went so far as even to commit indiscretions in order to be the first to read them.

But among all these lettered men, it was Caesar who had the most decided taste for letters : they suited his cultivated nature ; they seemed to him, no doubt, the most agreeable exercise and relaxation of an accomplished mind.   I should not, however, venture to say that his love for them was wholly disinterested, when I see that this taste assisted his policy so wonderfully.   He was compelled to gain public favour by every means ; now, nothing attracts the general judgment more than the superiority of intelligence united with that of force.   His principal works were composed with this intention, and we might say, from this point of view, that his writings were part of his actions.   It was not only to please a few idle men of letters that, during the latter part of his stay in Gaul, he wrote his *Commentaries* with such a

[1] *Ad Quint.* iii. 9.

rapidity as to astonish his friends. He wished to prevent
the Romans forgetting his victories; he wished, by his
admirable manner of narrating them, to renew, and if
possible, to increase, the effect they had produced. When
he composed his two books *De Analogia*, he calculated that
people would be struck by seeing the general of an army,
who, according to the expression of Fronto, "busied himself with the formation of words while arrows were cleaving
the air, and sought the laws of language amid the din of
clarions and trumpets." He knew very well the advantage
that his reputation would draw from these very diverse
performances, and how great would be the surprise and admiration at Rome when they received at the same moment
a treatise on grammar, and the news of a new victory, from
such a distance. The same thought also made him eager
for Cicero's friendship. If his refined and distinguished
nature found a great pleasure in keeping up some intercourse with a man of so much cultivation, he was not
ignorant of the power this man exercised over public
opinion, and how far his praises would resound when they
came from this eloquent mouth. We have lost the letters
that he wrote to Cicero; but as Cicero was delighted with
them, and it was not very easy to please him, we must
believe that they were filled with flatteries and caresses.
Cicero's answers were also full of the most lively protestations of friendship. He declared at that time that Caesar
came in his affections immediately after his children, and indeed almost in the same rank; he bitterly deplored all the
prejudices that had up till then kept him apart from him,
and he resolved to make him forget that he was one of the
last who had entered into his friendship. "I shall imitate,"
said he, "the travellers who have risen later than they wished
to do; they double their speed, and make such good haste
that they arrive at their destination before those who have

travelled part of the night." [1] They vied with each other, as it were, in compliments; they overwhelmed one another with flatteries, and emulated each other in works in verse and prose. On reading the first accounts of the expedition to Britain, Cicero exclaimed in a transport of enthusiasm: "What prodigious events! what a country! what people! what battles, and above all, what a general!" He wrote off immediately to his brother: "Give me Britain to paint; furnish me with the colours, I will use the brush." [2] And he had seriously taken in hand an epic poem on this conquest, which his occupations prevented him completing as quickly as he wished. Caesar, on his part, dedicated his treatise *De Analogia* to Cicero, and on this occasion said to him in splendid phrases: "You have discovered all the resources of eloquence, and are the first to use them. In virtue of this you have deserved well of the Roman name, and you do honour to our country. You have obtained the most illustrious of all honours, and a triumph preferable to those of the greatest generals, for it is better to extend the boundaries of the mind than to enlarge the limits of the empire!" [3] This, coming from a victorious general like Caesar, was the most delicate flattery for a man of letters.

Such were the relations that Cicero kept up with Caesar and his officers during the Gallic war. His correspondence, which preserves the memory of them, makes us better acquainted with the tastes and preferences of all these men of cultivation, and shows them to us in a very living fashion and draws us closer to them. This is, assuredly, one of the greatest services it could render to us. We seem, when we have read it, to be able to understand of what kind the meetings of these men must have been, and can imagine ourselves present at their conversations. We are entitled to

[1] *Ad Quint.* ii. 15. [2] *Ibid.* ii. 16.
[3] Cic. *Brut.* 72, and Pliny, *Hist. nat.* vii. 30.

suppose that Rome took up very much of their thoughts. From the depths of Gaul, they had their eyes upon it, and it was to make a little stir there that they took so much trouble. While marching over so many unknown countries from the Rhine to the Ocean, all these young men hoped that they would be talked about at those feasts and assemblies where men of the world discussed public affairs. Caesar himself, when he crossed the Rhine on his wooden bridge, reckoned upon striking the imaginations of all those idlers who met together in the Forum, at the rostrum, to learn the news. After the landing of his troops in Britain, we see him hastening to write to his friends, and especially to Cicero ;[1] not that he had much leisure at that moment, but he looked upon it no doubt as an honour to date his letter from a country where no Roman had yet set foot. If he was anxious to send glorious news to Rome, they were also very glad to receive it from Rome. All the letters that arrived were read with eagerness ; they seemed as it were to carry even to Germany and Britain a whiff of that fashionable life, which those who have enjoyed can never forget or cease to regret. It was not enough for Caesar to read the *journals of the Roman people*, which contained a dry summary of the principal political events, and a concise report of the proceedings of the assemblies of the people. His messengers constantly traversed Gaul, bringing him letters accurate and full of the most minute details. " He is told everything," said Cicero, " small as well as great." [2] This news, impatiently waited for, and commented on with pleasure, must have been the usual subject of his conversations with his friends. I

[1] Caesar wrote to Cicero twice from Britain. The first letter took twenty-six days to reach Rome, and the second twenty-eight. This was quick travelling for that time, and we see that Caesar must have organized his mail-service well. Furthermore, we know his stay in Britain was very short.

[2] *Ad Quint*. iii. I.

suppose that, at that sumptuous table of which I have spoken, after literature and grammar had been discussed, and they had listened to the verses of Matius or Quintus, the conversation turned especially upon Rome, of which these elegant young men, who regretted its pleasures, were never tired of talking. Certainly, if we could have heard them chatting about the last news, the political disorders, or, what interested them more, the private scandals of the city, telling the last rumours afloat, and quoting the most recent jokes, we should have found it difficult to believe that we were in the heart of the country of the Belgae, or near to the Rhine or the Ocean, or on the eve of a battle. I imagine that we should have rather fancied we were present at a party of clever men in some aristocratic house on the Palatine or in the rich quarter of Carinae.

Cicero's letters render us yet another service. They show us the prodigious effect that Caesar's victories produced at Rome. They excited as much surprise as admiration, for they were discoveries as well as conquests. What was known before him of those distant countries? A few ridiculous fables that traders related on their return, to give themselves importance. It was through Caesar that they were first really known. He first dared to attack, and he vanquished those Germans who have been depicted as giants, whose very looks caused terror; he first adventured as far as Britain, where it was said the night lasted three entire months, and all the wonders that had been related gave as it were a tinge of the marvellous to his victories. Nevertheless, not everybody willingly gave way to this fascination. The most clear-sighted of the aristocratic party, who felt, though indistinctly, that it was the fate of the republic that was being decided on the banks of the Rhine, wished to recall Caesar, and to appoint in his place another general, who might not perhaps complete the conquest of Gaul, but who would not be tempted to carry out that of his own country. Cato, who pushed everything to extremes, when the senate was asked to vote a thanksgiving to the gods for the defeat of Ariovistus, dared to propose, on the contrary, that they should deliver up the conqueror to the Germans. But these objections did not change public opinion, which declared itself in favour of him who had just conquered with such rapidity so many unknown countries. The knights, who had become the financiers and merchants of Rome, congratulated themselves on seeing immense countries opened up to their operations. Caesar, who wished to attach them to him, invited them to follow him, and his first care had been to open them a road across the Alps. The common people, who love military glory and who freely give way to enthusiasm, were never tired of admiring him who extended the limits of the Roman world. On the news of each victory, Rome had public rejoicings, and offered thanksgivings to the gods. After the defeat of the Belgae, the senate, under pressure of public opinion, was compelled to vote fifteen days of solemn thanksgiving, which had never been done for anybody. Twenty days was decreed, when the success of the expedition against Germany was reported, and twenty more after the taking of Alesia. Cicero usually demanded these honours for Caesar, and he became the mouthpiece of the public admiration when he said in his noble language : " This is the first time we have dared to attack the Gauls, hitherto we have been content to repulse them. The other generals of the Roman people regarded it as sufficient for their glory to prevent them invading us ; Caesar has gone to seek them out in their own homes. Our general, our legions, our arms have over-run those countries of which no history has ever spoken, of whose name the world was ignorant. We had only a foot-path in Gaul ; now the boundaries of these nations have become the frontiers of our own empire. It is not without the signal favour of Providence that nature gave the Alps for a rampart to Italy. If the entrance had been free to this multitude of barbarians, Rome never would have been the centre and the seat of the empire of the world. Now let insurmountable mountains sink. From the Alps to the Ocean Italy has nothing now to fear." [1]

These magnificent eulogies, for which Cicero has been so much blamed, are easily understood however, and, whatever politicians may say, it is easy to explain the enthusiasm that so many honest and sensible people then felt for Caesar. That which justified the unreserved admiration that his conquests caused, was less their grandeur than their necessity. They might threaten the future, at that moment they were indispensable. They later endangered the liberty of Rome, but they assured her existence then. [2] The patriotic instinct of the people let them divine what prejudice and fear, although quite legitimate, hid from the aristocracy. They understood in a confused way all the dangers that might soon come from Gaul, if they did not hasten to subdue it. It was not, in truth, the Gauls who were to be feared—their decadence had already commenced, and they no longer thought of making conquests—it was the Germans. Dio is quite wrong in asserting that Caesar wantonly stirred up wars for the sake of his glory. Whatever advantage he drew from them, we may certainly say that he rather submitted to them than provoked them. It was not Rome that went to seek the Germans at that time, but rather the Germans who came boldly towards her. When Caesar was appointed proconsul, Ariovistus occupied part of the country of the Sequani and wished to seize the rest. His compatriots, attracted by the fertility of this fine

[1] *De prov Cons.* 13, 14.
[2] M. Mommsen completely settles this in his *Roman History*.

country, were crossing the Rhine every day to join him,
and twenty-five thousand had come at one time. What
would have happened to Italy if, while Rome was losing
her strength in intestine struggles, the Suevi and the
Sicambri had established themselves on the Rhone and the
Alps? The invasion averted by Marius a century before
was recommencing; it might have caused the downfall of
Rome then as it did four centuries later, if Caesar had not
arrested it. His glory is to have thrown back the Germans
beyond the Rhine, as it was to the honour of the empire
to have kept them there for more than three hundred years.

But this was not the sole or even the greatest effect
of Caesar's victories. In conquering Gaul, he rendered it
entirely and for ever Roman. That marvellous rapidity
with which Rome then assimilated the Gauls can only be
understood, when we know in what a state she had found
them. They were not altogether barbarians like the
Germans; it is to be remarked that their conqueror, who
knew them well, does not call them so in his *Commentaries*.
They had great cities, a regular system of taxation, a body
of religious beliefs, an ambitious and powerful aristocracy,
and a sort of national education directed by the priests.
This culture, although imperfect, if it had not entirely
enlightened their minds, had at least awakened them.
They were frank and inquisitive, intelligent enough to know
what they were deficient in, and sufficiently free from
prejudice to give up their usages when they found better
ones. From the very beginning of the war, they succeeded in imitating the Roman tactics, in constructing
siege machines, and in working them with a skill to which
Caesar does justice. They were still rude and unpolished,
but already quite inclined for a superior civilization for
which they had the desire and instinct. This explains
how they did so readily accept it. They had fought for

ten years against the domination of the foreigner; they did not hesitate for a day to adopt his language and usages. We may say that Gaul resembled those lands, parched by a burning sun, which drink in with such avidity the first drops of rain; so completely did she imbibe the Roman civilization for which she longed before she knew it, that after so many centuries, and in spite of so many revolutions, she has not yet lost the mark of it; and this is the only thing that has endured to the present time in this country where everything changes. Caesar, then, did not only add a few new territories to the possessions of Rome; the present that he made her was greater and more useful; he gave her an entire people, intelligent, and civilized almost as soon as conquered, which, becoming Roman in heart as well as in language, sinking her interests in those of her new nationality, enlisting in her legions to defend her, and throwing herself with a remarkable ardour and talent into the study of the arts and letters, shed a new lustre over her, and for a long time gave a new youth and a return of vigour to the failing empire.

While these great events were passing in Gaul, Rome continued to be the theatre of the most shameful disorders. There was no longer any government; scarcely did they succeed in electing magistrates, and there was a fight every time the people assembled in the Forum or in the Campus Martius. These disorders, of which honest men were ashamed, added still more to the effect that Caesar's victories produced. What a contrast was there between the battles fought with Ariovistus or Vercingetorix and those combats of gladiators that stained the streets of Rome with blood! And how glorious appeared the taking of Agendicum or Alesia to people who were only occupied with the siege of Milo's house by Clodius or the assassination of Clodius by Milo! All the statesmen who had remained

in Rome, Pompey as well as Cicero, had lost something of
their dignity by mixing themselves up in these intrigues.
Caesar, who had withdrawn in time, was the only man who
had risen amidst the general degradation. Therefore all
those whose heart was wounded by these sad spectacles,
and who had some care for Roman honour, kept their eyes
fixed upon him and his army. As happened at certain
moments of our own revolution, military glory consoled
honest men for scandals and distress at home. At the
same time, the excess of the evil caused men to seek an
efficacious remedy everywhere. The idea began to spread
that, in order to obtain repose, it was necessary to create
a strong and durable power. After Cicero's exile, the
aruspices had predicted that the monarchy was about to
recommence,[1] and one did not need to be a prophet to anticipate this. A few years later, the evil having increased still
more, the republican party itself, notwithstanding its repugnance, was forced to have recourse to the violent remedy
of a temporary dictatorship. Pompey was appointed sole
consul, but Pompey had shown more than once that he had
neither the vigour nor the resolution necessary to overcome
anarchy entirely. A stronger arm and a more determined
will had to be sought elsewhere, and all eyes turned naturally
towards the conqueror of Gaul. His glory pointed him
out for this part; the hopes of some and the fears of others
called him to fulfil it; men's minds became accustomed
every day to the idea that he would be the heir of the
republic, and the revolution that delivered up Rome to him
was more than half accomplished when he crossed the
Rubicon.

[1] *De Arusp. resp.* 25.

II

THE VICTOR AND THE VANQUISHED

AFTER PHARSALIA

THE civil war interrupted the intercourse that Cicero had kept up with Caesar during the Gallic war. He hesitated for a long time to take part in it, and it was after long indecision that the stings of conscience, the fear of public opinion, and above all the example of his friends decided him at length to start for Pompey's camp. "As the ox follows the herd," said he, "I go to join the good citizens;" [1] but he went half-heartedly and without hope. After Pharsalia he did not think it was possible to continue the struggle : he said so openly in a council of the republican chiefs held at Dyrrhachium, and he hastened to return to Brundusium to hold himself at the disposal of the conqueror.

What regret must he not have felt, if his thoughts went back several years, and he remembered his triumphal return from exile ! In that very town, where he had been received with so much rejoicing, he was constrained to disembark furtively, to conceal his lictors, to avoid the crowd, and only go out at night. He passed eleven months there, the saddest of his life, in isolation and anxiety. He was distressed on all sides, and his domestic affairs did not cause him less sorrow than public events. His absence had completed the disorder of his pecuniary affairs. When they were most involved, he had been so imprudent as to lend

[1] *Ad Att.* vii. 7.

S

what ready money he had to Pompey : the poniard of the King of Egypt had at the same time carried off the debtor and put an end to his power of paying. While he was trying to procure some resources by selling his furniture and plate, he discovered that his wife was acting in concert with his freedmen to despoil him of what remained ; he learnt that his brother and his nephew, who had gone over to Caesar, sought to justify themselves at his expense, and were working to ruin him in order to save themselves ; he saw Tullia, his beloved daughter, again, but he found her sad and ill, lamenting at the same time the misfortunes of her father, and the infidelity of her husband. To these very real misfortunes were joined at the same time imaginary troubles, which caused him as much suffering ; above all, he was tormented by his habitual irresolution. Scarcely had he set foot in Italy when he repented having come. According to his habit, his restless imagination always puts things at their worst, and he is ingenious in finding some reason for discontent in everything that happens to him. He laments when Antony wishes to force him to leave Italy ; when he is allowed to remain, he still laments, because this exception made in his favour may injure his reputation. If Caesar neglects to write to him, he is alarmed ; if he receives a letter from him, however friendly it may be, he weighs all its expressions so carefully that he discovers at last some motive for fear ; even the broadest and most complete amnesty does not entirely remove his fears. " When a man pardons so easily," he says, " it is because he defers his vengeance."[1]

At last, after a sojourn of nearly a year in that noisy and pestilential town, he was permitted to leave Brundusium. He returned to his fine country houses that he liked so much,

[1] *Ad Att.* xi. 20. I read *cognitionem* instead of *notionem*, which does not seem to me to have any sense.

and where he had been so happy; he found his books again, he resumed his interrupted studies, he could appreciate again those precious things which we enjoy without thinking about them while they are ours, and only begin to appreciate when we have lost them for a moment, namely, security and leisure. He thought that nothing could equal the charm of those first days passed tranquilly at Tusculum after so many storms, and of that return to the quiet pleasures of the mind for which he felt then that he was in reality made. "Know," he wrote to his friend Varro, "that since my return I have been reconciled to my old friends: I mean my books. In truth, if I fled from them, it was not because I was angry with them, but I could not see them without some confusion. It seemed to me that in engaging in such stirring affairs, with doubtful allies, I have not followed their precepts faithfully enough. They forgive me, they recall me to their company; they tell me that you have been wiser than I not to leave them. Now that I am restored to their favour, I really hope that I shall support more easily the evils that oppress us and those with which we are threatened."[1]

His conduct henceforth was clearly marked out. He owed it to the great party he had served and defended to hold aloof from the new government. He must seek in philosophy and letters a useful employment for his activity, and create an honourable retreat far from public affairs in which he could no longer take part with honour. He well understood this when he said: "Let us preserve at least a partial liberty by knowing how to hide ourselves and keep silence."[2] To keep silence and hide, was indeed the programme that suited him best, as it did all those who had submitted after Pharsalia. We shall see how far he was faithful to it.

---

[1] *Ad fam.* ix. i.   [2] *Ad Att.* xvi. 31.

I.

It is very difficult to relinquish politics all at once. The conduct of public affairs and the exercise of power, even when they do not entirely content the mind, give a secondary importance to other things, and life appears aimless to him who can no longer employ himself in them. This is what happened to Cicero. He was certainly very sincere when, on leaving Brundusium, he undertook "to hide himself entirely in literature"; but he had promised more than he was able to perform. He soon wearied of repose, and the pleasures of study at length seemed a little too quiet; he listened with more curiosity to outside rumours, and, in order to hear them better, quitted Tusculum and returned to Rome. There he insensibly resumed his old habits; he returned to the senate; his house was again open to all who loved and cultivated letters; he began again to frequent the houses of the friends he had in Caesar's party, and by their means resumed intercourse with Caesar himself.

They were easily reconciled, notwithstanding all their motives for ill will. The taste for intellectual pleasures which united them was stronger than all political antipathy. The first irritation over, they approached each other with that ease that the habit and experience of society give, forgetting or appearing to forget all the disagreements that had separated them. Nevertheless these relations had become more difficult than ever for Cicero. It was not only a protector that he had found in his old fellow-student, it was a master. There was no longer between them, as formerly, an agreement or understanding that created reciprocal obligations; there was the victor to whom the laws of war permitted everything, and the vanquished who owed his life to his clemency. The difficulty of the position was greater, because the more right the conqueror had to be exacting the more public opinion commanded the conquered to be reserved. It may be supposed that, at the time of the Gallic war, Cicero defended Caesar's projects through friendship or conviction; but since he had shown that he disapproved his cause by boldly expressing his opinions during the civil war, the deference he might show to his wishes was nothing more than a sort of base flattery, and a discreditable way of earning his pardon. Already his sudden return from Pharsalia had been much blamed. "I am not forgiven for living,"[1] said he. He was forgiven still less for his familiar relations with Caesar's friends. Good citizens murmured at seeing him visit so assiduously the house of Balbus, go and dine with the voluptuous Eutrapelus in company with Pansa or Antony, and by the side of the actress Cytheris, take part in the sumptuous feasts that Dolabella gave with the money of the vanquished; on all sides the malevolent had their eyes open to his weaknesses. He had, then, to satisfy at once all parties, to hold with the conquerors and the conquered for the sake of his reputation or his safety, to live near the master without being too confident, and without ever offending him, and in these dangerous relations to make what he owed to his honour agree with what was needful for his repose. It was a delicate situation, from which an ordinary man would have had perhaps some trouble to extricate himself, but which was not beyond the dexterity of Cicero. To get out of it he had in his favour one marvellous quality which prevented him from appearing too humble and too base, even when he was constrained to flatter. Madame de Sévigné has said somewhere: "Wit is a dignity." This saying is true in every sense; nothing helps one more to pass through difficult times without baseness. When a man preserves his wit before an absolute master, when he dares to

[1] *Ad fam.* ix. 5.

joke and smile in the midst of the silence and terror of others, he shows by this that the greatness of him to whom he speaks does not intimidate him, and that he feels himself sufficiently strong to support it. To remain master of one-self in his presence is still a way of braving him, and it seems to me that an exacting and suspicious despot ought to be almost as displeased with those who dare to be witty before him as with those he may suspect of having courage. There is, then, below that courage of the soul that inspires energetic resolutions, but near it, that courage of the mind which is not to be despised, for it is often the sole courage possible. After the defeat of the men of resolution, the men of wit have their turn, and they still do some service when the others can no longer do anything. As they are crafty and supple, as they can raise their head quickly after necessity has forced them to bend it, they maintain themselves with a certain amount of honour in the ruin of their party. Their raillery, however discreet it may be, is a sort of protestation against the silence imposed on all, and it at least prevents the loss of liberty of speech after having lost the liberty of action. Wit is not then such a trivial thing as people affect to consider it; it also has its grandeur, and it may be that, after a great disaster, when all is silent, downcast, and discouraged, it alone maintains human dignity, which is in great danger of perishing.

Such was, very nearly, the part Cicero played at this time, and we must acknowledge that it was not wanting in import-ance. In that great city, submissive and mute, he alone dared to speak. He began to do so early, he was still at Brundusium, not knowing if he should obtain his pardon, when he frightened Atticus by the freedom of his re-marks. Impunity naturally rendered him bolder, and after his return to Rome he took scarcely any other precaution than to make his raillery as agreeable and as witty as possible. Caesar liked wit even when it was exercised at his own expense. Instead of getting angry at Cicero's jokes, he made a collection of them, and in the midst of the war in Spain, he ordered his correspondents to send them to him. Cicero, who knew this, spoke without constraint. This freedom, then so rare, drew all eyes upon him. He had never had more society round him. The friends of Caesar frequented his society readily to give themselves an air of liberality and tolerance, after the example of their chief. As he was the most illustrious survivor of the republican party after the death of Pompey and Cato, the remaining partisans of the republic crowded around him. People came to see him from all sides, and all parties met in the mornings in his vestibule. "I receive at the same time," said he, "the visits of many good citizens who are downcast, and those of our joyful conquerors." [1]

This attention no doubt had something flattering in it, and nothing must have given him more pleasure than to have regained his importance. Let us remark, however, that in regaining his position as a person of eminence, whose friendship was sought and whose house was frequented, he had already fallen short of the first part of the programme that he had laid down for himself; the share he had, about the same time, in the return of the exiles, soon made him forget the other. He had given up hiding to respond to Caesar's advances. We are going to see how he ceased to keep silence in order to thank him for his clemency.

Caesar's clemency is admired with good reason, and it deserves the praises awarded to it. For the first time a ray of humanity had been seen to shine in the midst of the pitiless wars of the ancient world.

No doubt about the extent of his rights had hitherto entered the mind of the conqueror; he believed them to

[1] *Ad Att.* ix. 20.

have no limit, and exercised them without scruple. Who, before Caesar, had thought of proclaiming and practising consideration for the vanquished? He was the first who declared that his vengeance would not outlast his victory, and that he would not strike a disarmed enemy. What adds to the admiration his conduct inspires is that he gave this fine example of mildness and moderation in a time of violence, between the proscriptions of Sulla and those of Octavius; that he pardoned his enemies at the very moment that they were massacring his soldiers who were prisoners, and burning his sailors alive with their ships. We must not, however, exaggerate, and history should not be a panegyric. Without attempting to diminish Caesar's glory, we may be allowed to ask what motive he had in pardoning the vanquished, and it is right to inquire how and within what limits he exercised his clemency.

Curio, one of his closest friends, said one day to Cicero, in a private conversation, that Caesar was cruel by nature, and that he had only spared his enemies to preserve the affection of the people;[1] but the sceptic Curio was very much disposed, like Caelius, to look at people always on their bad side: he has certainly calumniated his chief. The truth is that Caesar was clement both by nature and policy: *bro natura et pro instituto;*[2] the continuator of his *Commentaries*, who knew him well, says so. Now, if the heart does not change, policy often changes with circumstances. When a man is good solely by nature he is good always; but when the reflection which calculates the good effect clemency will produce, and the advantage which may be drawn from it, is added to the natural instinct that inclines to clemency, it may happen that a man may become less clement as soon as he has less interest to be so. He who becomes gentle and humane, by policy, in order to draw

[1] *Ad Att.* x. 4.   [2] *Bell. Afric.* 88.

men towards him, would become cruel, by policy also, if he had need of intimidating them. This happened to Caesar, and when we study his life closely we find that his clemency suffered more than one eclipse. I do not think that he committed any gratuitous cruelties for the sake of committing them, as so many of his contemporaries did; but neither did he refrain when he found some advantage in them. While he was praetor in Spain he sometimes stormed towns which were willing to surrender, in order to have a pretext for sacking them. In Gaul he never hesitated to terrify his enemies by fearful vengeance; we see him behead the whole senate of the Veneti, massacre the Usipetes and the Tencteri, sell the forty thousand inhabitants of Genabum for slaves at one time, and cut off the hands of all in Uxellodunum who had taken up arms against him. And did he not keep in prison five whole years that heroic chief of the Arverni, that Vercingetorix who was an adversary so worthy of him, that he might coolly give the order to slaughter him on the day of his triumph? Even at the time of the civil war and when he was fighting his fellow-citizens, he got tired of pardoning. When he saw that his system of clemency did not disarm his enemies, he gave it up, and their obstinacy, which surprised him, at last made him cruel. As the struggle was prolonged it took darker colours on both sides. The war between the republicans exasperated by their defeats and the conqueror furious at their resistance, became merciless. After Thapsus, Caesar set the example of punishments, and his army, inspired by his anger, slaughtered the vanquished before his face. He had proclaimed, when starting on his last expedition into Spain, that his clemency was exhausted, and that all who did not lay down their arms should be put to death. Therefore the battle of Munda was terrible. Dio relates that both armies attacked with silent rage, and that instead of the war-songs that usually resounded, one only heard at intervals the words: "strike and kill." When the fight was over the massacre began. The eldest son of Pompey, who had succeeded in escaping, was tracked in the forest for several days and killed without mercy, like the Vendean chiefs in our wars of the Bocage.

The most glorious moment of Caesar's clemency was just after the battle of Pharsalia. He had proclaimed in advance when he entered Italy that the proscriptions would not recommence. "I will not imitate Sulla," said he in a celebrated letter, which no doubt was widely circulated. "Let us introduce a new way of conquering, and seek our safety in clemency and mildness."[1] At first he did not belie these fair words. After the victory, he ordered the soldiers to spare their fellow-citizens, and on the battle-field itself he gave his hand to Brutus and many others. It is wrong however to think that there was a general amnesty at that moment.[2] On the contrary, an edict of Antony, who governed Rome in the absence of Caesar, strictly forbade any Pompeian to return to Italy without having obtained permission. Cicero and Laelius, from whom there was nothing to fear, were alone excepted. Many others returned afterwards, but they were only recalled individually and by special decree. This was a means for Caesar to make the most of his clemency. Usually pardons thus given separately were not given gratuitously, they were almost always bought by the exiles with a part of their property. Besides, they were seldom complete at first; the exiles were allowed to return to Sicily, then to Italy, before opening to them completely the gates of Rome. These steps cleverly managed, by multiplying the number of favours granted by

---

[1] *Ad Att.* ix. 7.
[2] The general amnesty that Suetonius speaks of did not take place till much later.

Caesar, did not allow public admiration to cool. Each time the chorus of flatterers recommenced their praises, and did not cease to celebrate the generosity of the victor.

There was, then, after Pharsalia, a certain number of exiles in Greece and in Asia who were waiting impatiently for permission to return home, and who did not all obtain it. Cicero's letters do us the good office of making us acquainted with some of them. They are people of all conditions and fortunes, merchants and farmers of the taxes as well as great nobles. By the side of a Marcellus, a Torquatus and a Domitius there are entirely unknown persons like Trebianus and Toranius, which shows that Caesar's vengeance did not stop at the heads of the party. We find also among them three writers, and it is worthy of notice that they were perhaps the most hardly treated. One of them, T. Ampius, was a fiery republican who did not show so much firmness in exile as one would have expected. He was occupied in writing a history of illustrious men, and it seems that he did not profit much by the good examples he found there. We know the other two, who are not much alike, better : they were the Etruscan Caecina, a merchant and a wit, and the scholar Nigidius Figulus. Nigidius, who was compared with Varro for the extent of his attainments, and who was, like him, at once philosopher, grammarian, astronomer, physicist, rhetorician and lawyer, had particularly struck his contemporaries by the extent of his theological researches. As he was seen to be much occupied with the doctrines of the Chaldeans and the followers of Orpheus, he passed for a great magician. It was believed that he predicted the future, and he was suspected of raising the dead. So many occupations, of such various kinds, did not prevent him taking an interest in the affairs of his country. It was not thought, then, that a scholar was excused from performing the duties of a citizen. He solicited and obtained public

offices : he was praetor in difficult times, and was noticed
for his energy. When Caesar entered Italy, Nigidius, faithful to the maxim of his master Pythagoras, which commands
the sage to carry help to the law when it is menaced,
hastened to leave his books, and was one of the principal combatants at Pharsalia. Caecina had appeared at first as firm
as Nigidius, and like him was conspicuous for his republican
ardour. Not content with taking up arms against Caesar,
he had, besides, insulted him in a pamphlet at the beginning
of the war : but he was as weak as he was violent, he could
not bear exile. This frivolous and worldly man had need
of the pleasures of Rome, and was disconsolate at being
deprived of them. To obtain his pardon, he formed the
idea of writing a new work destined to contradict the old
one, and to obliterate its bad effect. He had called it his
Querelae, and this title indicates well enough its character.
In it he lavished eulogies on Caesar without measure, and
yet he was always afraid he had not said enough. " I
tremble in all my limbs," said he to Cicero, " when I ask
myself if he will be satisfied." [1] So much humiliation and
baseness succeeded in softening the victor, and while he
relentlessly left the energetic Nigidius, who could not flatter,
to die in exile, he allowed Caecina to approach Italy, and
settle down in Sicily.

Cicero had become the consoler of all these exiles, and
employed his influence in ameliorating their condition. He
served them all with the same zeal, although there were
some among them of whom he had reason to complain ;
but he no longer remembered their offences when he saw
their misfortunes. In writing to them he showed a graceful
tact in accommodating his language to their situation and
feelings, caring little whether he was consistent with himself,
provided he could console them and be useful to them.

[1] *Ad fam.* vii. 7.

He told those who lamented that they were kept away from Rome, that they were wrong in wishing to return, and that it was better simply to hear reports of the misfortunes of the republic than to see them with their eyes; he wrote in the opposite strain to those who supported exile too courageously, and would not beg for recall, to the great despair of their families. When he met with a too servile eagerness in anticipating and entreating Caesar's kindness, he did not hesitate to blame it, and with infinite tact recalled the unfortunate to that self-respect which they had forgotten. If, on the contrary, he saw some one disposed to commit a heroic imprudence and to attempt a useless and dangerous move, he hastened to restrain this burst of idle courage, and preached prudence and resignation. He did not spare his pains during this time. He went to see the friends of the master, or if necessary, he tried to see the master himself, although it was very difficult to approach a man who had the affairs of the whole world on his shoulders. He begged, he promised, he wearied with his supplications and was almost always successful, for Caesar was anxious to draw him more and more into his party by the favours he granted him. The favour once obtained, he wished to be the first to announce it to the exile, who impatiently awaited it; he heartily congratulated him and added to his compliments a few of those counsels of moderation and silence which he readily gave to others, but which he did not always follow himself.

There was no more important personage among these exiles than the former consul Marcellus; neither was there any whom Caesar had so much reason to hate. By a sort of cruel bravado, Marcellus had had an inhabitant of Como beaten with rods, in order to show what value he set upon the rights that Caesar had granted to that city. After Pharsalia, he had retired to Mitylene and did not think of returning, when his relatives and Cicero took it into their heads to obtain his pardon. While taking the first steps they met with an unexpected obstacle : they thought they only had to entreat Caesar, and they had to begin by appeasing Marcellus. He was an energetic man whom the ill success of his cause had not dispirited, a veritable philosopher, who had reconciled himself to exile, an obstinate republican, who would not return to Rome to see her a slave. Quite a long negotiation was necessary before he would consent to allow them to crave anything for him from the conqueror, and even then he allowed it with a very bad grace. When we read the letters that Cicero wrote to him on this occasion, we greatly admire his skill, but have some difficulty in understanding the motives of his persistence. We ask with surprise why he took more interest in the return of Marcellus than did Marcellus himself. They had never been very closely connected ; Cicero did not stand upon ceremony in blaming his obstinacy, and we know that those stiff and self-willed characters did not suit him. He must have had then some stronger motive than affection to be so anxious for Marcellus' return to Rome. This motive, which he does not mention, but which we can guess, was the fear he had of public opinion. He well knew that he was reproached with not having done enough for his cause, and at times he accused himself of having abandoned it too quickly. When, in the midst of Rome, where he passed his time so gaily at those sumptuous dinners that Hirtius and Dolabella gave him, and to which he went, he said, to enliven his slavery a little; when he came to think of those brave men who had been killed in Africa and Spain, or who were living in exile in some dull and unknown town in Greece, he was angry with himself for not being with them, and the thought of their sufferings often troubled his pleasures. That is the reason why he worked with so much ardour for their return. It was of importance to him to diminish the number of those whose miseries formed a disagreeable contrast to the happiness that he enjoyed, or who appeared to condemn his submission by their haughty attitude. Every time that an exile returned to Rome, it seemed to Cicero as though he got rid of some remorse and escaped the reproaches of the ill-natured. Therefore, when he had obtained, contrary to his expectation, the pardon of Marcellus, his joy knew no bounds. It went so far as to make him forget that resolution he had taken to keep silence to which he had been faithful during two years. He spoke in the senate to thank Caesar, and delivered the celebrated speech which remains to us.[1]

The reputation of this speech has had very diverse fortunes. It was long unreservedly admired, and, in the last century, the worthy Rollin regarded it as the model and perfection of eloquence ; but this enthusiasm has much diminished since we have become less appreciative of the art of praising princes with delicacy, and value free and open speech more highly than the most ingenious flattery. We should certainly sometimes wish for a little more dignity in this speech, and we are especially shocked at the manner in which embarrassing recollections of the civil war are treated in it. He should have said nothing of them, or have spoken out more boldly. Ought he, for example, to hide the motives that the republicans had for taking up arms and reduce the whole struggle to a conflict between two eminent men ? Was it the time, after the defeat of Pompey,

---

[1] It is unnecessary to say that I believe in the authenticity of this speech : it has been disputed for reasons that seem to me futile. Further on I shall reply to those drawn from the character of the speech, by showing that it is less base and servile than has been asserted.

to sacrifice him to Caesar, and to assert with so much assurance that he would have used the victory less well? That we may be able to judge less severely the concessions that Cicero thought himself obliged to make to the victorious party, we must recall the circumstances in which this speech was delivered. It was the first time he had spoken in public since Pharsalia. In that senate, purged by Caesar and filled with his creatures, free speech had not yet been heard. The friends and admirers of the master alone spoke, and whatever excess we may find in the praises that Cicero gives him, we may rest assured that all these flatteries must have seemed lukewarm compared with those heard every day. Let us add that, as no one had yet dared to make a trial of Caesar's forbearance, its limits were not exactly known. Now it is natural, that he who does not exactly know where rashness begins has a little dread of becoming rash. When one does not know the bounds of the liberty that is permitted, the fear of overstepping them sometimes prevents their being reached at all. Besides, this orator who spoke for an exile was himself one of the vanquished. He knew the whole extent of the rights that victory then conferred, and he did not try to hide it. "We have been defeated," he said to Caesar, "you might legitimately put us all to death."[1] At the present time things are quite different. Humanity has lessened these pitiless rights, and the conquered, who knows it, does not give way so completely; from the moment that he does not run the same risks it is easy for him to have more courage; but when he found himself before a master who had absolute power over him, when he knew that he only held liberty and life by a favour always revocable, he could not speak with the same boldness, and it would not be just to call the reserve imposed by such a perilous position, timidity. There is yet

[1] *Pro Marc.* 4.

one other way, simpler and probably truer than the others, of explaining these rather too exaggerated praises with which Cicero has been reproached, namely, to acknowledge that they were sincere. The greater the rights of the conqueror, the more becoming it was in him to renounce them, and the merit was still greater when they were renounced in favour of a man whom there were legitimate reasons for hating. Accordingly, the excitement was very great among the senators when they saw Caesar pardon his personal enemy, and Cicero shared it. What proves that all these effusions of joy and thankfulness, with which his speech is filled, were not simply oratorical embellishments, is that we find them in a letter which he addressed to Sulpicius, and which was not written for the public. "That day seemed to me so grand," said he, relating that memorable sitting of the senate, "that I thought I saw the republic rise again."[1] This was going very far, and indeed nothing less resembled the revival of the republic than this arbitrary act of a despot in pardoning men who were only guilty of having served their country. This violent hyperbole is none the less a proof of the deep and sincere emotion that Caesar's clemency caused Cicero. We know how open that sensitive nature was to the impressions of the moment. He usually allows himself to be seized so forcibly by admiration or hatred, that he seldom keeps within bounds in expressing them. Hence came, in the speech for Marcellus, some hyperbolical eulogies and an excess of complimentary phrases which it is easy to account for, although one would rather not have found them there.

These reservations being made, nothing remains but to admire. Cicero's speech does not contain only flatteries, as is asserted, and those who read it carefully and without prejudice will find something else. After thanking Caesar for his

[1] *Ad fam.* iv. 4.

T

clemency, he takes the liberty of telling him a few truths and giving him some advice. This second part, which is somewhat hidden now under the splendour of the other, is much more curious, although less striking, and must have produced more effect in its time. Although he revised his work before publishing it, as was usual with him, he must have preserved the movement of improvisation. If he had not at first found those grand periods, the most sonorous and pompous of the Latin tongue, it is at least probable that he has not changed very much the order of the ideas and the coherency of the speech. We feel that he becomes excited and warmed by degrees, and in proportion as he advances he becomes more daring. The success of his eloquence, of which they had been deprived so long, the applause of his friends, the admiration and surprise of the new senators who had not yet heard him, that sort of transport a man feels in speaking when he perceives he is listened to ; in sum, the place itself where he was speaking, those walls of the senate house to which he alluded in his discourse, and which guarded the memory of so many eloquent and free voices,—all this put him in heart again. He forgot the timid precautions of the commencement, and boldness came with success. Was it not attacking absolute power indirectly when he said : " I am grieved to think that the destiny of the republic, which ought to be immortal, depends entirely on the life of one man who must some time die." [1] And what can we think of that other saying, still sharper, almost cruel ? " You have done much to gain the admiration of men ; you have not done enough to deserve their praises." [2] What must Caesar do in order that the future may praise him as much as it admires him ? He must change that which exists : " The republic cannot remain as it is." He does not explain himself, but we guess what he

[1] *Pro Marc.* 7.   [2] *Ibid.* 8.

wants. He wants liberty, not that entire liberty that they had enjoyed up to Pharsalia, but a moderate and regulated liberty, compatible with a strong and victorious government, the sole liberty that Rome could support. It is plain that at this moment Cicero did not think it impossible to make a compromise between Caesar and liberty. Could not a man who so ostentatiously renounced one of the least disputed rights of victory be tempted to renounce the others later? And when he was seen to be so clement and generous towards private individuals, was it forbidden to think that he might one day show the same liberality to his country? However weak this hope might be, as there was then no other, an honest man and a good citizen would not let it be lost, and it was his duty to encourage Caesar by all possible means to realize it. They were not then to blame in praising him without restraint for what he had done, in order to urge him to do still more, and it seems to me that the praises Cicero heaps on him, when we think of the intention he had in giving them, lose a little of that look of slavishness with which they have been reproached.

Caesar listened to the compliments with pleasure and to the advice without anger. He was too pleased that Cicero had at last broken silence to think of being angry at what he had said. It was important to him that this statesman, on whom all eyes were fixed, should re-enter public life in some way or other. While that powerful voice persisted in remaining mute it seemed to protest against the new government. By not even attempting to contradict him, it let it be thought it had not the liberty to do so, and made the slavery appear heavier. He was then so content to hear Cicero's voice again that he let him say what he liked. Cicero quickly perceived it and took advantage of it. From this moment, when he speaks in public, we feel that he is more at his ease. His tone becomes firmer, and he concerns himself less about compliments and eulogies. With the speech for Marcellus, he had tried what liberties he could take. Having once felt his ground, he was more sure of his steps and walked with confidence.

Such was the position of Cicero during Caesar's dictatorship ; we see clearly that it was not so humble as has been asserted, and that, in a time of despotism, he was able to render some services to liberty. These services have been generally ill appreciated, and I am not surprised at it. It is with men something as it is with works of art : when we see them at a distance we are only struck with the bold situations and well-drawn attitudes ; the details and finer shades escape us. We can well understand those who give themselves up entirely to the conqueror like Curio or Antony, or those who constantly resist him like Labienus and Cato. As to those ingenious and flexible minds who fly from all extremes, who live adroitly between submission and revolt, who turn difficulties rather than force them, who do not refuse to pay with a few flatteries for the right of telling a few truths, we are always tempted to be severe towards them. As we cannot clearly distinguish their attitude at the distance from which we regard them, their smallest subserviencies appear to be cowardice, and they seem to be prostrating themselves when they are only bowing. It is only by drawing near them, that is to say by studying the facts closer, that we succeed in rendering them justice. I think that this minute study is not unfavourable to Cicero, and that he was not mistaken when he said later, speaking of this period of his life, that his slavery had not been without some honour : *quievi cum aliqua dignitate.*[1]

[1] *Philipp.* iii. 11.

II.

In giving an account of the relations of Cicero and Caesar after Pharsalia, I have purposely omitted to speak of the courteous contest they had about Cato. It was such a curious incident that it seems to me to be worth the trouble of being studied apart, and in order to understand better the sentiments that each of the two brought into this contest, perhaps it will not be amiss to begin by making the acquaintance of the person who was the subject of the dispute.

A sufficiently correct idea is generally formed of Cato by us, and those who attack him as well as those who admire him are very nearly agreed upon the principal features of his character. He was not one of those elusive and many-sided natures like Cicero, that it is so difficult to seize. On the contrary, no one was ever more outspoken, more uniform, than he, and there is no figure in history whose good and bad qualities are so clearly marked. The only danger for those who study him is to be tempted to ex-aggerate still more this bold relief. With a little intention it is easy to make an obstinate block of this obstinate man, a boor and brute of this frank and sincere man ; that is to say, to draw the caricature and not the portrait of Cato. To avoid falling into this extreme, it will be proper, before speaking of him, to read again a short letter that he addressed to Cicero when proconsul of Cilicia.[1] This note is all that remains to us of Cato, and I should be surprised if it did not very much astonish those who have a pre-conceived notion of him. There is neither rudeness nor brutality in it, but on the contrary much refinement and wit. The occasion of the letter was a very difficult one : it was a

[1] *Ad fam.* xv. 5.

question of refusing Cicero a favour that he very much wished to obtain. He had had in his old age the aspiration to become a conqueror, and he asked the senate to vote a thanksgiving to the gods for the success of the campaign he had just made. The senate in general showed deference to this caprice, Cato almost alone resisted; but he did not wish to fall out with Cicero, and the letter he wrote to justify his refusal is a masterpiece of dexterity. He shows him that in opposing his demand, he understands the interests of his glory, better than he does himself. If he will not thank the gods for the successes Cicero has obtained, it is because he thinks that Cicero owes them to himself alone. Is it not better to give him all the honour than to attribute it to chance, or the protection of heaven? This is certainly a very amiable way of refusing, and one that did not leave Cicero an excuse for getting angry, discontented though he was. Cato, then, was a man of wit at odd moments, although at first sight we might have some difficulty in supposing so. His character had become supple by the study of Greek literature; he lived in the midst of an elegant society, and he had unconsciously taken something from it. This is what that witty letter makes us suspect, and we must remember it, and take care to read it again every time we are tempted to fancy him an ill-bred rustic.

We must, however, admit that usually he was stiff and stubborn, hard to himself, and severe on others. That was the turn of his humour; he added to it by his self-will. Nature is not alone to blame for those self-willed and absolute characters that we meet with; a certain pursuit of quaint originality and a little self-complacency, very often make us aid nature and bring it out more vigorously. Cato was led into this defect by the very name he bore. The example of his illustrious grandfather was always before his eyes, and his single study was to resemble him, without taking into account the difference of times and men. In imitating we exaggerate. There is always a little effort and excess in the virtues we try to reproduce. We take only the most salient points of the model, and neglect the others which tone them down. This happened with Cato, and Cicero justly blames him for imitating only the rough and hard sides of his grandfather. " If you let the austerity of your behaviour take a few tints of his gay and easy manners, your good qualities would be more pleasing." [1]   It is certain that there was in the old Cato a dash of piquant animation, of rustic gaiety, of bantering good-nature, that his grandson did not have. He only shared with him his roughness and obstinacy, which he pushed to extremes.

Of all excesses the most dangerous perhaps is the excess of good ; it is at least that of which it is most difficult to correct oneself, for the culprit applauds himself, and no one dares to blame him. Cato's great defect was that he never knew moderation. By dint of wishing to be firm in his opinion, he became deaf to the advice of his friends and the lessons of experience. The practical conduct of life, that imperious mistress, to speak like Bossuet, had no hold upon him. His energy often went to the length of obstinacy, and his sense of honour was sometimes in fault by being too scrupulous. This extreme delicacy prevented him succeeding when he canvassed for public offices. The people were very exacting towards those who asked for their votes. During the rest of the year they allowed themselves to be driven and ill-used, but on election day they knew they were masters and took pleasure in showing it. They could only be gained by flattering all their caprices. Cicero often laughed at those unfortunate and deferential candidates (*natio officiosissima candidatorum*), who go in the

[1] *Pro Muraen.* 31.

morning knocking at every door, who pass their time in
paying visits and compliments, who make it a duty to
accompany the generals when they enter or leave Rome,
who form the retinue of all the influential orators, and who
are forced to have infinite consideration and respect for
everybody. Among the common people, upon whom after
all the election depended, the more honest wished to be
flattered, the rest required to be bought. Cato was not the
man to do either the one or the other. He would neither
flatter nor lie ; still less would he consent to pay. When
he was pressed to offer those repasts and those presents
that for so long candidates had not dared to refuse, he
answered bluntly : " Are you bargaining for pleasures with
debauched young men, or asking the government of the
world of the Roman people ? " And he did not cease
repeating this maxim, " that it is only a man's merits which
must solicit." [1] A hard saying ! said Cicero, and one they
were not accustomed to hear at a time when all offices
were for sale. It displeased the people, who profited by
this venality, and Cato, who persisted in only soliciting on
his merits, was almost always vanquished by those who
solicited with their money.

Characters of this sort, honest and outspoken, are met
with, in different degrees, in private as well as in public
life, and for this reason they belong to the domain of
comedy as well as to that of history. If I were not afraid
of failing in respect towards the gravity of the personage I
am studying, I should say that this haughty response that I
have just quoted, makes me think involuntarily of one of
the finest creations of our theatre. It is a Cato that
Molière wished to paint in the *Misanthrope*. We are here
only concerned with the fortune of a private individual, and
not with the government of the world, we have only to do

[1] *Pro Muraen.* 35.

with a lawsuit; but in his position, the Cato of the Comedy speaks just like the other. He will not submit to customs that he does not approve of. Even at the risk of losing his case he will not visit the judges, and when people say to him : " And who do you then intend to solicit for you ? " he answers as haughtily as Cato : " Who do I intend ? Reason, my just cause, and equity." Whatever we may feel, these personages always inspire a great respect. We have not the heart to blame them, but, nevertheless, we must have the courage to do so. Honesty, honour, liberty, all noble causes in fine, cannot well be defended with this exaggerated and strait-laced rigour. They have disadvantages enough by themselves in their struggle with corruption and licence, without making them more unpleasing still by a useless stiffness and severity. To multiply scruples is to disarm virtue. It is quite enough that she is forced to be grave ; why wish to make her repulsive ? Without sacrificing any- thing of principle, there are points on which she ought to give way to men in order to rule them. What proves that those men, who boast of never giving way, are wrong is that they are not as inflexible as they suppose, and that, in spite of their resistance, they always end by making some con- cessions. That austere, that stern Alceste, is a member of society after all, and of the best. He lives at court, and we can see very well what he is. I do not say only by his manners and appearance, although I imagine *the man with the green ribbons* dressed with taste and elegance, but by those turns of phrase he employs, by those polite evasions which are also lies, and which he will not endure in Philinte. Before breaking out against the nobleman of the sonnet he uses adroit formulas where we only catch a glimpse of the truth :

" Do you find anything amiss in my sonnet ? "

" I do not say that."

What is this "*I do not say that*," which he repeats so often, but a blameworthy compliance and weakness, if we judge it with the rigour of the misanthrope? Rousseau severely reproaches Alceste for it, and I do not think that Alceste, if he remains faithful to his principles, can find any reply to Rousseau; it would not be difficult either to point out contradictions of the same kind in Cato. This stern enemy of intrigue, who at first will do nothing for the success of his candidature, ends by canvassing: he went to the Campus Martius like everybody else, to shake hands with the citizens and ask for their votes. "What!" says Cicero to him ironically, whom these inconsistencies put into good humour, "is it your business to come and ask for my vote? Is it not rather I who ought to thank a man of your merit who wishes to brave fatigue and dangers for me?"[1] This stern enemy of lying did more: he had one of those slaves called *nomenclatores* who knew the name and profession of every citizen of Rome, and he used him like the rest, to make the poor electors believe that he knew them. "Is not this cheating and deceiving the public?" said Cicero, and he was not wrong. The saddest thing is that these concessions, that compromise the dignity and unity of a character, are of no use: they are generally made with a bad grace, and too late; they do not efface the remembrance of past rudeness, and gain nobody. Notwithstanding his tardy solicitations and the aid of his *nomenclator*, Cato did not attain the consulship, and Cicero severely blames the awkwardness that made him fail. No doubt he could do without being consul; but the republic had need that he should be consul, and in the eyes of many good citizens, to favour by refinements of scrupulosity and exaggerations of honour the triumph of the worst men was almost to abandon and betray it.

[1] *Pro Mur.* 36.

It is easy to understand these excesses and exaggerations in a man who intends *to fly the approach of humankind,* like Alceste; but they are unpardonable in one who wishes to live with men, and still more so in one who aspires to govern them. The government of men is a nice and difficult matter which requires a man not to begin by repelling those whom he is desirous of leading. Certainly he ought to intend to make them better, but it is necessary to begin by taking them as they are. The first law of politics is to aim only at the possible. Cato often overlooked this law. He could not condescend to those attentions without which one cannot govern the people; he had not sufficient flexibility of character nor that turn for honourable intrigue which make a man succeed in the things he undertakes; he wanted some of that pliancy that brings opposing pretensions together, calms jealous rivalries, and groups people divided by humours, opinions and interests around one man. He could only be a striking protest against the manners of his time; he was not the head of a party. Let us venture to say, notwithstanding the respect we feel for him, that his spirit was obstinate because his mind was narrow. He did not at first distinguish the points on which a man should give way and those that ought to be defended to the last. A disciple of the Stoics, who said that all faults are equal, that is, according to Cicero's joke, that it is as wrong to kill a fowl needlessly as to strangle one's father, he had applied this hard and strange theory to politics. His mind being restricted to the merest legality, he defended the smallest things with tiresome obstinacy. His admiration of the past knew no discrimination. He imitated the ancient costumes as he followed the old maxims, and he affected not to wear a tunic under his toga because Camillus did not wear one. His want of breadth of mind, his narrow and obstinate zeal were more than once hurtful to the republic.

Plutarch reproaches him with having thrown Pompey into Caesar's arms by refusing some unimportant gratifications of his vanity. Cicero blames him for having dissatisfied the knights whom he had had so much trouble to conciliate with the senate. No doubt the knights made unreasonable demands, but he should have conceded everything rather than let them give Caesar the support of their immense wealth. It was on this occasion that Cicero said of him: " He thinks he is in the republic of Plato and not in the mud of Romulus,"[1] and this saying is still that which best characterizes that clumsy policy that, by asking too much of men, ends by getting nothing.

Cato's natural character was that of opposition. He did not understand how to discipline and lead a party, but he was admirable when it was a question of making head against an adversary. To conquer him, he employed a tactic in which he often succeeded : when he saw that a decision that seemed to him fatal, was about to be taken, and that it was necessary at any price to prevent the people voting, he began to speak and did not leave off. Plutarch says that he could speak for a whole day without fatigue. Nothing deterred him, neither murmurs, cries, nor threats. Sometimes a lictor would pull him down from the rostrum, but as soon as he was free he went up again. One day the tribune Trebonius got so much out of patience with this resistance that he had him led off to prison : Cato, without being disconcerted, continued his speech while going along, and the crowd followed him to listen. It is to be remarked that he was never really unpopular : the common people, who love courage, were at last mastered by this steady coolness and this unconquerable energy. It sometimes happened that they declared themselves in his favour, contrary to their interests and preferences, and Caesar,

[1] *Ad Att.* ii. 1.

all-powerful with the populace, dreaded nevertheless the freaks of Cato.

It is none the less true, as I have already said, that Cato could not be the head of a party, and what is more deplorable is, that the party for which he fought had no head. It was an assemblage of men of capacity and of dignified personages, none of whom had the necessary qualities to take the lead of the rest. Not to mention Pompey, who was only a doubtful and distrusted ally, among the others, Scipio repelled every one by his haughtiness and cruelty; Appius Claudius was only a credulous augur who believed in the sacred chickens; Marcellus was wanting in pliability and urbanity, and was himself aware that scarcely anybody liked him; Servius Sulpicius had all the weaknesses of a punctilious lawyer; and lastly, Cicero and Cato erred in opposite directions, and it would have been necessary to unite them both, or modify them one by the other in order to have a complete politician. There were, therefore, only brilliant personalities and no head in the republican party before Pharsalia, and we may even say that, as this jealous selfishness and these rival vanities were ill blended, there was scarcely a party.

The civil war, which was a stumbling-block for so many others, which laid bare so many littlenesses and so much cowardice, revealed, on the other hand, all the goodness and all the greatness of Cato. A sort of crisis then took place in his character. As in certain maladies the approach of the last moments gives more elevation and lucidity to the mind, so, it seems, that at the threat of that great catastrophe which was about to engulf the free institutions of Rome, Cato's honest soul was yet further purified, and that his intelligence took a juster view of the situation from the feeling of the public dangers. While fear makes others go to extremes, he restrains the usual violence of his conduct, and, while thinking of the dangers the republic is running, he becomes all at once discreet and moderate. He who was always ready to attempt useless resistance, advises giving way to Caesar; he wishes them to grant all his demands; he resigns himself to all concessions in order to avoid civil war. When it breaks out he submits to it with sorrow, and tries by all means to diminish its horrors. Every time he is consulted he is on the side of moderation and mildness. In the midst of those young men, the heroes of the polished society of Rome, among those lettered and elegant wits, it is the rugged Cato who defends the cause of humanity. He compelled the decision, in spite of the outbursts of the fiery Pompeians, that no town shall be sacked, no citizen be killed off the field of battle. It seems that the approach of the calamities he foresaw, softened that energetic heart. On the evening of the battle of Dyrrhachium, while every one was rejoicing in Pompey's camp, Cato alone, seeing the corpses of so many Romans lying on the ground, wept: noble tears, worthy of being compared with those that Scipio shed over the ruins of Carthage, the memory of which antiquity so often recalled! In the camp at Pharsalia, he severely blamed those who spoke only of massacre and proscription and divided among themselves in advance the houses and lands of the conquered. It is true that after the defeat, when the greater number of those wild schemers were at Caesar's knees, Cato went everywhere to stir him up enemies and to revive the civil wars in all the ends of the earth. Just as he had wished them to yield before the battle, so was he determined not to submit when there was no more hope of freedom. We know his heroic resistance in Africa, not only against Caesar, but against the furious men of the re-publican party, who were always ready to commit some excess. We know how he would not accept the pardon of the victor after Thapsus, when he saw that all was lost, and killed himself at Utica.

His death made an immense impression in all the Roman world. It put to the blush those who were beginning to accustom themselves to slavery; it gave a sort of new impulse to the discouraged republicans, and revived opposition. During his life-time, Cato had not always rendered good service to his party ; he was very useful to it after his death. The proscribed cause had henceforth its ideal and its martyr. Its remaining partisans united and sheltered themselves under that great name. At Rome especially, in that great, unquiet, restless city, where so many men bowed the head without submitting, his glorification became the ordinary theme of the discontented. " The battle raged round the body of Cato," says M. Mommsen, " as at Troy it had raged around that of Patroclus." Fabius Gallus, Brutus, Cicero, and many others no doubt whom we do not know, wrote his eulogy. Cicero began his at the request of Brutus. At first he was repelled by the difficulty of the subject : " This is a work for Archimedes," said he ; [1] but as he advanced, he took a liking to his work and finished it with a sort of enthusiasm. This book has not come down to us : we only know that Cicero made a complete and unreserved apology for Cato : " he raises him to the skies," [2] says Tacitus. They had, however, disagreed more than once, and he speaks of him without much consideration in many passages of his correspondence ; but, as often happens, death reconciled everything. Besides, Cicero, who reproached himself with not having done enough for his party, was happy to find an opportunity of paying his debt. His book, that the name of the author and that of the hero recommended at once, had so great a success that Caesar was uneasy and discontented about it. He took care, however, not to show his ill humour ; on the contrary, he hastened to write a flattering letter to Cicero to congratulate him on the talent

[1] *Ad Att.* xii. 4.   [2] *Ann.* iv. 34.

he had displayed in his work. "In reading it," he told him, "I feel that I become more eloquent." [1] Instead of employing any rigorous measure, as was to be feared, he thought that the pen alone, according to the expression of Tacitus, ought to avenge the attacks that the pen had made. By his order, his lieutenant and friend Hirtius addressed a long letter to Cicero, which was published, and in which he controverted his book. Later, as this answer was not thought sufficient, Caesar himself entered the lists, and, in the midst of the anxieties of the war in Spain, he composed the *Anti-Cato*.

This moderation of Caesar has been justly praised : it is not common with men who possess unlimited authority, and the Romans justly said, that it is seldom a man is contented to write when he can proscribe. The fact that he detested Cato adds to the merit of his generous conduct. He always speaks of him with bitterness in his *Commentaries*, and although he was accustomed to do justice to his enemies, he never misses an opportunity of decrying him. Has he not dared to assert that in taking up arms against him, Cato gave way to personal rancour and to the desire of revenging his electoral defeats,[2] when he well knew that no one had more generously forgotten himself in order to think only of his country ! This was because there was more than political disagreement between them, there was antipathy of character. The defects of Cato must have been particularly disagreeable to Caesar, and his virtues were those that Caesar not only did not seek to acquire, but which he could not even understand. How could he have any feeling for his strict respect for law, for his almost servile attachment to old customs? he who found a lively pleasure in laughing at ancient usages. How could a prodigal, who had formed the habit of squandering the money of the state and his own without reckoning,

---

[1] *Ad Att.* xiii. 46.   [2] Caes. *Bell. civ.* i. 4.

how could he do justice to those rigorous scruples that Cato had in the handling of the public funds, to the attention he gave to his private affairs, and to that ambition, so strange for that time, of not having more debts than assets? These were, I repeat, qualities that Caesar could not comprehend. He was, then, sincere and convinced when he attacked them. A man of wit and pleasure, indifferent to principles, sceptical in opinion, accustomed to live in a frivolous and polished society, Cato could scarcely appear to him anything else than fanatical and brutal. As there was nothing that he put above refinement and politeness of manners, an elegant vice suited him better than a savage virtue. Cato, on the contrary, although he was not a stranger to literary culture and the spirit of society, had none the less remained at bottom an old-fashioned Roman. Notwithstanding their power, society and letters could not entirely overcome that bluntness, or if you will, that brutality of manner that he owed to his constitution and his race, and of which we find something even in his finest actions. To cite only one example; Plutarch, in the admirable narrative that he has given of his last moments, relates that, when a slave refused, through affection for Cato, to give him his sword, he knocked him down with a furious blow by which his hand was covered with blood. To the eyes of a fastidious man like Caesar, this blow revealed a vulgar nature, and I am afraid prevented him understanding the grandeur of this death. The same contrast, or rather the same antipathy, is found in all their private conduct. While Caesar's maxim was to pardon everything in his friends, and he therefore pushed complacency so far as to shut his eyes to their treasons, Cato was too exacting and particular with regard to his. At Cyprus he did not hesitate to fall out with Munatius, his life-long companion, by showing an offensive distrust of him. He was, no doubt, in his household, a model of honour and

U

fidelity ; yet he did not always maintain that respect and regard for his wife that she deserved. We know how he gave her up without ceremony to Hortensius, who had asked him for her, to take her again without scruple after Hortensius' death. How different was Caesar's conduct with regard to his, although he had reason to complain of her ! A man had been surprised at night in his house, the affair came before the courts, he might have avenged the outrage, but he preferred rather to forget it. Called as a witness before the judges, he declared he knew nothing about it, thus saving his rival in order to preserve his wife's reputation. He only divorced her later, when the report of the intrigue had blown over. This was acting like a well-bred man of the world. Here again, between Cato and him, it is the least scrupulous and in the main the least honourable of the two, the fickle and libertine husband, who, by reason of a certain natural delicacy, appears in a more advantageous light.

This contrast in conduct, this opposition of character, seem to me to explain the way in which Caesar writes of Cato in his book, even better than all their political disagreements. The fragments of it that survive and the testimony of Plutarch, show that he attacked him with extreme violence, and that he tried to make him at once ridiculous and odious. But it was useless, it was lost labour. People continued, notwithstanding his efforts, to read and admire Cicero's book. Not only did Cato's reputation survive Caesar's insults, it increased still more under the empire. In Nero's time, when despotism was heaviest, Thrasea wrote his history again, Seneca quotes him on every page of his books, and to the end he was the pride and model of honest men who preserved some feeling of honour and dignity in the general abasement of character. They studied his death even more than his life, for they needed then, above all, to learn how to die, and when this sad necessity presented itself, it was his example they set before their eyes, and his name that was in their mouths. To have sustained and consoled so many noble hearts in these cruel trials is assuredly a great glory, and I think that Cato would not have desired any other.

III.

The conclusion to be drawn from Caesar's conduct after Pharsalia, and from his relations with Cicero, is, that he wished at that time to draw nearer to the republican party. It was difficult for him to act otherwise. As long as it was a question of overturning the republic, he had accepted the support of everybody, and the worst men had come to him by preference. " When a man was eaten up with debts and in want of everything," said Cicero, " and if, besides, he was shown to be a scoundrel capable of daring anything, Caesar made him his friend; "[1] but all these unprincipled and unscrupulous men, excellent for upsetting an established power, were worth nothing in setting up a new one. It was impossible that Caesar's government should inspire any confidence as long as some honourable persons, whom men were accustomed to respect, were not seen with the master and alongside these adventurers, whom they had learnt to fear. Now, honourable men were chiefly found among the vanquished. We must add that it was not Caesar's idea that one party alone should profit by his victory. He had no ambition to work, like Marius or Sulla, for the triumph of a faction : he wished to found a new government, and he invited men of different opinions to aid him in the enterprise. It has been asserted that he sought to reconcile parties, and great compliments have been paid him for it. The praise is not altogether just:

[1] *Philipp.* ii. 32.

he did not reconcile them, he annihilated them. In the monarchical system, that he wished to establish,[1] the old parties of the republic had no place. He had cleverly used the dissensions of the people and the senate to dominate both; the first result of his victory was to put them both aside, and we may say that after Pharsalia, there was only Caesar on one side, and the vanquished on the other. This explains how it was that, once victorious, he made use indifferently of the partisans of the senate and those of the democrats. This equality which he established between them was natural, since they had all become, equally and without distinction, his subjects. Only he well knew that in accepting the services of the old republicans he should not have instruments always tractable, and that he would be obliged to allow them a certain independence of action and speech, to preserve, at least outwardly, some appearance of a republic; but that in itself did not give him much uneasiness. He had not that invincible repugnance for liberty that princes have who are born to an absolute throne, and who only know its name to dread and detest it. He had lived with it for twenty-three years, he had become accustomed to it, he knew its importance. Therefore he did not seek to destroy it entirely. He did not silence, as he might have done, the eloquent voices that regretted the past; he did not even impose silence on that harassing opposition that tried

---

[1] It is not easy to say what Caesar's projects were, as his work was interrupted by his death. Some insist that he only desired a sort of dictatorship for life; the greater number suppose that he thought of permanently establishing monarchical rule. The question is too grave to be entered upon incidentally, and settled in a few words. I will simply say that perhaps he only thought at first of the dictatorship; but in proportion as he became more powerful, the idea of founding a monarchy seemed to take more consistency in his mind. Yet it may be inferred from a passage in Plutarch (*Brut.* 7), that he was not decided on the question of an hereditary succession when he died.

to respond to his victories by jeers. He allowed some acts of his administration to be criticized, and permitted men to give him advice. This great mind well knew that a country becomes enervated when the citizens are rendered indifferent to public affairs, and lose the taste for attending to them. He did not think that anything solid could be established on passive and silent obedience, and in the government that he founded he wished to preserve something of public life. Cicero tells us this in a curious passage of his correspondence : " We enjoy here a profound calm," he writes to one of his friends ; " I should rather prefer, however, a little honest and salutary agitation ; " and he adds : " I see that Caesar is of my opinion." [1]

All these reasons decided him to take one step further on that path of generosity and clemency on which he had entered after Pharsalia. He had pardoned the greater number of those who had borne arms against him ; he invited some of them to share his power. At the very time that he was recalling the greater part of the exiles, he appointed Cassius his lieutenant ; he gave Brutus the government of Cisalpine Gaul, and Sulpicius that of Greece. We shall speak further on of the first two ; it is important, the better to appreciate Caesar's policy, to rapidly make known the third, and to inquire how he had become worthy of the favours of the conqueror, and in what manner he profited by them.

Servius Sulpicius belonged to an important Roman family, and was the most celebrated lawyer of his time. Cicero gives him this great praise, namely, that he was the first to bring philosophy into the law, that is to say, that he bound together all those minute rules and precise formulas of which this science is composed, by general principles and comprehensive views. [2] Accordingly he does not hesitate to place him much above his predecessors, and more especi-

[1] *Ad fam.* xii. 17. [2] *Brut.* 51.

ally, over that great family of the Scaevolas, in which as it
seemed Roman jurisprudence had been up to that time
incarnate.　There was, however, a difference between them
and Sulpicius, which it is important to notice : the Scaevolas
had given to Rome, lawyers, augurs, pontifs, that is to say,
they excelled in the arts that are friendly to tranquillity and
peace ; but they were also very active citizens, resolute
politicians, valiant soldiers who courageously defended their
country against conspirators and against the foreigner.
They showed themselves, in their busy life, competent for
all affairs and equal to all situations.　Scaevola the augur,
when Cicero knew him, was still, notwithstanding his age,
a vigorous old man, who rose at daybreak to meet his
country clients.　He was the first to arrive at the Curia,
and he had always some book with him, that he read so as
not to remain idle while waiting for his colleagues ; but
the day that Saturninus threatened the public tranquillity,
this learned man who loved study so much, this infirm old
man who supported himself with difficulty, and could only
use one arm, seized a javelin with that arm, and marched
at the head of the people to the assault of the Capitol.[1]
Scaevola the pontif was not only an able lawyer, he was
also an upright administrator whose memory Asia never
forgot.　When the farmers of the taxes attacked his quaestor
Rutilius, guilty of having wished to prevent them ruining
the province, he defended him with an admirable eloquence
and vigour that no threat could shake.　He refused to leave
Rome at the time of the first proscriptions, and abandon
his clients and their business, although he knew the fate
that was awaiting him.　Wounded at the funeral of Marius,
he was dispatched a few days later near the temple of
Vesta.[2]　However, such men were not exceptional at
Rome.　In the best times of the republic, the complete

[1] *Pro Rabir.* 7.　　　　　[2] *Pro Rosc. Am.* 12.

citizen had to be at once agriculturist, soldier, administrator, financier, advocate, and even jurist. There were no specialists then, and we should be forced to make now-a-days four or five different persons out of one ancient Roman ; but in the period of which we are now speaking, these diverse aptitudes that were then required in a single man were separated : each man gave himself to a special science, and we can begin to divide men of study from men of action. It is difficult to say whether the reason of this was that men had lost the energy of their character ; or perhaps we should think that since the masterpieces of Greece had been made known, and each science had become more complicated, one man could not any longer bear the burden of all united ? However this may be, if Sulpicius was above the Scaevolas as a lawyer, he was far from having their firmness as a citizen. Praetor or consul, he was never anything more than a man of learning and chamber practice. In circumstances that require resolution, every time it was necessary to decide and to act, he was ill at ease. We feel that this honest and gentle soul was not made to be the first magistrate of a republic in a period of revolution. His fondness for always playing the part of conciliator and arbitrator in that time of violence ended by exciting laughter. Cicero himself, although he was his friend, quizzes him a little, when he shows us this great peacemaker starting off with his little secretary, after having looked over all his lawyers' rules, to intervene between the parties at the time these parties only desired to destroy one another.

Caesar had always thought that Sulpicius was not of a character to oppose him vigorously, and had early worked to attach him to himself. He began by making an ally in his house, and a powerful ally. It was a matter of common talk at Rome, that the worthy Sulpicius allowed himself to be led by his wife Postumia ; Cicero, who likes to repeat scandals, several times tells us this. Now, Postumia's reputation was not spotless, and Suetonius places her name on the list of those women who were loved by Caesar. She is one of a very numerous company ; but this fickle man, who passed so quickly from one mistress to another, had this singular privilege, that all the women whom he abandoned, remained none the less his devoted friends. They forgave his infidelities, they continued to take an interest in all his successes, they put those immense resources of ingenuity and persistency which belong only to a woman who is in love, at the service of his policy. It was no doubt Postumia who decided Sulpicius to work for Caesar during the whole time that he was consul, and to oppose the vehemence of his colleague Marcellus who wished another governor of Gaul to be appointed. However, notwithstanding all his weaknesses, Sulpicius was none the less a sincere republican, and when the war had broken out, he declared against Caesar, and left Italy. After the defeat, he submitted like the rest, and he had resumed his usual occupations, when Caesar sought him out in his retreat in order to appoint him governor of Greece. It was certainly impossible to find a government that suited him better. A residence in Athens, at all times agreeable to the rich Romans, must have been especially so at this time when that city was the asylum of so many illustrious exiles. Sulpicius could at the same time have the pleasure of hearing the most celebrated rhetoricians and philosophers of the world, and could talk of Rome and the republic with eminent persons like Marcellus and Torquatus, and thus satisfy all his tastes at once. Nothing could have been more pleasing, we should have thought, to this scholar and man of letters, whom chance had made a statesman, than the exercise of extensive power, without danger, combined with the most refined intellectual pleasures in one of the grandest and most beautiful countries in the world. We should, therefore, have thought that Caesar had done the most agreeable thing for him, in sending him on duty to that city where the Romans usually went for pleasure. Yet it does not seem that Sulpicius appreciated these advantages. He had scarcely arrived in Greece, when he was discontented at having gone, and longed to depart. Evidently it was not the country that displeased him, he would not have thought himself better off anywhere else ; but he regretted the republic. After having so timidly defended it, he could not console himself for its fall, and blamed himself for serving him who had overturned it. These feelings are clearly expressed in a letter that he wrote to Cicero from Greece. " Fortune," he tells him, " has taken from us our most precious possessions ; we have lost our honour, our dignity, and our country. . . . In the times in which we live, those are most happy who are dead." [1]

When a timid and moderate man like Sulpicius dared speak thus, what must others not have said and thought ! We can guess this when we see how Cicero writes to the greater number of them. Although he is addressing officials of the new government, he does not take the trouble to hide his opinions ; he freely expresses his regrets, because he well knows they are shared by those to whom he is writing. He speaks to Servilius Isauricus, the proconsul of Asia, as to a man whom the absolute power of one does not satisfy, and who wishes some restraints to be put on it.[2] He tells Cornificius, the governor of Africa, that affairs are going ill at Rome, and that many things happen there which would pain him.[3] " I know what you think of the lot of honest people, and of the misfortunes of the republic," he writes to Furfanius, the proconsul of Sicily, in recommending an exile to him.[4] These persons, however, had

[1] *Ad fam.* iv. 5.   [2] *Ibid.* xiii. 68.   [3] *Ibid.* xii. 18.   [4] *Ibid.* vi. 9.

accepted important offices from Caesar: they shared his power, they passed for his friends; but all the favours they had received from him had not thoroughly attached them to his cause. They made their reservations while serving him, and only half gave themselves up to him. Whence could this opposition come, that the new government met with among men who had at first agreed to take a share in it? It proceeded from different motives which it is easy to point out. The first, perhaps the most important, was that this government, even while loading them with honours, could not give them what the old republic would have given them. With the establishment of the monarchy an important change in all public employments was accomplished: the magistrates became subordinate officials. Formerly, those elected by the popular vote had the right to act as they pleased within the sphere of their functions. A fertile power of initiative inspired every rank of this hierarchy of republican dignitaries. From the aedile to the consul all were supreme within their own limits. They could not be so under an absolute government. Instead of governing on their own account, they were only the channels, so to say, by which the will of a single man acted to the ends of the earth. Certainly public security gained much by the cessation of those conflicts of authorities, which had continually troubled it, and it was a great advantage for the provinces that absolute power had been taken away from their greedy governors. Nevertheless, if the governed profited by these reforms, it was natural that the governors should be discontented with them. From the moment that they were only entrusted with the execution of the orders of another man the importance of their functions diminished, and this sovereign and absolute authority whose weight they always felt, finally vexed even the most submissive. If ambitious men complained of the diminution of their power, honest people did not get accustomed so easily as might have been expected to the loss of their liberty. In proportion as they left Pharsalia behind, their regrets became more lively. They began to get over the surprise of the defeat, and gradually recovered from the fear it had caused them. During the moments that immediately follow those great disasters in which men have expected to perish, they give themselves up entirely to the pleasure of living, but this pleasure is one of those to which men accustom themselves so quickly, and which are taken so much as a matter of course, that they soon cease to be sensible of it. All those terrified people who on the morrow of Pharsalia desired only tranquillity, when it had been given them, wished for something else. As long as men are uncertain of their life, they do not trouble themselves to know if they shall live free, but when once life is assured, the desire for liberty returns to all hearts, and those who served Caesar felt it like the rest. Caesar, we know, partly satisfied this desire, but this satisfaction did not last long. It is as difficult to halt on the road to liberty as on that to absolutism. One favour granted makes men desire another, and men think less of enjoying what they have obtained than of lamenting what they lack. It was thus that Cicero, who had welcomed Caesar's clemency with transports of joy, and who saluted the return of Marcellus as a sort of restoration of the republic, soon changed his opinion and language. As we get on further in his correspondence, he becomes more bitter and more revolutionary. He who had so severely condemned those who "after having disarmed their hands did not disarm their hearts," [1] had his own heart filled with the bitterest resentment. He said on every opportunity that all was lost, that he blushed to be a slave, that he was ashamed to

[1] *Pro Marc.* 10.

live. He attacked with his pitiless raillery the most useful measures and the most just acts. He laughed at the reform of the calendar, and pretended to appear scandalized at the enlargement of Rome. He went further. On the day that the senate ordered Caesar's statue to be placed beside those of the ancient kings, he could not avoid making a cruel allusion to the manner in which the first of these kings had perished. "I am very glad," said he, "to see Caesar so near to Romulus!"[1] And yet it was scarcely a year since, in his speech for Marcellus, he had implored him in the name of the country to watch over his life, and had said with much feeling, "Your safety is ours!"

Caesar, then, had only malcontents around him. The moderate republicans, on whom he reckoned to aid him in his work, could not resign themselves to the loss of the republic. The exiles whom he had recalled to Rome were more humiliated by his clemency than grateful for it, and did not give up their resentment. His own generals, whom he loaded with riches and honours, without being able to satisfy their cupidity, reproached him for his ingratitude, and even plotted his death. The common people, at last, of whom he was the idol, and who had so cheerfully granted all his demands, the people themselves began to withdraw from him ; they no longer welcomed his victories with the same applause as formerly, and seemed to be afraid that they had made him too great. When his statue was placed beside those of the kings, the multitude, who saw it pass, remained mute, and we know that the news of this unusual silence was spread by the messengers of the allied kings and nations in all the countries of the world, and caused it to be believed everywhere that a revolution was at hand.[2] In the provinces of the East, where the last soldiers of Pompey were hiding, the fire of civil war, which was smouldering rather than

[1] *Ad Att.* xii. 45.   [2] *Pro Dejot.* 12.

extinct, constantly revived, and these perpetual alarms, without leading to serious danger, prevented the public tranquillity becoming settled. At Rome, Cicero's works, in which he celebrated the glories of the republic, were read with enthusiasm ; anonymous pamphlets, which had never been more violent or more numerous, were eagerly sought. As happens on the eve of great crises, every one was discontented with the present, unquiet about the future, and prepared for the unforeseen. We know in how tragical a manner this strained situation terminated. The stab of Brutus' dagger was not altogether, as has been said, an unpremeditated incident and a chance ; it was the general uneasiness of men's minds which led to and which explains such a terrible catastrophe. The conspirators were but little over sixty in number, but they had all Rome for their accomplice.[1] All this disquietude and rancour, those bitter regrets for the past, those disappointed ambitions, this baffled cupidity, this open or secret hatred, those bad or generous passions of which men's hearts were full, armed their hands, and the Ides of March were only the deadly explosion of so much stored-up anger. Thus events frustrated all Caesar's projects. He did not find safety in his clemency, as he thought ; he failed in that work of conciliation that he had attempted with the applause of the world : he did not succeed in disarming parties. This glory was reserved for a man who had neither his breadth of genius, nor his generosity of character—for the crafty and cruel Octavius. This is not the only time that history shows us the sad spectacle of the success of ordinary men where the greatest have failed ; but in enterprises of this nature success depends above all on circumstances, and it must be admitted

---

[1] " All the honest men," said Cicero (*Phil.* ii. 12), " in so far as they could, have killed Caesar. Some wanted the means, others the resolution, several the opportunity ; no one wanted the will."

that they singularly favoured Augustus. Tacitus tells us
the principal cause of his good fortune, when he says,
speaking of the establishment of the empire : " There was
almost no one left who had seen the republic." [1]   The men
over whom Caesar aspired to reign, on the contrary, had all
seen it.   Many cursed it when it troubled the tranquillity
of their lives by its storms and agitations ; almost all regretted it as soon as they had lost it.   There is, notwithstanding the perils to which it exposes men, a singular
charm and attraction in the habit and exercise of liberty
which cannot be forgotten when once it has been known.
It was against this inextinguishable memory that the genius
of Caesar was shattered.   But after the battle of Actium,
the men who had looked upon the grand scenes of liberty,
and who had seen the republic, no longer existed.   A civil
war of twenty years, the most murderous of all those that
have ever depopulated the world, had destroyed them
almost all.   The recollections of the new generation did
not go further back than Caesar.   The first sounds it had
heard were the acclamations that saluted the conqueror of
Pharsalia, of Thapsus, and of Munda ; the first spectacle
that had struck its eyes was that of the proscriptions.   It
had grown up among pillage and massacres.   During twenty
years it had daily trembled for its property or its life.   It
thirsted for security, and was ready to sacrifice everything
for repose.   Nothing attracted it towards the past, as the
contemporaries of Caesar had been attracted.   On the contrary, all the memories of the past which survived only
attached it more to the government under which it lived,
and when by chance it turned its eyes backwards it found
many subjects for fear without any subject for regret.
It was only under these circumstances that absolute power
could peaceably succeed the republic.

[1] *Ann.* i. 3.

BRUTUS

HIS RELATIONS WITH CICERO

WE should not know Brutus without Cicero's letters. As he has never been spoken of with composure, and as political parties have been accustomed to screen their hatred or their hopes under his name, the true features of his character were early effaced. Amid the heated discussions that his mere name raises, while some, like Lucan, exalt him almost to heaven, and others, like Dante, resolutely place him in hell, it was not long before he became a sort of legendary personage. To read Cicero brings us back to the reality. Thanks to him, this striking but indistinct figure, that admiration or terror have immoderately enlarged, becomes more defined and takes human proportions. If it loses in grandeur by being viewed so close, at least it gains something by becoming true and living.

The connection between Cicero and Brutus lasted ten years. The collection of letters they wrote to each other during this interval must have been voluminous, since a grammarian quotes the ninth book of them. They are all lost, with the exception of twenty-five which were written after the death of Caesar.[1] Notwithstanding the loss of the

[1] The authenticity of these letters has been often called in question since the last century, and has been debated in Germany quite recently with much warmth, and a distinguished critic, F. Hermann of Göttingen, has published some remarkable essays, to which it seems to me difficult to reply, in order to prove that they are really letters of Brutus and Cicero. I have summed up his principal arguments in *Recherches sur la manière dont furent recueillies les lettres de Cicéron*, ch. v.

rest, Brutus still holds such a large place in the surviving works of Cicero, and especially in his correspondence, that we find in it all the elements necessary for becoming well acquainted with him. I am going to collect these references, and to re-write, not the narrative of Brutus' entire life, which would oblige me to dwell upon very well-known events, but only the history of his relations with Cicero.

I.

Atticus, the friend of everybody, brought them together. It was about the year 700, a short time after Cicero's return from exile, and in the midst of the troubles stirred up by Clodius, one of those vulgar agitators like Catiline, by whose means Caesar exhausted the strength of the Roman aristocracy that he might one day overcome it more easily. Cicero and Brutus occupied at that time very different positions in the republic. Cicero had filled the highest offices, and in them had rendered eminent services. His talents and his probity made him a valuable auxiliary for the aristocratical party to which he was attached; he was not without influence with the people whom his eloquence charmed; the provinces loved him, as they had seen him more than once defend their interests against greedy governors, and still more recently Italy had shown her affection by carrying him in triumph from Brundusium to Rome. Brutus was only thirty-one; a great part of his life had been passed away from Rome, at Athens, where we know that he devoted himself earnestly to the study of Greek philosophy, in Cyprus, and in the East, where he had followed Cato. He had not yet filled any of those offices which gave political importance, and he had to wait more than ten years before thinking of the consulship. Nevertheless Brutus was already an important person. In his early relations with Cicero, notwithstanding the distance that age and official position set between them, it is Cicero who makes the advances, who treats Brutus with consideration, and who seeks his friendship. One would say that this young man had given rise to singular expectations, and that it was already vaguely felt that he was destined for great things. While Cicero was in Cilicia, Atticus, pressing him to do justice to certain claims of Brutus, said: " It would be something if you only brought back his friendship from that province." [1] And Cicero wrote of him at the same period : " He is already the first among the young men ; he will soon be, I hope, the first in the city." [2]

Everything in fact seemed to promise a splendid future for Brutus. A descendant of one of the most illustrious families of Rome, the nephew of Cato, the brother-in-law of Cassius and Lepidus, he had just married one of the daughters of Appius Claudius ; another was already married to Pompey's eldest son. By these alliances he was connected on all sides with the most influential families ; but his character and manners distinguished him even more than his birth. His youth had been austere : he had studied philosophy, not merely as a *dilettante* and as being a most useful discipline for the mind, but like a wise man who wishes to apply the lessons that it gives. He had returned from Athens with a great reputation for wisdom, which his virtuous and regular life confirmed. The admiration that his virtue excited was redoubled when his surroundings and the detestable examples he had resisted were considered. His mother Servilia had been the object of one of the most violent passions of Caesar, perhaps his first love. She always held a great sway over him, and took advantage of

---

[1] *Ad Att.* vi. 1.   [2] *Ad fam.* iii. 11.

x

it to enrich herself after Pharsalia by getting the property of the conquered awarded to her. When she became old, and felt the powerful dictator slipping from her, in order to continue to rule him, she favoured, it is said, his amours with one of her daughters, the wife of Cassius. The daughter who had married Lepidus, had no better reputation, and Cicero tells a merry tale about her. A young Roman fop, C. Vedius, going through Cilicia with a great train, found it convenient to leave part of his baggage with one of his hosts. Unfortunately this host died; seals were put on the traveller's baggage along with the rest, and to begin with, the portraits of five great ladies were found in it, and among them that of Brutus' sister. "It must be admitted," said Cicero, who did not lose an opportunity for a joke, "that the brother and the husband well deserve their names. The brother is very stupid (*brutus*) who perceives nothing, and the husband very easy-going (*lepidus*) who endures all without complaint."[1] Such was the family of Brutus. As to his friends, there is no need to say much about them. We know how the rich young men of Rome lived at that time, and what Caelius, Curio, and Dolabella were. Among all this dissipation the rigid integrity of Brutus, his application to business, that disdain for pleasures, that taste for study to which his pale and serious countenance bore witness, stood out in higher relief by the contrast. Accordingly all eyes were fixed on this grave young man who resembled the others so little. In approaching him men could not help a feeling that seemed ill suited to his age: he inspired respect. Even those who were his elders and his superiors, Cicero and Caesar, notwithstanding their glory, Antony who resembled him so little, his opponents and his enemies, could not escape this impression in his presence. What is most surprising is, that it has survived

[1] *Ad Att.* vi. 1.

him. It has been felt in presence of his memory as it was before his person; living and dead he has commanded respect. The official historians of the empire, Dio, who has so roughly handled Cicero, Velleius, the flatterer of Tiberius, all have respected Brutus. It seems that political rancour, the wish to flatter, and the violence of party have felt themselves disarmed before this austere figure.

While respecting him, they loved him. These are sentiments which do not always go together. Aristotle forbids us to represent heroes perfect in all points in the drama, lest they should not interest the public. Things go in ordinary life very much as they do on the stage; a sort of instinctive dread holds us aloof from irreproachable characters, and as it is usually by our common failings that we are drawn together, we feel very little attraction towards a man who has no failings, and are content to respect perfection at a distance. Yet it was not so in the case of Brutus, and Cicero could say of him with truth in one of the works that he addresses to him: "Who was ever more respected and loved than you?"[1] And yet this man without weaknesses was weak for those he loved. His mother and sisters had great influence over him, and made him commit more than one fault. He had many friends, and Cicero blames him for listening too readily to their advice; they were worthy men who understood nothing of public affairs; but Brutus was so much attached to them that he could not protect himself against them. His last sorrow at Philippi was to learn of the death of Flavius, his overseer of works, and that of Labeo, his lieutenant; he forgot his own self to weep for them. His last words before his death were to congratulate himself that none of his friends had betrayed him: this fidelity, so rare at that time, consoled his last moments. His legions also, although they were partly

[1] *Orat.* 10.

composed of old soldiers of Caesar, and he kept them
tightly in hand, punishing plunderers and marauders, his very
legions loved him and remained faithful to him. Even the
people of Rome themselves, who were in general enemies
of the cause he defended, showed their sympathy for him
more than once. When Octavius proclaimed the assassins
of Caesar public enemies, every one sadly bowed their
heads when they heard the name of Brutus pronounced
from the rostrum, and in the midst of the terrified senate
which foresaw the proscriptions, a voice dared to declare
that it would never condemn Brutus.

Cicero fell under the charm like the rest, but not without
resistance. His friendship with Brutus was troubled and
stormy, and, notwithstanding the general agreement of their
opinions, violent dissensions arose between them more than
once. Their disagreements are explained by the diversity
of their characters. Never did two friends resemble each
other less. There never was a man who seemed made for
society more than Cicero ; he brought into it all the qualities
that are necessary for success, great flexibility of opinion,
much toleration for others, allowance enough for himself,
the talent of steering with ease between all parties, and a
certain natural indulgence that made him understand and
almost accept everything. Although he made bad verses,
he had the temperament of a poet, a strange mobility of
impression, an irritable sensitiveness, a supple, broad, and
quick intellect which conceived promptly, but quickly
abandoned its ideas, and passed from one extreme to
another at a bound. He did not make a single serious
resolution of which he did not repent the next day. When-
ever he joined a party he was only quick and decided at
the beginning, and gradually cooled down. Brutus, on the
contrary, had not a quick intelligence : he usually hesitated
at the commencement of an enterprise and did not decide

at once. Slow and serious, he advanced step by step in everything, but, once resolved, he was so absorbed in his conviction that nothing could divert him : he isolated and concentrated himself in it, he excited and inflamed himself for it by reflection, and at last listened only to that inflexible logic that drove him to realize his purpose. He was one of those minds of which Saint-Simon says that they have an almost ferocious consistency. His obstinacy was the real source of his strength, and Caesar well understood it when he said of him : " All that he wills he means." [1]

Two friends who resembled each other so little must naturally have clashed at every opportunity. Their first differences were literary. It was a custom then at the bar to divide an important case among several orators ; each took the part best suited to his talents. Cicero, obliged to appear often before the judges, went with his friends and pupils, and gave out to them part of his work in order to be able to get through it. He was often satisfied with keeping the peroration for himself, in which his copious

---

[1] *Ad Att.* xiv. 1.—A very curious statue of Brutus is to be seen at the Campana Museum. The artist has not tried to idealize his model, and seems to have aimed at nothing but a vulgar exactness ; but we can very well recognize in it the real Brutus. We can trace in that low forehead and the heavy bones of the face a narrow mind and an obstinate will. The face has a feverish and sickly look ; it is at once young and old, as is the case with those who have never really been young. Above all we perceive in it a strange sadness, that of a man overwhelmed by the weight of a great and fateful destiny. In the fine bust of Brutus preserved in the Museum of the Capitol, the face is fuller and handsomer. The sweetness and sadness remain ; the sickly look has disappeared. The features exactly resemble those on the famous medal struck during Brutus' last years, and which bears on the reverse a Phrygian cap between two daggers, with the threatening legend, *Idus Martiae.* Michael Angelo commenced a bust of Brutus, of which the admirable rough model may be seen at the Uffizi in Florence. It was not a fancy study, and we see that he had made use of ancient portraits while idealizing them.

and impassioned eloquence was at home, and left them
the rest. It was thus that Brutus pleaded at his side and
under his direction. Brutus, however, was not of his
school: a fanatical admirer of Demosthenes, whose statue
he had placed among those of his ancestors, and nurtured
on the study of the Attic masters, he sought to reproduce
their graceful severity and vigorous strength. Tacitus says
that his efforts were not always happy: by dint of avoiding
ornament and pathos he was dull and cold, and by too
eagerly seeking precision and strength he became dry and
stiff. These faults were repugnant to Cicero, who always
saw in this type of eloquence, which was founding a school,
a criticism of his own, and tried by every means to convert
Brutus; but he did not succeed, and on this point they
never agreed. After the death of Caesar, and when something else than literary discussions was in question, Brutus
sent his friend the speech he had just delivered in the
Capitol, and begged him to correct it. Cicero took good
care not to do so: he knew too well by experience the
self-esteem of the literary man to run the risk of offending
Brutus by trying to do better than he. Besides, the speech
seemed to him very fine, and he wrote to Atticus that
nothing could have been more graceful or better written.
"Yet," added he, "if I had had to make it I should have
put more passion in it."[1] Assuredly Brutus did not lack
passion, but it was in him a secret and repressed flame that
only touched the nearest, and he disliked to give the rein
to those powerful emotions and that fiery pathos without
which one cannot carry away the multitude.

He was not then a docile follower of Cicero, and we may
add that neither was he an accommodating friend. He
lacked pliancy in his relations with others, and his tone
was always rough and abrupt. At the commencement of

[1] *Ad Att.* xv. 1, B.

their intercourse, Cicero, accustomed to be treated with great respect even by the highest personages, thought the letters of this young man were curt and haughty, and felt hurt. This was not the only complaint he had to make of him. We know the great consular's irritable, suspicious and exacting vanity; we know to what a degree he loved praise; he gave it to himself liberally and he expected it from others, and if they were slow in giving it he was not ashamed to ask for it. His friends were generally indulgent to this harmless failing, and did not wait to be invited by him to praise him. Brutus alone resisted; he prided himself on his candour, and spoke out what he thought. Accordingly Cicero often complains that he was chary of his praises; one day indeed he was seriously angry with him. It was a question of the great consulship, and of the discussion in consequence of which Lentulus and the accomplices of Catiline were executed. This was the most vigorous action of Cicero's life, and he had a right to be proud of it, since he had paid for it with exile. In the narrative that Brutus gave of the events of this day he depreciated the part that Cicero had played in them to the advantage of his uncle Cato. He only praised him for having punished the conspiracy, without saying that he had discovered it, and contented himself with calling him an *excellent consul.* "Poor praise!" said Cicero angrily; "one would think it came from an enemy."[1] But those were only small differences arising from wounded self-esteem, which might easily be made up; we must now mention a graver disagreement that deserves to be dwelt upon, for it suggests some serious reflections on the Roman society of that period.

In 702, that is to say, a short time after the commencement of his relations with Brutus, Cicero went out as pro-

[1] *Ad Att.* xii. 21.

consul to Cilicia. He had not sought this office, for he knew what difficulties he should find in it. He set out decided to do his duty, and he could not do it without bringing on his hands at the same time the patricians, his protectors, and the knights, his *protégés* and clients. In fact, patricians and knights, usually enemies, agreed, with a singular unanimity, in plundering the provinces. The knights, farmers of the public revenue, had only one thought : to make a fortune in five years, the usual duration of their contract. Consequently they exacted without mercy the tax of a tenth on the productions of the soil, a twentieth on merchandise at the ports, the harbour dues, the tax on pasture-lands in the interior ; in fact, all the tribute that Rome had imposed on the conquered nations. Their greed respected nothing. Livy wrote this terrible sentence about them : "Wherever the 'publican' penetrates, there is no more justice or liberty for any one."[1] It was very difficult for the wretched cities to satisfy these insatiable financiers ; almost everywhere the municipal coffers, ill administered by incompetent, or pillaged by dishonest magistrates, were empty. Money, however, had to be found at any price. Now, of whom could they borrow it, except of the bankers of Rome, who had been for a century the bankers of the whole world ? It was to them therefore that they applied. Some were rich enough to draw from their private fortune money to lend to foreign cities, or sovereigns, like that Rabirius Postumus, for whom Cicero had pleaded, who furnished the king of Egypt with the money necessary to reconquer his kingdom. Others, in order to run less risk, formed financial companies, in which the most illustrious Romans invested their funds. Thus, Pompey had a share for a considerable sum in one of those joint-stock companies founded by Cluvius of

[1] Liv. xlv. 18.

Puteoli. All these money-lenders, whether private individuals or companies, knights or patricians, were very unscrupulous, and only advanced their money at enormous
interest, generally 4 or 5 per cent. per month. Their
difficulty consisted in getting paid. As it is only men who
are quite ruined who accept these hard terms, the money
lent on such high interest is always subject to risk. When
the date of payment arrived the poor city was less than ever
in a position to pay : it employed a thousand pettifogging
tricks, spoke of complaining to the senate, and began by
appealing to the proconsul. Unfortunately for it, the proconsul was usually an accomplice of its enemies, and took
his share of their profits. The creditors who had secured
his co-operation by paying him well, had then only to send
into the province some freedman or agent who represented
them ; the proconsul placed the public forces at the service
of private interests, gave this agent the title of his lieutenant,
some soldiers, and full powers, and if the insolvent town
did not quickly come to some satisfactory arrangement, it
suffered the horrors of a siege and of official pillage in time
of peace. The proconsul who refused to lend himself to
these abuses, and who intended, according to Cicero's
expression, to prevent the provinces perishing, naturally
aroused the anger of all those who lived by the ruin of the
provinces. The knights, the nobles, who no longer got
their money, became his deadly enemies. It is true he
had the gratitude of his province, but this did not amount
to much. It had been remarked that, in those Eastern
countries " trained by a long servitude to loathsome
flattery,"[1] the governors who received most adulation, and
to whom they raised most statues were precisely those who
had robbed the most, because they were the most dreaded.
Cicero's predecessor had completely ruined Cilicia : con-

[1] Cic. *Ad Quint.* i. 1.

sequently they thought of building him a temple. These
were some of the difficulties to which an upright governor
exposed himself. Cicero extricated himself with honour.
Seldom was a province so well administered as his under
the Roman republic; but he only brought back from it
some gratitude, little money, and many enemies, and very
nearly quarrelled with Brutus.

Brutus, though we can scarcely believe it, had a hand in
this traffic. He had lent money to Ariobarzanes, king of
Armenia, one of those small princes that Rome charitably
allowed to live, and to the town of Salamis in the island
of Cyprus. At the moment of Cicero's departure for his
province, Atticus, who himself, as we know, did not despise
this species of gain, recommended these two affairs to him
very warmly; but Brutus had invested his money badly,
and it was not possible for Cicero to get him repaid.
Ariobarzanes had many creditors and paid none. "I cannot imagine," said Cicero, "any one poorer than this king,
and anything more miserable than this kingdom." [1] Nothing could be got from him. As to the business of
Salamis, it was from the first still graver. Brutus had not
dared, at the beginning, to acknowledge that he was directly
interested in it, the usury was so enormous and the circumstances so scandalous. A certain Scaptius, a friend of
Brutus, had lent a large sum to the inhabitants of Salamis
at 4 per cent. per month. As they could not repay it he
had, according to custom, obtained from Appius, Cicero's
predecessor, a company of cavalry, with which he held the
senate of Salamis so closely besieged that five senators had
died of hunger. On learning of this conduct Cicero was
shocked, and hastened to recall the soldiers of whom such
bad use had been made. He only thought he was hurting
a *protégé* of Brutus; but as the affair took a more serious

[1] *Ad Att.* vi. I.

turn, Brutus showed his hand more openly, so that Cicero might show himself more accommodating in arranging matters. As he saw that he had no hope of being paid, except at a great reduction, he became quite offended, and decided to let it be known that Scaptius was only a man of straw, and that he himself was the real creditor of the Salaminians. Cicero's astonishment when he learnt this will be shared by everybody, so much does Brutus' action seem at variance with his whole conduct. Certainly no one could doubt his disinterestedness and honesty. Some years before, Cato had paid them a splendid tribute, when, not knowing whom to trust, so rare were men of honour, he had appointed him to collect the treasure of the king of Cyprus, and to carry it to Rome. Let us be assured then, that if Brutus conducted himself as he had done towards the Salaminians, it was because he thought he might legitimately do so. He followed the example of others, he yielded to an opinion that was universal around him. The provinces were still considered as conquered countries by the Romans of that time. They had been conquered too short a time for the remembrance of their defeat to be obliterated. It was supposed that they also had not forgotten it, which led to distrust of them ; in any case it was remembered, and the conquerors always thought themselves armed with those terrible laws of war against which no one in antiquity had protested. The property of the vanquished belonging to the victor, far from blaming themselves for taking what they took, they thought they gave whatever they did not take, and perhaps at the bottom of their heart they thought they were generous in leaving them anything. The provinces were regarded as the domains and property of the Roman people (*praedia, agri fructuarii populi Romani*), and they were treated accordingly. When they consented to spare them it was not through pity or affection, but through prudence, and in imitation of good landowners who take care not to exhaust their fields by over-cultivation. This was the meaning of the laws made under the republic to protect the provinces; humanity had a smaller share in them than well-considered interest, which, in exercising a certain restraint on the present, is mindful of the future. Evidently Brutus fully accepted this way of looking at the rights of the conqueror and the condition of the vanquished. In this we touch one of the greatest failings of this upright but narrow soul. Brought up in the selfish ideas of the Roman aristocracy, he had not sufficient breadth or elevation of mind to perceive their iniquity; he followed them without hesitation till the time that his natural mildness and humanity got the better of the recollections of his education, and the traditions of his class. The mode in which he behaved in the provinces that he governed shows that all his life there was a struggle between the integrity of his nature and these imperious prejudices. After having ruined the Salaminians by his usury, he governed Cisalpine Gaul with a disinterestedness that did him honour, and while he had made himself detested in the island of Cyprus, the remembrance of his beneficent administration was preserved in Milan even to the time of Augustus. The same contrast is found in the last campaign; he wept with grief at seeing the inhabitants of Xanthus persist in destroying their city, and on the eve of Philippi he promised his soldiers the pillage of Thessalonica and Lacedaemon. This is the single grave fault that Plutarch finds to censure in his whole life; it was the last awakening of an inveterate prejudice of which he could never get rid notwithstanding his uprightness of mind, and which shows the sway that the society in which his birth had placed him, exercised over him to the last.

Yet this influence was not felt then by everybody. Cicero,

who, being a " new man," could more easily protect himself
against the tyranny of tradition, had always shown more
humanity towards the provinces, and blamed the scandalous
gains that were drawn from them. In a letter to his
brother he boldly proclaimed this principle,[1] then altogether
new, that they must not be governed in the exclusive interest
of the Roman people, but also in their own interest, and in
such a manner as to give them the greatest amount of
happiness and well-being that was possible. This is what
he tried to do in Cilicia : accordingly he was very much hurt
by the action of Brutus, and flatly refused to have anything
to do with it, although Atticus, whose conscience was more
elastic, warmly begged him to do so. " I am sorry," he
replied, " that I am not able to please Brutus, and still more
so to find him so different from what I had thought him." [2]
" If he condemns me," he said elsewhere, " I do not want
such friends. At least I am certain that his uncle Cato will
not condemn me." [3]

These were bitter words, and their friendship would no
doubt have suffered much from these disputes if the grave
events which supervened had not drawn them together again.
Cicero had scarcely returned to Italy when the civil war, so
long foreseen, broke out. Private differences had to disappear
before this great conflict. Besides, Cicero and Brutus were
united by a singular community of feelings. Both had gone
to Pompey's camp, but both had done so without enthusiasm
or eagerness, as a sacrifice demanded by duty. Brutus
loved Caesar, who showed him a paternal affection on all
occasions, and moreover he detested Pompey. Besides the
fact that his pompous vanity displeased him, he could not
forgive the death of his father, killed during the civil wars of
Sulla. Yet, in this public danger, he forgot his personal
likings and hatreds, and went to Thessaly, where the consuls

[1] *Ad Quint.* i. 1.　　　[2] *Ad Att.* vi. 1.　　　[3] *Ibid.* v. 21.

and senate were already. We know that he made himself remarked for his zeal in Pompey's camp;[1] many things however happened there which must have displeased him, and no doubt he thought that too many personal rancours and ambitions were mixed up with the cause of liberty which alone he wished to defend. This also displeased his friend Cicero and his brother-in-law Cassius, and these two last, indignant at the language of those madmen who surrounded Pompey, resolved not to pursue the war to extremes as others wished to do. "I still remember," Cicero wrote later to Cassius, "those familiar conversations in which, after long deliberation, we made up our minds to allow our action, if not the abstract justice of our cause, to be determined by the result of a single battle."[2] We do not know whether Brutus was present at these conversations of his two friends; but it is certain that all three behaved in the same manner. Cicero, on the day after Pharsalia, refused the command of the republican army; Cassius hastened to hand over the fleet he commanded to Caesar; as to Brutus, he did his duty as a brave man during the battle; but, the battle over, he thought he had done enough, and went over to the conqueror, who welcomed him joyfully, took him apart in confidential conversation, and succeeded in obtaining some information about Pompey's retreat. After this conversation Brutus was completely gained over; not only did he not go and rejoin the republicans who were fighting in Africa, but he followed Caesar to the conquest of Egypt and of Asia.

II.

Brutus was thirty-seven years old at the battle of Pharsalia. This was the age of political activity among the Romans. Usually a man had then just been quaestor or aedile; he

[1] *Ad Att.* xi. 4.   [2] *Ad fam.* xv. 15.

might look forward to the praetorship and the consulship, and acquired a right to gain them by courageously contending in the Forum or the Curia. The brightest hope of every young man on entering public life was to obtain these high honours at the age appointed by law, the praetorship at forty and the consulship at forty-three, and nothing was thought to give greater distinction than to be able to say, "I was praetor or consul as soon as I had the right to be so (*meo anno*)." If by good luck, while a man held these offices, fortune favoured him by some considerable war that gave an opportunity of killing five thousand enemies, he obtained a triumph and had nothing more to wish for.

There is no doubt that Brutus had conceived this hope like the rest, and it is certain that his birth and his talents would have permitted him to realize it ; Pharsalia upset all these projects. He was not precluded from honours, for he was the friend of him who distributed them ; but these honours were now only empty titles, since one man had seized all real power. This man really aimed at being sole master, and admitted no one to share his authority. "He does not even consult his own friends," says Cicero, "and only takes counsel of himself." [1] Political life did not exist for the rest, and even those whom the new government employed felt time hang heavy on their hands, especially after the violent agitations of the preceding years. God, according to Virgil's expression, gave leisure to everybody. Brutus employed this leisure by returning to the studies of his youth, which he had rather interrupted than forsaken. To return to them was to draw still nearer to Cicero.

He had not indeed forgotten him ; while following Caesar in Asia he had learnt that his friend, having retired to Brundusium, suffered at once from the threats of the Caesarians, who did not forgive his going to Pharsalia, and

[1] *Ad fam.* iv. 9.

from the ill-will of the Pompeians, who blamed him for having returned too quickly. Amidst all this irritation, Cicero, who, as we know, had not much energy, was very downcast. Brutus wrote to him to encourage him. "You have performed actions," said he, "which will speak of you, notwithstanding your silence, which will live after your death, and which, by the safety of the state, if the state is saved, by its loss, if it is not saved, will for ever bear witness in favour of your political conduct."[1] Cicero says that in reading this letter he seemed to recover from a long illness, and to open his eyes to the light. When Brutus returned to Rome, their intercourse became more frequent. Knowing each other better they appreciated each other more. Cicero, whose imagination was so lively, whose heart was so youthful, in spite of his sixty years, became entirely enamoured of Brutus. This constant communication with a mind so inquiring and a soul so upright, reanimated and revived his talents. His friend always holds a large place in the fine works that he published at that time, which succeeded each other so rapidly. We see that his heart is full of him, he speaks of him as often as he can, he is never weary of praising him, he wishes to please him before everything; one would almost say that he cares only for the praises and friendship of Brutus.

It was the study of philosophy that united them above all. Both loved and cultivated it from their youth, both seemed to love it more and to cultivate it more ardently when the concentration of the government in one hand had removed them from public life. Cicero, who could not accustom himself to repose, turned all his activity towards it. "Greece is getting old," he said to his pupils and friends, "let us snatch from her her philosophical glory;"[2] and he at once set about the work. He groped about for some time, and

[1] Cic. *Brut.* 96.   [2] *Tusc.* ii. 2.

did not immediately hit upon the philosophy that was suitable to his fellow-countrymen. He had been tempted for a moment to direct their attention towards those subtle metaphysical questions that were repugnant to the practical good sense of the Romans. He had translated the *Timaeus*, that is to say, the most obscure thing in Plato's philosophy; but he quickly perceived that he was mistaken, and hastened to quit that path in which he would have walked alone. In the Tusculan Disputations he returned to questions of applied morality and did not leave them again. The diverse characters of the passions, the real nature of virtue, the relative rank of duties, all those problems that a virtuous man proposes to himself during his life; above all, that before which he so often draws back, but which always returns with a terrible persistency and troubles at times the most gross and earthly souls, the future after death; this is what he studies without tricks of dialectical skill, without the prejudices of a school, without a preconceived system, and with less anxiety to discover new ideas than to accept practical and sensible principles wherever he found them. Such is the character of Roman philosophy, of which we must be careful not to speak ill, for it has played a great part in the world, and it is through it that the wisdom of the Greeks, rendered at once more solid and yet more clear, has come down to the nations of the West. This philosophy dates from Pharsalia, like the empire, and owes much to the victory of Caesar, who, by suppressing political life, forced inquiring minds to seek other subjects for their activity. Welcomed at first, with enthusiasm, by all minds unoccupied and ill at ease, it became more and more popular in proportion as the authority of the emperors became more oppressive. To the absolute authority that the government exercised over external actions they were glad to oppose the entire self-possession that philosophy gives; to study oneself, to withdraw into oneself was to escape on one side from the tyranny of the master, and in seeking to know oneself the ground to which his power had no access seemed to be enlarged. The emperors understood this well; and were the mortal enemies of a science that was so bold as to limit their authority. Along with history, which recalled disagreeable memories, it soon fell under their suspicion; they were two names, said Tacitus, unpleasing to princes, *ingrata principibus nomina.*

I have not here to show why all the philosophical works composed at the end of the republic or under the empire have a much greater importance than the books we write now on the same subjects : this has been too well told already for me to have need to return to it.[1] It is certain that during that time when religion was confined to ritual, when its books only contained collections of formulae and the minute regulations of observances, and when it did not go beyond teaching its adepts the science of sacrificing according to the rites, philosophy alone could give to all virtuous and troubled souls which were tossed about without definite aim and were desirous of finding one, that teaching of which they had need. We must not forget, then, when we read an ethical treatise of that time, that it was written not only for lettered idlers who are delighted with fine discourses, but for those whom Lucretius represents as groping after the way of life ; we must remind ourselves that these precepts have been practised, that theories became rules of conduct, and that, so to say, all this ethical theory was once alive. Let us take for example the first Tusculan Disputation : Cicero wishes to prove in it that death is not an evil. What a trite remark in appearance, and how difficult it is not to regard all this elaborated treatment as an oratorical exercise and an

[1] See on this question the very interesting work of M. Martha, *Les Moralistes sous l'Empire Romain.*

essay for the schools ! It is nothing of the kind however, and the generation for whom it was written found something else in it. Men read it on the eve of the proscriptions to renew their strength, and came from their reading firmer, more resolute, better prepared to support the great misfortunes that they foresaw. Atticus himself, the egotist Atticus, so far removed from risking his life for anybody, found in them the source of an unusual energy. " You tell me," Cicero writes to him, " that my Tusculans give you courage : so much the better. There is no surer and speedier resource against circumstances than that which I indicate." [1] This resource was death. How many people accordingly availed themselves of it ! Never has a more incredible contempt of life been seen, never has death caused less fear. Since Cato, suicide became a contagion, a frenzy. The vanquished, Juba, Petreius, Scipio, know no other way of escaping the conqueror. Laterensis kills himself through regret when he sees his friend Lepidus betray the republic ; Scapula, who can no longer hold out in Cordova, has a funeral pyre constructed, and burns himself alive ; when Decimus Brutus, a fugitive, hesitates to choose this heroic remedy, his friend Blasius kills himself before him in order to set him an example. It was a veritable delirium at Philippi. Even those who might have escaped did not seek to survive their defeat. Quintilius Varus put on the insignia of his rank, and had himself killed by a slave ; Labeo dug his own grave and killed himself on its brink ; Cato the younger, for fear of being spared, threw away his helmet and shouted his name ; Cassius was impatient, and killed himself too soon ; Brutus closes the list by a suicide, astonishing by its calmness and dignity. What a strange and frightful commentary on the Tusculans, and how clearly this general truth,

---

[1] *Ad Att.* xv. 2

thus put in practice by so many men of spirit, ceases to
be a mere platitude !

We must study in the same spirit the very short fragments that remain of the philosophical works of Brutus.
The general thoughts that we find in them will no longer
appear insignificant and vague when we think that he who
formulated them also intended to put them in practice in
his life.   The most celebrated of all these writings of
Brutus, the treatise *On Virtue*, was addressed to Cicero, and
is worthy of them both.   It was a fine work that was especially pleasing because it was felt that the writer was thoroughly
convinced of all that he said.[1] An important passage preserved
by Seneca survives.   In this passage Brutus relates that he
had just seen M. Marcellus at Mitylene, the same whom
Caesar pardoned later at the request of Cicero.   He found
him employed in serious studies, easily forgetting Rome
and its pleasures, and enjoying in this tranquillity and leisure
a happiness that he had never known before.   "When I
had to leave him," says he, " and saw that I was going away
without him, it seemed to me that it was I who was going into
exile, and not Marcellus, who remained there." [2]   From this
example he concludes that a man must not complain of being
exiled since he can carry all his virtue with him.   The moral
of the book was that to live happily one need not go outside of oneself.   This is another truism, if you like ; but, in
trying to conform his whole life to this maxim, Brutus made
it a living truth.   It was not a philosophical thesis that he
developed, but a rule of conduct that he proposed to others
and took for himself.   He was early accustomed to com-
mune with his own thoughts, and to place in this his
pleasures and pains.   Thence came that freedom of mind
that he preserved in the gravest affairs, that contempt for outward things that all his contemporaries remarked, and the

[1] Quint. x. i.   [2] Sen. *Cons. ad Helv.* 9.

ease with which he detached himself from them. On the eve of Pharsalia, when every one was restless and uneasy, he was tranquilly reading Polybius and taking notes while awaiting the moment of combat. After the Ides of March, in the midst of the excitement and fears of his friends, he alone preserved a constant serenity that rather annoyed Cicero. Driven away from Rome and threatened by Caesar's veterans, he consoled himself for everything by saying: "There is nothing better than to rest upon the memory of one's good actions, and not to busy oneself with events or men."[1] This capacity for abstraction from outward things and this self-sufficingness are certainly valuable qualities in a man of reflection and study: it is the ideal that a philosopher proposes to himself; but is it not a danger and a fault in a man of action and a politician? Is it right for a man to hold himself aloof from the opinions of others when the success of the things he undertakes depends upon their opinions? Under pretence of listening to one's conscience, and resolutely following it, ought a man to take no account of circumstances, and risk himself heedlessly in useless adventures? Indeed, by wishing to keep aloof from the multitude, and preserve himself entirely from its passions, does he not risk the loss of the tie that binds him to it and becoming incapable of leading it? Appian, in the narrative that he gives of the last campaign of the Republican army, relates that Brutus was always self-possessed, and that he kept himself almost aloof from the grave affairs that were discussed. He liked conversation and reading; he visited as a connoisseur the places they passed through, and made the people of the country talk to him: he was a philosopher in the midst of camps. Cassius, on the contrary, occupied solely with the war, never allowing himself to be turned aside, and, so to say, wholly intent upon that

[1] *Epist. Brut.* i. 16.

end, resembled a fighting gladiator.[1] I suspect that Brutus must have rather disdained that feverish activity entirely confined to ordinary duties, and that this *rôle* of gladiator made him smile. He was wrong; success in human things belongs to the gladiator, and a man only succeeds by throwing his whole soul into them. As to those speculative men, wrapped up in themselves, who wish to keep outside of and above the passions of the day, they astonish the multitude but do not lead it ; they may be sages, they make very bad party leaders.

And further, it is very possible that Brutus, if left to himself, would not have thought of becoming a party leader. He was not hostile to the new government, and Caesar had neglected no opportunity of attaching him to himself by granting him the pardon of some of the very much compromised Pompeians. On his return to Rome he confided to him the government of one of the finest provinces of the empire, Cisalpine Gaul. About the same time the news came of the defeat of the republican army at Thapsus, and the death of Cato. No doubt Brutus felt it very much. He himself wrote and persuaded Cicero to compose the eulogy of his uncle ; but we know from Plutarch that he blamed him for refusing Caesar's clemency. When Marcellus, who had just obtained his pardon, was assassinated near Athens, some persons affected to believe and to say that Caesar might well have been an accomplice in this crime. Brutus hastened to write, with a warmth that surprised Cicero, to exculpate him. He was at that time, then, quite under the spell of Caesar. We may add that he had taken a horror of civil war in Pompey's camp. It had carried off some of his dearest friends, for instance Torquatus and Triarius, two young men of great promise, whose loss he bitterly regretted. In thinking of the dis-

[1] App. *De bell. civ.* iv. 133.

orders it had caused, and of the victims it had made, he no doubt said with his friend, the philosopher Favonius : " It is better to endure arbitrary power than to revive impious wars."[1] How, then, did he allow himself to be drawn on to recommence them ? By what clever conspiracy did his friends succeed in overcoming his repugnance, in arming him against a man he loved, in involving him in an enterprise that was to throw the world into confusion ? This deserves to be related, and Cicero's letters allow us to catch a glimpse of it.

III.

After Pharsalia, there was no want of malcontents. That great aristocracy that had governed the world so long, could not consider itself beaten after a single defeat. It was so much the more natural that it should wish to make a last effort, as it was well aware that, the first time, it had not fought under favourable conditions, and that, in uniting its cause to Pompey's, it had placed itself in a bad position. Pompey inspired little more confidence in those who desired liberty than Caesar. It was known that he had a taste for extraordinary powers, and that he liked to concentrate all public authority in his hands. At the commencement of the civil war he had rejected the most just proposals with so much haughtiness, and shown so much ardour in precipitating the crisis, that he seemed rather to wish to get rid of a rival who hampered him than to come to the aid of the threatened republic. His friend Cicero tells us that when the insolence of his associates, and his own persistency in not taking advice from any one, were seen in his camp, it was suspected that a man who took

[1] Plut. *Brut.* 12.

counsel so ill before the battle would wish to make himself master after the victory. That is why so many good citizens, and Cicero among the chief, had hesitated so long to take his part ; that is, above all, why intrepid men like Brutus had hastened to lay down their arms after the first defeat. It must be added that, if they were not perfectly satisfied about Pompey's intentions, it was also possible they might be mistaken about Caesar's projects. No one was ignorant that he wished for power ; but what kind of power ? Was it only one of those temporary dictatorships, necessary in free states after a period of anarchy, which suspend liberty but do not annihilate it ? Was it a question of repeating the history of Marius and Sulla, whom the republic had survived ? In strictness it might be thought so, and nothing prevents us supposing that several of Caesar's officers, those especially who, when undeceived later, conspired against him, did not think so then.

But after Pharsalia there was no longer any means of preserving this illusion. Caesar did not demand an exceptional authority ; he aspired to found a new government. Had he not been heard to say that "republic" was a word void of meaning, and that Sulla was a fool to have abdicated the dictatorship ? His measures for regulating the exercise of the popular suffrage in his own interest, the choice that he had made in advance of consuls and praetors for several years running, the delivery of the public treasure and the administration of the revenue of the state by his freedmen and slaves, the union of all dignities in his own person, the censorship under the name of praefecture of morals, the perpetual dictatorship, which did not prevent him getting himself appointed consul every year ; everything, in fine, in his laws and in his conduct indicated a definitive taking possession of power. Far from taking any of those precautions to hide the extent of his authority that Augustus employed later, he seemed to exhibit it with complacency, and without concerning himself about the enemies that his frankness might make him. On the contrary, by a sort of ironical scepticism and bold impertinence, that betrayed the great nobleman, he loved to shock the fanatical partisans of ancient usages. He smiled at seeing pontifs and augurs scared when he dared to deny the gods in full senate, and it was his amusement to disconcert those ceremonious old men, the superstitious guardians of ancient practices. Further, as he was a man of pleasure before all things, he loved power not only for the sake of exercising it, but also to enjoy its fruits; he was not contented with the reality of sovereign authority, he wished also for its outward signs, the splendour that surrounds it, the homage it exacts, the pomp that sets it off, and even the name that designates it. He knew well how much that title of king that he so ardently desired frightened the Romans; but his hardihood took pleasure in braving old prejudices at the same time that his candour no doubt thought it more honourable to give its real name to the power he exercised. The result of this conduct of Caesar was to dissipate all doubts. Thanks to it, illusion or misunderstanding was no longer possible. The question was now, not between two ambitious rivals, as at the time of Pharsalia, but between two opposite forms of government. Opinions, as sometimes happens, became clearly defined one by the other, and the intention of founding a monarchy, which Caesar openly avowed, brought about the creation of a great republican party.

How was it that in this party the boldest and most violent men formed the idea of uniting and organizing themselves? How, with growing confidence, did they come to form a plot against the life of the dictator? It is impossible to find this out exactly. All that we know is that the first idea

of the plot had been formed at the same time in two quite
opposite parties, among the vanquished of Pharsalia, and,
what is more surprising, among Caesar's generals themselves. These two conspiracies were probably distinct in
origin, and each acted on its own account : while Cassius
was thinking of killing Caesar on the banks of the Cydnus,
Trebonius had been on the point of assassinating him at
Narbonne. They finally united.

Every party begins by seeking a leader. If they had
wished to continue the traditions of the preceding war, this
leader was already at hand. Sextus, a son of Pompey, remained. He had escaped by a miracle from Pharsalia and
Munda, and had survived all his family. Conquered, but
not discouraged, he wandered in the mountains or along the
shores, by turns an able partisan or a bold pirate, and the
obstinate Pompeians united around him. But men no
longer desired to be of a Pompeian party. They wished to
have some one for chief who represented not merely a name
but a principle, one who should represent the republic and
liberty without any personal reservations. It was necessary
that he should be in complete opposition to the government
they were going to attack, by his life, his manners, and his
character. He must be upright, because the power was corrupt, disinterested, in order to protest against the insatiable
greed that surrounded Caesar, already illustrious, in order
that the different elements of which the party was composed
should give way to him, and still young, for they had need of
a bold stroke. Now, there was only one man who united all
these qualities, namely Brutus. Consequently, the eyes of
every one were fixed on him. The public voice marked him
out as the chief of the republican party while he was still
the friend of Caesar. When the first conspirators went to
all quarters seeking accomplices, they always received the
same answer : "We will join you if Brutus will lead us."

Caesar himself, notwithstanding his confidence and his friendship, seemed sometimes to have a presentiment whence the danger would come to him. One day when they were trying to alarm him with the discontent and threats of Antony and Dolabella: "No," he replied, "those debauchees are not to be feared; it is the thin and pale men." He meant chiefly to indicate Brutus.

To this pressure of public opinion, which wished to direct the action of Brutus, and to implicate him without his assent, it was necessary to add more formal exhortations in order to persuade him; they came to him from all sides. I have no need to recall those notes that he found in his tribunal, those inscriptions that were placed at the foot of his grandfather's statue,[1] and all those clever manœuvres that Plutarch has so well narrated. But no one better served the designs of those who wished to make Brutus a conspirator than Cicero, who, however, did not know them. His letters show us the disposition of his mind at that time. Spite, anger, regret for lost liberty break out in them with singular vivacity. "I am ashamed of being a slave,"[2] he wrote one day to Cassius, without suspecting that at that very moment Cassius was secretly searching for the means of being so no longer. It was impossible that these sentiments should not come to light in the books he published at that time. We find them there now that we read them in cold blood; much more must they have been seen when these books were commented on by hatred and read with eyes rendered penetrating by passion. How many epigrams were then appreciated

[1] Those who employed these manœuvres well knew that they were taking Brutus on his weak side. His descent from him who expelled the kings was much contested. The more it was regarded as doubtful the more anxious he was to prove it. To say to him: "No, you are not Brutus," was to put on him the necessity or the temptation of proving his origin by his actions.

[2] *Ad fam.* xv. 18.

which now escape us ! What stinging and bitter words,
unperceived now, were then applauded and maliciously
repeated in those conversations where the master and
his friends were pulled to pieces ! There was in them
what Cicero wittily calls " the bite of liberty which never
tears better than when she has been muzzled for some
time." [1] With a little effort we find allusions everywhere.
If the author spoke with so much admiration of the ancient
eloquence, it was because he wished to put to shame that
deserted Forum and that mute senate ; the memories of the
old government were only recalled in order to attack the
new one, and the praise of the dead became the satire of
the living. Cicero well understood the whole import of his
books when he said of them later : " They served me as a
senate or a rostrum from which I could speak." [2] Nothing
served more to stir up public opinion, to put regret for the
past and disgust for the present into men's minds, and thus
to prepare the events which were to follow.

Brutus must have been more moved than any one else
in reading Cicero's writings ; they were dedicated to him ;
they were written for him. Although they were meant to
influence the whole public, they contained passages addressed more directly to him. Cicero not only sought to
arouse his patriotic sentiments ; he recalled the memories
and hopes of his youth. With perfidious skill he even interested his vanity in the restoration of the ancient government by pointing out what a position he might make for
himself in it. " Brutus," he said, " I feel my grief revive
when I look upon you and consider how the unhappy fate
of the republic has arrested the rapid advance to glory
which we anticipated in your youth. This is the true
cause of my sorrow, this is the cause of my cares and of
those of Atticus, who shares in my esteem and affection for

---

[1] *De Offic.* ii. 7.   [2] *De Divin.* ii. 2.

you. You are the object of all our interest, we desire that you should reap the fruits of your virtue ; our most earnest wishes are that the conditions of the republic may permit you one day to revive and increase the glory of the two illustrious houses you represent. You ought to be master in the Forum and reign there without a rival ; we are, in truth, doubly afflicted, that the republic is lost for you, and you for the republic." [1] Such regrets, expressed in this fashion, and with this mixture of private and public interests, were well calculated to disturb Brutus. Antony was not altogether wrong when he accused Cicero of having been an accomplice in the death of Caesar. If he did not himself strike, he armed the hands that struck, and the conspirators were perfectly right when, on coming from the senate house, after the Ides of March, they brandished their bloody swords and called aloud upon Cicero.

To these incitements from without there were added others of a still more powerful kind from Brutus' own household. His mother had always used the influence she had over him to draw him towards Caesar ; but just at this critical time Servilia's influence was lessened by the marriage of Brutus with his cousin Porcia. Daughter of Cato and widow of Bibulus, Porcia brought into her new home, all the passions of her father and her first husband, and especially hatred of Caesar, who had caused all her misfortunes. She had scarcely entered when disagreements arose between her and her mother-in-law. Cicero, who tells us of them, does not relate to us their cause ; but it is not rash to suppose that these two women contended for the affection of Brutus, and that they wished to rule him that they might draw him in different directions. Servilia's influence no doubt lost something in these domestic discussions, and her voice, opposed by the advice of a new and

[1] *Brut.* 97.

beloved wife, had no longer the same authority when it spoke for Caesar.

Thus everything combined to lead Brutus on. Let us conceive this hesitating and scrupulous man attacked on so many sides at once, by the incitements of public opinion, by memories of the past, by the traditions of his family and the very name he bore, by those secret reproaches placed under his hands and scattered on his path, which came every moment to strike his inattentive eyes, to murmur in his heedless ear, and then finding at home the same memories and the same reproaches under the form of legitimate sorrows and touching regrets. Must he not at last give way to this daily assault? Nevertheless it is probable that he resisted before giving in, that he had violent struggles during those sleepless nights that Plutarch speaks of; but as these private struggles could have no confidants they have left no trace in the historians.

All that we can do if we wish to know them is, to try and find their faint impression in the letters that Brutus wrote later, and that are preserved. We see, for instance, that he returns at two different times to this same thought: " Our ancestors thought that we ought not to endure a tyrant even if he were our own father.[1] . . . To have more authority than the laws and the senate is a right that I would not grant to my father himself." [2] Is not this the answer which he made every time he felt himself moved by the memory of Caesar's paternal affection, when he reflected that this man against whom he was about to take arms called him his child? As to the favours that he had received or that he might expect from him, they might have been able to disarm another, but he hardened and stiffened himself against them. " No slavery is advantageous enough to make me abandon the resolution to be free." [3] It was with such con-

---

[1] _Epis. Brut._ i. 17.   [2] _Ibid._ i. 16.   [3] _Ibid._ i. 17.

siderations that he defended himself against the friends of the dictator, perhaps against his mother, when in order to dazzle him she pointed out to him that, if he would acquiesce in the kingship of Caesar he might hope to share it. He would never have consented to pay with his liberty the right to domineer over others; the bargain would have been too disadvantageous. " It is better to command no one than to be a slave," he wrote. "A man can live without commanding, but life as a slave is worthless." [1]

In the midst of all these anxieties of which no one could know, an event happened which very much surprised the public, and which Cicero's letters relate without explanation. When it was known that Caesar was returning to Rome after his victory over Pompey, Brutus went to meet him with an alacrity that everybody remarked, and that many people blamed. What was his intention? A few words of Cicero, to which sufficient attention has not been paid, allow us to guess. Before taking a definite resolution, Brutus wished to make a last appeal to Caesar, and to try once more to draw him towards the republic. He made a point of commending to him the men of the vanquished party, and especially Cicero, in the hope that they might be recalled to public office. Caesar listened kindly to these praises, welcomed Brutus, and did not discourage him too much. The latter, with too easy confidence, hastened to return to Rome, and announce to every one that Caesar was coming back to the party of honest men. He went so far as to advise Cicero to address a political letter to the dictator, which should contain some good advice and make some advances; but Cicero did not share in his friend's hopes, and after a little hesitation, refused to write. In truth, Brutus' illusions did not last long. Antony had anticipated him with Caesar. Antony, who by his follies had

[1] Quint. ix. 3.

disturbed the tranquillity of Rome, had much to be pardoned for ; but he well knew the means of succeeding in this. While Brutus was trying to bring Caesar and the republicans together, and thought he had succeeded, Antony, in order to soften his master, flattered his most cherished wishes, and no doubt made that crown which he so anxiously desired, glitter before his eyes. The scene of the Lupercalia showed clearly that Antony had carried the day and it was no longer possible for Brutus to doubt Caesar's intentions. Antony's plan, indeed, did not succeed this time : the cries of the multitude, and the opposition of the two tribunes, forced Caesar to refuse the diadem that was offered him ; but it was well known that this check had not discouraged him. The occasion was only deferred, and was about to present itself again. With regard to the Parthian war, an old Sybilline oracle which said that the Parthians would only be conquered by a king was to be brought before the senate, and this title was to be demanded for Caesar. Now there were too many foreigners and too many cowards in the senate to admit of the answer being doubtful. This was the moment that Cassius chose to reveal to Brutus the plot that was being hatched, and to ask him to be its head.

Cassius, whose name becomes from this moment inseparable from that of Brutus, formed a complete contrast to him. He had gained a great military reputation by saving the remains of Crassus' army and driving the Parthians from Syria ; but at the same time he was charged with being fond of pleasure, an epicurean in doctrine and conduct, eager for power, and not very scrupulous about the means of gaining it. He had pillaged the province he governed, like almost all the proconsuls ; it was said that Syria had found little advantage in being saved by him, and would almost as soon have passed into the hands of the Parthians. Cassius was bitter in raillery, uneven in temper, hasty, sometimes cruel,[1] and we can well understand that he would not have shrunk from an assassination; but whence came the idea of killing Caesar? Plutarch says that it was through spite at not having obtained the urban praetorship which the dictator's favour had accorded to Brutus, and indeed, nothing prevents us thinking that personal resentment had embittered that impetuous spirit. Yet if Cassius had only this insult to avenge it is not probable that he would have acted in concert with the man who had been a party to it and had profited by it. He had quite other motives for hating Caesar. An aristocrat by birth and temper, his heart was full of the hatred felt by the vanquished aristocracy; he must have a bloody revenge for the defeat of his party, and Caesar's pardon had not extinguished the anger that the sight of his oppressed caste aroused in him. Thus, while Brutus sought to be the man of a principle, Cassius was openly the man of a party. It seems that he early had the idea of avenging Pharsalia by an assassination. At least, Cicero says that, a very few months after he had obtained his pardon, he waited for Caesar on one bank of the Cydnus to kill him, and that Caesar was saved only by the accident that made him land on the other bank. He resumed his purpose at Rome, notwithstanding the favours of which he had been the object. It was he who got up the conspiracy, sought out the malcontents, and brought them together in secret meetings; and as he saw that they all demanded Brutus for leader, he took upon himself to speak to him.

They were still at variance in consequence of their rivalry for the urban praetorship. Cassius put his resentment aside and visited his brother-in-law. "He took him by the

[1] It must, however, be noticed that there are several of Cassius' letters in Cicero's correspondence, and that some of them are witty and very lively. There are even puns in them.—(*Ad fam.* xv. 19.)

Z

hand," as Appian relates, and said : "'What shall we do if Caesar's flatterers propose to make him king?' Brutus answered that he purposed not to go to the senate. 'What?' replied Cassius. 'If we are summoned in our capacity as praetors, what must we do then?' 'I will defend the republic,' said the other, 'to the last.' 'Will you not then,' replied Cassius, embracing him, 'take some of the senators, as parties to your designs? Do you think it is worthless and mercenary people, or the chief citizens of Rome who place on your tribunal the writings you find there? They expect games, races or hunting spectacles from the other praetors; what they demand of you is that you should restore liberty to Rome, as your ancestors did.'" [1] These words completely gained over a mind that so many private and public solicitations had unsettled for so long. Still hesitating, but already almost gained, it only waited to find itself face to face with a firm resolution in order to yield.

At last the conspiracy had a leader, and there was no longer any reason to hesitate or to wait. To avoid indiscretions or weaknesses it was necessary to act quickly. Cassius had revealed everything to Brutus a short time after the feast of the Lupercalia, which was kept on February 15, and less than a month after, on March 15, Caesar was struck down in the curia of Pompey.

IV.

Brutus was in reality the head of the conspiracy, although he had not formed the first idea of it. Cassius alone, who had formed it, could dispute the right of conducting it with him, and perhaps he had for an instant the intention

[1] *De Bell. civ.* ii. 113. Plutarch relates the same thing, and almost in the same words.

of doing so. We see that at first he proposed a plan in which all the violence of his character is shown. He wished that, with Caesar, they should kill his chief friends, and especially Antony. Brutus refused, and the other conspirators were of his mind. Cassius himself yielded at last, for it must be remarked that, although imperious and haughty, he submitted to the ascendency of Brutus. He tried several times to escape from it; but after many threats and fits of anger, he felt himself overcome by the cold reasoning of his friend, and it was Brutus who really conducted the whole enterprise.

This is clearly seen, and in the manner in which it was conceived and executed we find his character and turn of mind. We have not an ordinary conspiracy before us, we have not to do with professional conspirators, with men of violence and adventures. They are not vulgarly ambitious men who covet the fortune or honours of others, nor even madmen whom political hatred misleads even to frenzy. No doubt these sentiments were found in the hearts of many of the conspirators; historians say so, but Brutus forced them to lie hid. He made a point of accomplishing his action with a sort of quiet dignity. It was the system alone that he aimed at; he was animated by no hatred against the man. After having struck him he does not insult him; he permits, in spite of many objections, his funeral to be celebrated, and his will to be read to the people. What occupies his thoughts most of all is that he should not appear to work for himself or his friends, and to avoid all suspicion of personal ambition or party interest. Such was this conspiracy in which men of very different characters took part, but which bears the imprint of Brutus' own mind. His influence is not less perceptible on the events that followed it. He did not act at random, although Cicero accused him of doing so, and everybody repeats it; he had formed in advance a rule of conduct for the future, he had a well-defined plan. Unfortunately it was found that this plan, conceived in solitary reflection, far from the intercourse and acquaintance of men, could not be followed out. It was the work of a logician who reasons, who purposes to conduct himself in the midst of a revolution as in ordinary times, and wishes to introduce the narrow respect for legality even into a work of violence. He acknowledged that he was mistaken, and he had to give up successively all his scruples; but, as he had not the pliability of the politician who knows how to submit to necessity he gave way too late, with a bad grace, and always looked back with regret to the fine projects he had been forced to abandon. Thence came his hesitation and incoherence. It has been said that he failed through not having had an exact plan in advance; I think, on the contrary, that he did not succeed through wishing to be too faithful to the chimerical plan he had conceived, notwithstanding the lessons given by events. A rapid recital of the facts will suffice to show that it was this which caused the loss of himself and his party, and made the blood that was shed useless.

After the death of Caesar, the conspirators came out of the senate house, brandishing their swords, and calling on the people. The people listened to them with surprise, without much anger, but without any sympathy. Seeing themselves alone, they went up to the Capitol, where they could defend themselves, and shut themselves in under the guard of some gladiators. They were joined only by some doubtful friends who always join parties when they are successful. If there had been little eagerness to follow them there was still less desire to attack them. Caesar's partisans were scared. Antony had thrown off his consul's robe and hidden himself. Dolabella affected to appear joyful, and let it be understood that he also was one of the conspirators. Many left Rome in haste, and fled into the country; yet, when they saw that all remained quiet, and that the conspirators were contented with making speeches in the Capitol, courage returned to the most timid. The fear that this bold action had caused gave place to surprise at such strange inaction. The next day Antony had resumed his consular robes, reassembled his friends, and recovered his audacity, and it was necessary to reckon with him.

"They have acted," said Cicero, "with manly courage, but childish judgment; *animo virili, consilio puerili.*" [1] It is certain that they seemed to have prepared nothing, and to have foreseen nothing. On the evening of the Ides of March they were awaiting events without having done anything to guide them. Was it, as has been said, improvidence and levity? No, it was system and deliberate intention. Brutus had only joined the others to deliver the republic from the man who prevented the free play of the institutions. He being dead, the people regained their rights, and became free again to use them. The conspirators would have appeared to be working for themselves in keeping even for a day that authority that they had torn from Caesar. Now, to prepare decrees or laws in advance, to arrange about regulating the future, to consider the means of giving affairs the direction they wished, was not this to take upon themselves in some sort the duty of the entire republic? And what more had Caesar done? Thus, on pain of appearing to imitate him, and to have acted only through the rivalry of ambition, once the great blow struck, the conspirators had to abdicate. This is how I think their conduct must be explained. It was by a strange prejudice of disinterestedness and of legality that they remained voluntarily disarmed. They thought it

[1] *Ad Att.* xv. 4.

glorious to act in concert only so far as to kill Caesar.
That act accomplished, they were to restore to the people
the direction of their affairs, and the choice of their government, leaving them free to express their gratitude to those
who had delivered them, or if they so willed it, to repay
them by forgetfulness.

There the illusion commenced : they thought there was
only Caesar between the people and liberty, and that when
Caesar no longer existed liberty would naturally reappear ;
but on the day that they called on the citizens to resume
their rights, no one answered, and no one could answer, for
there were no longer any citizens. "For a very long time,"
says Appian on this occasion, "the Roman people was only a
mixture of all the nations. The freedmen were confounded
with the citizens, the slave had no longer anything to
distinguish him from his master. In sum, the distributions
of corn that were made at Rome gathered the beggars, the
idle, and the scoundrels from all Italy." [1] This cosmopo-
litan population, without a past and without traditions, was
not the Roman people. The evil was old, and clear-sighted
minds must have perceived it for a long time. Cicero
seems to suspect it sometimes, especially when he sees
with what facility they traffic in votes at the elections.
Nevertheless everything continued with apparent regularity,
and things went on from the impulse they had received.
In such a condition of affairs, and when a state only moves
through habit, all is lost if this movement is arrested for a
single day. Now, with Caesar, the old machinery ceased to
act. The interruption was not long, but the machine was
so dilapidated that in stopping it fell to pieces entirely.
Thus the conspirators could not restore what was existing
before the civil war, and this last shadow of the republic,
imperfect as it was, disappeared for ever.

[1] *De Bell. civ.* ii. 120.

This is why no one either listened to or followed them.
Courage must have failed more than one of them in that
Capitol where they were left alone, at the sight of the indifference of the populace. Cicero especially was distressed
at seeing that they did nothing but make fine speeches.
He wished them to act, to profit by the occasion, to die if
need were : " Would not death be glorious for such a great
cause ? " This old man, usually irresolute, had then more
resolution than all those young men who had just struck so
bold a stroke. And yet, what did he suggest after all ?
" You must rouse the people again," he said. We have
just seen that the people would not respond. " You must
convoke the senate, and take advantage of its fears, to
extort some favourable decrees." [1] Assuredly the senate
would have voted whatever they wished : but when the
decrees had been made, how were they to be executed ?
All these schemes were insufficient, and it was hardly
possible to propose anything more practical to men who
were determined not to overstep the law. The only
possible chance was boldly to seize the government, to
hold it by violence and illegality, not even flinching from
proscription, and to replace by an aristocratic dictatorship
that popular tyranny they had just destroyed ; in a word, to
recommence the history of Sulla. Cassius perhaps would
have done this, but Brutus had a horror of violence.
Tyranny, from whatever side it might come, seemed to
him a crime ; he would rather have perished with the
republic than save it by these means.

The few succeeding days passed in strange alternations.
There was a sort of interregnum during which the parties
contended with varying success. The people, who had not
followed the conspirators, did not support their enemies
either. As they did not know on what to rely men acted on

[1] *Ad Att.* xiv. 10, and xv. 11.

both sides at random, and frequently in a contradictory and surprising manner. One day an amnesty was proclaimed, and Brutus went to dine with Lepidus; the next, the conspirators' houses were set on fire. After having abolished the dictatorship they ratified the acts of the dictator. The friends of Caesar erected a column and an altar to him on the Forum; another friend of Caesar had them thrown down. It was in the midst of this confusion, while the two parties were wavering, undecided and hesitating, without daring to strike, while each was looking around it to see where the real forces were, that those who henceforth were to be the masters appeared.

For a long time a secret revolution had been in operation at Rome, which had been scarcely perceived because its progress was slow and continuous, but which, when it was complete, changed the character of the state. Campaigns had been short while they had only been fought in the neighbourhood of Rome and in Italy. The citizens had not had time to lose the traditions of civil life in the camp; there had not been a family either soldiers by trade, or generals by profession. But in proportion as wars were more distant, and lasted longer, the men who carried them on became accustomed to living at a distance from Rome. They lost sight of the Forum for so long a time that they forgot its controversies and customs. At the same time, as the right of citizenship was extended, the legion was thrown open to men of all races. This medley completed the destruction of the ties that bound the soldier to the city; he acquired the habit of isolating himself from it, of having separate interests, and of looking on the camp as his country. After the great Gallic war, which lasted ten years, Caesar's veterans no longer remembered that they were citizens, and their recollections did not go back beyond Ariovistus and Vercingetorix. When it had become necessary to reward them, Caesar, who was not ungrateful, distributed the finest lands of Italy among them; and this partition was made under new conditions. Up to that time the soldiers, after the war, returned into the mass of the people : when they were sent to a colony, they were lost, and, as it were, absorbed among the other citizens; but now they passed without transition from their camp to the domains that had been given them, and thus the military spirit was preserved among them. As they were not far removed from one another, and could communicate with each other, they did not altogether lose the taste for a life of adventure. "They compared," says Appian, "the toilsome labour of agriculture with the brilliant and lucrative chances of battles." [1] They formed then in the heart of Italy a population of soldiers, listening for rumours of war, and ready to answer the first call.

Precisely at that time there were many in Rome, whom Caesar had called there while they were waiting for him to grant them lands. Others were close at hand, in Campania, busied in settling themselves down, and perhaps disgusted with these preliminary toils of their settlement. Some among them had returned to Rome on the rumour of the events that were taking place, the rest were waiting to be well paid before deciding, and put themselves up to auction. Now, there was no want of buyers. The heritage of the great dictator tempted every one's cupidity. Thanks to those soldiers who were ready to sell their services, each of the competitors had his partisans and his chances. Antony was predominant over all by the lustre of his consular authority, and the memory of Caesar's friendship; but near him was the debauchee Dolabella, who had held out hopes to all parties, and the young Octavius, who came from Epirus to receive the inheritance of his uncle. There was

[1] *De Bell. civ.* iii. 42.

no one, even to the incapable Lepidus, who had not got several legions in his interest, and who did not make some figure among these ambitious men. And all, surrounded by soldiers whom they had bought, masters of important provinces, watched each other mistrustfully while waiting to fight.

What was Brutus doing in the meantime? The opportunity of the Ides of March having failed, he might still have taken advantage of the quarrels of the Caesarians to throw himself upon them and crush them. The resolute men of his party advised him to try this, and to call to arms all those young men who, in Italy and the provinces, had applauded the death of Caesar; but Brutus hated civil war and could not resolve to give the signal anew. As he had fancied that the people would hasten to accept the liberty that was given back to them, he had thought that the restoration of the republic could be made without violence. One illusion led him to another, and that stab which began a frightful war of twelve years seemed to him bound to assure public tranquillity for ever. It was in this belief that, on coming out of the curia of Pompey where he had just killed Caesar, he ran through the streets crying, "Peace! peace!" And this word was henceforth his motto. When his friends, on learning the dangers he was running, came from the neighbouring municipia to defend him, he sent them back. He preferred to remain shut up in his house rather than give any pretext for the commencement of violence. Forced to leave Rome, he remained hidden in the gardens of the neighbourhood, disturbed by the soldiers, only going out at night, but always expecting that great popular movement that he persisted in hoping for. No one moved. He removed still further and took refuge in his villas of Lanuvium and Antium. There he heard the rumours of war with which Italy resounded, and saw all parties preparing to fight. He alone always resisted. He passed six entire months shrinking from this terrible necessity that became more clearly inevitable every day. He could not resolve to accept it, and asked advice of everybody.

Cicero even tells, in his letters,[1] of a sort of council that was held at Antium, to consider what it was needful to do. Servilia was there with Porcia, Brutus with Cassius, and a few of the most faithful friends had been invited, among whom were Favonius and Cicero. Servilia, more anxious for the safety than the honour of her son, wished him to withdraw. She had obtained from Antony, who had remained her friend, for her son and her son-in-law, a *legatio*, that is a commission to go and collect corn in Sicily. It was a specious and safe pretext for quitting Italy; but what a disgrace! to leave with a permission signed by Antony, to accept exile as a favour. Cassius would not consent; he spoke with passion, he was indignant, he threatened, "one would have said he breathed only war." Brutus, on the contrary, calm and resigned, questioned his friends, being resolved to satisfy them at the risk of his life. Did they wish him to return to Rome? He was ready to go there. Every one cried out at this proposition. Rome was full of danger for the conspirators, and they would not uselessly expose the last hopes of liberty. What should they do then? They only agreed in bitterly regretting the course they had followed. Cassius regretted that they had not killed Antony as he had demanded, and Cicero did not care to contradict him.

Unfortunately these recriminations were of no use; it was not a question of complaining of the past, the moment had arrived for regulating the future, and they did not know what to resolve upon.

Brutus did not immediately decide after this meeting.

[1] *Ad Att.* xv. 11.

He persisted in remaining as long as he could in his villa at Lanuvium, reading and discussing, under his handsome porticoes, with the Greek philosophers, his usual society. It was necessary to go away, however. Italy was becoming less and less safe, the veterans infested the roads and pillaged the country houses. Brutus went to Velia to join some vessels that were waiting to conduct him to Greece. He called his departure an exile, and, by a last illusion, he hoped that it would not be the signal for war. As Antony accused him of preparing for this, he replied to him in Cassius' name and his own, by an admirable letter of which this is the end : " Do not flatter yourself that you have frightened us, fear is beneath our character. If other motives were capable of giving us any leaning towards civil war your letter would not take it from us, for threats have no power over free hearts ; but you well know that we hate war, that nothing can drag us into it, and you put on a threatening air, no doubt to make men believe that our resolution is the effect of our fears. These are our sentiments ; we wish to see you live with distinction in a free state ; we do not wish to be your enemies, but we have more regard for liberty than for your friendship. We therefore pray the gods to inspire you with counsels salutary for the republic and for yourself. If not, we desire that your own party may hurt you as little as possible, and that Rome may be free and glorious ! " [1]

At Velia, Brutus was joined by Cicero, who also thought of leaving. Discouraged by the inaction of his friends, terrified by the threats of his enemies, he had already attempted to fly to Greece : but the wind had thrown him back on the coast of Italy. When he learnt that Brutus was going to leave, he wished to see him again and if possible start with him. Cicero often spoke with a heartrending accent

[1] *Ad fam.* xi. 3.

of the emotions of this last interview. "I saw him," he
related to the people later, " I saw him depart from Italy in
order not to cause a civil war there. O sorrowful spectacle,
I do not say for men only, but for the waves and the shores.
The saviour of his country was forced to flee, its destroyers
remained all-powerful."[1]

The last thought of Brutus at this sad moment was still
for the public peace. Notwithstanding so many disappointments he still reckoned upon the people of Rome; he
thought enough had not been done to arouse their ardour ;
he could not resign himself to believe that there were no
longer any citizens. He started with the regret that he had
not essayed another struggle by legal means. Doubtless it
was not possible for him to return to Rome and to reappear
in the senate ; but Cicero was less compromised, his fame
extorted respect ; men liked to listen to his words. Could
not he attempt this last struggle? Brutus had always
thought so ; at this moment he dared to say so. He
pointed out to Cicero a great duty to accomplish, a great
part to play ; his advice, his reproaches, his prayers, determined him to give up his voyage and return to Rome. He
seemed to hear, as he said later, "the voice of his country
recalling him!"[2] And they separated not to meet again.

It was useless, however, for Brutus to resist; the inevitable tendency of the events against which he had been
struggling for six months, dragged him into civil war. On
leaving Italy he had come to Athens, where he passed his
time in hearing the academician Theomnestes and the peri-
patetic Cratippus. Plutarch sees a clever dissimulation in
this conduct. "He was preparing for war," he says, "in
secret." Cicero's letters prove that, on the contrary, it was
the war that went to seek him. Thessaly and Macedonia were
full of Pompey's old soldiers, who had remained there after

[1] *Philipp.* x. 4.   [2] *Ad fam.* x. 1.

Pharsalia ; the islands of the Aegean, the towns of Greece, which were regarded as a sort of asylum for the exiles, contained many malcontents who had refused to submit to Caesar, and since the Ides of March they were the refuge of all who fled from the domination of Antony. Athens, in truth, was full of young men of the greatest families of Rome, republicans by their birth and their age, who went there to finish their education. They were only waiting for Brutus in order to take up arms. On his arrival, there was a great and irresistible movement on all sides, to which he was constrained to give way himself. Apuleius and Vatinius brought him the troops that they commanded. The old soldiers of Macedonia assembled under the command of Q. Hortensius ; so many came from Italy, that the consul Pansa at last complained and threatened to stop the recruits of Brutus on their passage. The students of Athens, and among them Cicero's son and the young Horace, deserted their studies and enrolled themselves under him. In a few months Brutus was master of all Greece, and had eight legions.

At this moment the republican party seemed to awaken everywhere at once. Cicero had succeeded better than he had hoped at Rome, and had raised up enemies to Antony, who had defeated him before Modena. Brutus had just formed a considerable army in Greece. Cassius went over Asia recruiting legions on his passage, and all the East had declared for him. Hope returned to the most timid, and it seemed that everything was to be hoped for the republic from the co-operation of so many generous defenders. It was, however, at this very moment, when it was so necessary to be united, that the most serious disagreement broke out between Cicero and Brutus. Whatever vexation it may cause us, it must be told, for it completes our knowledge of both.

Cicero was the first to complain. This man, usually so weak and hesitating, had become singularly energetic since the death of Caesar. Prudence, clemency, moderation, great qualities that he appreciated much and readily practised, seemed no longer suitable to the circumstances of the time. This great preacher of pacific victories preached war to everybody; this stern friend of legality asked everybody to overstep it. "Do not wait for the decrees of the senate," [1] he said to one. "Be your own senate," [2] he wrote to another. To gain his ends, all means, even the most violent, seemed good to him; all alliances pleased him, even that of men whom he did not esteem. Brutus, on the contrary, even while deciding to take up arms, remained scrupulous and hesitating, and continued to dislike violence. Although his name has become famous chiefly through an assassination, blood was repugnant to him. He spared his enemies when they were in his power, in opposition to those inhuman laws, accepted by everybody, which delivered up the vanquished unreservedly to the will of the victor. He had just given an instance, by sparing the life of Antony's brother after having conquered him. Although he was a bad man, who had shown his gratitude by attempting to corrupt the soldiers who guarded him, Brutus had persisted in treating him with kindness. We should not consider this a great crime, nevertheless they were very much irritated about it at Rome. The furious threats of Antony, from whom they had just escaped with so much difficulty, the remembrance of the terrors they had endured, and the terrible alternations they had passed through for six months, had exasperated the most peaceable. Nothing is more violent than the anger of moderate men when they are driven to extremities. They wish to make an end at any price and as soon as possible. They recalled

[1] *Ad fam.* xi. 7. [2] *Ibid.* x. 16.

the repugnance and slowness with which Brutus had begun the war. Seeing him so yielding, so clement, they were afraid of seeing him fall back into his hesitation, and still further defer the moment of vengeance and security. Cicero undertook to let Brutus know of their discontent. In his letter, which we still possess, he enumerates with much force the mistakes that had been made since the death of Caesar ; he recalls all the weaknesses and hesitations that had dis- couraged resolute men, and, what must have especially wounded Brutus, the absurdity of wishing to establish public tranquillity by speeches. "Are you ignorant," said he, "what is in question at this moment ? A band of scoundrels and wretches threatens even the temples of the gods, and it is our life or death that is at stake in this war. Whom are we sparing ? What are we doing ? Is it wise to treat gently men who, if they are conquerors, will wipe out the very traces of our existence ? " [1]

These reproaches provoked Brutus, and he answered with recriminations. He also was discontented with the senate and Cicero. Whatever admiration he may have felt for the eloquence of the *Philippics*, many things must have annoyed him in them. The general tone of these speeches, their bitter personalities, their fiery invectives, could not be pleasing to a man who, in striking down Caesar, had wished to appear passionless, and rather the enemy of a principle than of a man. Now, if there is a great love of liberty in the *Philippics*, there is also a violent personal hatred. We feel that this enemy of the country is, at the same time, a private and personal adversary. He had attempted to enslave Rome, but he had also taken the liberty of quizzing the weaknesses of the old consular in a very amusing speech. Cicero's irritable vanity was roused when he read this invective : "he took the bit between his teeth," [2]

[1] *Ad Brut.* ii. 7.   [2] *Ad fam.* xi. 23.

according to the expression of a contemporary. The generous hatred he felt against a public enemy was inflamed by private rancour; a mortal struggle began, followed up with increasing energy through fourteen orations. "I am resolved," said he, "to overwhelm him with invectives, and to give him over dishonoured to the eternal contempt of posterity;"[1] and he kept his word. This passionate persistence, this impetuous and violent tone must have annoyed Brutus. Cicero's flatteries were no less displeasing to him than his anger. He bore him a grudge for the exaggerated eulogies that he gave to men who little deserved them, to those generals who had served every cause, to those statesmen who had submitted to every government, to those men of ambition and intrigue of every sort, whom Cicero had united with so much trouble, to form what he called the party of the honest men; he was specially vexed at seeing him lavish praises on the young Octavius, and lay the republic at his feet; and when he heard him call him "a divine young man, sent by the gods for the defence of the country," he could scarcely contain his anger.

Which of the two was right? Brutus assuredly if we think of the end. We see clearly that Octavius could not be anything but an ambitious man and a traitor. The name he bore was an irresistible temptation for him; to deliver the republic to him was to destroy it. Brutus was right in thinking that Octavius was more to be dreaded than Antony, and his hatred did not mislead him, when he foresaw in this *divine young man*, who was so much praised by Cicero, the future master of the empire, the heir and successor of him whom he had slain. Was it really Cicero who was to blame, or only the circumstances? When he accepted the aid of Octavius was he at liberty to refuse it? The republic had not, at that time, a single

[1] *Philipp.* xiii. 19.

A A

soldier to oppose Antony, they had to take those of
Octavius or to perish. After he had saved the republic, it
would have been ungracious to haggle with him over thanks
and dignities. Besides, his veterans demanded them in a
way that did not brook refusal, and often gave them to him
in advance. The senate sanctioned everything as quickly
as possible, for fear that they would do without its assent.
" Circumstances," says Cicero somewhere, " gave him the
command, we have only added the fasces." [1] Thus, before
blaming Cicero's compliance, or complaining of his weakness, they should have thought of the difficulties of his
position. He tried to re-establish the republic by the help
of men who had [fought against it and did not love it.
What reliance could he place on Hirtius, the framer of a
severe law against the Pompeians, on Plancus and Pollio,
old lieutenants of Caesar, on Lepidus and Octavius, each
of whom wished to take his place? and yet he had no
other support than they. To that great and ambitious
man who, on the morrow of the Ides of March, wished
to make himself master, he could only oppose a coalition
of inferior or concealed ambitions. Nothing was more
difficult than to steer one's way in the midst of all these
open or secret rivalries. It was necessary to curb one by
the other, to flatter them in order to lead them, to content
them in part in order to keep them within bounds. Hence
those lavish grants or promises of honours, that profusion of
praises and titles, and those exaggerated official thanks.
This was a necessity imposed by the circumstances; instead
of considering it a crime in Cicero to have submitted to it,
they should have drawn this conclusion, namely, that to
attempt another struggle by legal means, to return to Rome
to arouse the ardour of the populace, to trust again in
the force of memories, and the supreme power of oratory,

[1] *Philipp.* xi. 8.

was to expose oneself to useless dangers and certain disappointment. Cicero knew this well. Sometimes, no
doubt, in the heat of combat, he might allow himself to be
carried away by the triumphs of his eloquence, as on that
day, when he wrote naïvely to Cassius : "If one could
speak oftener it would not be very difficult to re-establish
the republic and liberty." [1]   But this illusion never lasted
long.   The momentary intoxication over, he was not long
in recognizing the impotence of oratory, and was the first to
say they could only place their hopes on the republican
army.   He never changed that opinion.   "You tell me," he
wrote to Atticus, "that I am wrong in thinking that the
republic depends entirely upon Brutus ; nothing is more certainly true.   If it can be saved at all, it can only be by him
and his friends." [2]   Cicero had undertaken this last enterprise
without illusions and without hope, and solely to yield to
the wishes of Brutus, who persisted in his love of consti-
tutional resistance and pacific struggles.   Brutus, then, had
less right than any one to reproach him with having
succumbed.   Cicero was right in often recalling that interview at Velia, when his friend persuaded him, notwithstanding his hesitation, to return to Rome.   This recollection was his defence ; it should have prevented Brutus
uttering any bitter word against him, whom he had himself
led into a useless enterprise.

Cicero must have deeply felt these reproaches, yet his
friendship for Brutus remained unaltered by them.   He
still looks to him, he calls upon him, when all seems lost
in Italy.   Nothing is more touching than his last cry of
alarm : "We are the sport, my dear Brutus, of the licence
of the soldiers and the insolence of their leader.   Every one
wishes to have as much authority in the republic as he has
force.   Men no longer know reason, measure, law, nor

[1] *Ad fam.* xii. 2.   [2] *Ad Att.* xiv. 20.

duty; they no longer care for public opinion or the judgment of posterity. Come, then, and give at length to the republic that liberty which you have gained for it by your courage, but which we cannot yet enjoy. Every one will press around you; liberty has no refuge but in your tents. This is our position at this moment; would that it might become better! If it chances otherwise I shall only weep for the republic; it ought to be immortal. As for myself, I have but a little time to live!"[1]

A very few months afterwards, Lepidus, Antony, and Octavius, triumvirs to reconstitute the republic, as they called themselves, assembled near Bologna. They knew each other too well not to be aware that they were capable of anything, consequently they had taken minute precautions against each other. The interview took place on an island, and they arrived with an equal number of troops who were not to lose sight of them. For still greater security, and for fear that any one should carry a hidden dagger, they went so far as to search each other. After having thus reassured themselves, they held a long conference. There was no longer any question of reconstituting the republic; what occupied their attention most, besides the division of power, was vengeance, and they carefully drew up a list of those who were to be slain. Dio Cassius remarks that, as they detested each other profoundly, a man was sure, if he was closely connected with one of them, to be the mortal enemy of the other two, so that each demanded precisely the heads of the best friends of his new allies. But this difficulty did not stop them; their gratitude was much less exacting than their hatred, and in purchasing the death of an enemy with that of a few friends or even relations, they thought they made a good bargain. Thanks to these mutual concessions, they soon came to an

[1] *Ad Brut.* i. 10.

agreement, and the list was drawn up. Cicero was not
forgotten in it, as we can well understand; Antony urgently
demanded him, and it is not probable, whatever the writers
of the empire may say, that Octavius defended him with
much zeal; he would have constantly recalled to him a
troublesome gratitude and a glaring act of perjury.

With the death of Cicero we have reached the end of
this work, since we only proposed to study the relations of
Cicero and Brutus. If we wished to carry it further, and to
know Brutus' end as well, it would suffice to read the
admirable narrative of Plutarch. I should be afraid of
spoiling it by abridging it. In it we see that Brutus felt
intense sorrow on learning that Cicero had perished. He
regretted more than a friend that with him he had
lost a cherished hope, which he had been unwilling to
surrender. This time, however, he was bound to acknowledge that there were no longer citizens at Rome, and to
despair of that base populace who thus allowed its defenders
to perish. "If they are slaves," said he sadly, "it is their
own fault rather than that of their tyrants." No confession
could have cost him more. Since he had killed Caesar, his
life had been nothing but a series of disappointments, and
events seemed to play with all the plans he had formed.
His scruples about legality had caused him to lose the
opportunity of saving the republic; his horror of civil war
had only served to make him begin it too late. It was not
enough that he found himself forced, in spite of himself, to
violate the law and fight against his fellow-citizens, he was
constrained to acknowledge, to his great regret, that in
expecting too much of men he was mistaken. He had a
good opinion of them when he studied them from a distance
with his beloved philosophers. His opinions changed when
he came to deal closely with them, when he had to be
a witness of the debasement of character, to detect the

secret greed, the senseless hatreds, the cowardly fears of those whom he regarded as the bravest and most honest! He was so deeply grieved that, on learning of the last weaknesses of Cicero, he came to doubt of philosophy itself, his favourite science, which had been the delight of his life. "Of what use has it been to him," said he, "to have written with so much eloquence for the liberty of his country, upon honour, death, exile, or poverty? In truth, I begin to have no more confidence in those studies in which Cicero was so much occupied."[1] In reading these bitter words, we think of those which he spoke before his death; the one explains the other, and each is a symptom of the same internal trouble, which becomes great in proportion as the experience of public affairs disenchants him more and more with men and with life. He hesitated about philosophy, when he saw the weakness of those who had studied it most deeply; when he saw the party of the proscribers triumphing, he doubted of virtue.

It was fitting that thus should perish this man of thought, who had reluctantly become a man of action, and who was thrown by the force of events out of his natural element.

[1] *Epist. Brut.* i. 17.

OCTAVIUS

THE POLITICAL TESTAMENT OF AUGUSTUS

CICERO liked young men; he willingly frequented their society and readily became young again with them. Just after he had been praetor and consul, we see him surrounding himself with promising young men like Caelius, Curio, and Brutus, whom he took with him to the Forum and taught to plead at his side. Later, when the defeat of Pharsalia had removed him from the government of his country, he began to live familiarly with those light-hearted young men who had followed the party of the conqueror, and even consented, as a pastime, to give them lessons in oratory. "They are my pupils in the art of speaking well," he merrily wrote, "and my masters in the art of dining well." [1] After the death of Caesar events brought him into connection with a still younger generation, which then began to appear in political life. Plancus, Pollio, Messala, whom fate destined to become high dignitaries of a new government, sought his friendship, and the founder of the empire called him father.

The correspondence of Octavius and Cicero was published, and we know that it formed at least three books. It would have been very interesting had it been preserved. In reading it we might follow all the phases of that friendship of

[1] *Ad fam.* ix. 16.

a few months which was to end in such a terrible manner. Probably the earlier letters of Cicero would show him distrustful at first, doubtful and coldly polite. Nothwithstanding what has been said, it was not he who called Octavius to the help of the republic. Octavius came of his own accord. He wrote to Cicero every day;[1] he overwhelmed him with protestations and promises, he assured him of a devotion that could not fail. Cicero hesitated for a long time to put this devotion to the proof. He thought Octavius was intelligent and resolute, but rather young. He dreaded his name and his friends. " He has too many bad men around him," said he, " he will never be a good citizen."[2] Nevertheless he allowed himself to be gained over; he forgot his mistrust, and when the *boy*, as he affected to call him, had raised the siege of Modena, his gratitude was carried to an excess that the prudent Atticus disapproved, and which displeased Brutus. The joy that he felt at the defeat of Antony made him forget all restraint ; he was blinded and carried away by his hatred. When he saw "that drunkard fall into the snares of Octavius, on coming from his debauches,"[3] he was beside himself. But this joy did not last long, for he learnt of the treason of the general almost at the same time as of his victory. It is at this moment above all that his letters would become interesting. They would throw a light on the last months of his life, the history of which we do not know well. The efforts that he then made to soften his old friend have been imputed to him as a crime, and I admit that, consulting only his dignity, it would have been better not to have asked anything from him who had so basely betrayed him.

---

[1] *Ad Att.* xvi. 11.   [2] *Ibid.* xiv. 12.
[3] *Ad fam.* xii. 25 : *Quem ructantem et nauseantem conjeci in Caesaris Octaviani plagas.*

But it was not a question of himself alone. Rome had no soldiers to oppose to those of Octavius. The sole resource that remained in order to disarm him, was to remind him of the promises he had made. No hope remained of success in reviving any sparks of patriotism in that selfish mind; but the attempt at least should be made. The republic was in danger as well as the life of Cicero, and what it was not proper for him to do to prolong his own life, it was necessary to attempt in order to save the republic. Supplication is not base when a man defends the liberty of his country, and there is no other way of defending it. It was, no doubt, at this terrible moment that he wrote those very humble words to Octavius that we find in the fragments of his letters: "Let me know for the future what you wish me to do, I shall exceed your expectation."[1] Far from reproaching him for his entreaties, I admit that I cannot see without emotion this glorious old man humble himself thus before *the boy* who had betrayed his confidence, who had played with his credulity, but who has the power to save or destroy the republic!

Unfortunately there only remain fragments of these letters, which can teach us nothing. If we wish to know him who held so great a place in the last events of Cicero's life we must look elsewhere. It would be easy and instructive to reproduce here the opinions that the historians of the empire give of him. But I prefer to keep to the method that I have followed in this work to the end, and if it is possible, to judge Octavius, like Cicero, by what he tells us himself, by his admissions and his confidences. In the absence of his correspondence and memoirs which are lost, let us take the great inscription at Ancyra, which is sometimes called the political testament of

[1] Orelli, *Fragm. Cic.* p. 465.

Augustus, because he sums up his whole life in it. Fortunately it has come down to us. We know from Suetonius that he had ordered it to be engraven on brass plates fixed on his tomb.[1] It is probable that it was very widely diffused in the first century of the Christian era, and that flattery or gratitude had multiplied copies everywhere, at the same time that the worship of the founder of the empire extended throughout the universe. Fragments have been found among the ruins of Apollonia, and it still exists entire at Angora, the ancient Ancyra. When the inhabitants of Ancyra erected a temple to Augustus, who had been their benefactor, they thought they could not honour his memory better than by engraving this account, or rather this glorification of his life that he had himself composed. Since that time, the monument consecrated to Augustus has more than once changed its destination; to the Greek temple a Byzantine church succeeded, and to the church a Turkish school. The roof has fallen in, dragging with it the ornaments of the summit, the columns of the porticoes have disappeared, and to the ancient ruins has been added the rubbish of the Byzantine and Turkish buildings, which are already also in ruins. But by singular good fortune the slabs of marble which recount the actions of Augustus have remained solidly attached to the indestructible walls.

This is a favourable opportunity for studying this monument. M. Perrot[2] has just brought from Galatia a more

---

[1] Suet. *Aug.* 101.

[2] *Exploration archéologique de la Galatie*, etc., par MM. Perrot, Guillaume et Delbet. Paris, 1863. Didot. As the Galatians spoke Greek and understood Latin ill, the official text was put in the place of honour, in the temple itself, and the translation was placed outside where every one might read it, in order to bring the narrative of Augustus within their reach. But the exterior of the temple has not been any more respected than the interior. The Turks have fixed their

correct copy of the Latin text, and an altogether new part of the Greek translation which elucidates and completes the Latin. Thanks to him, with the exception of a few lacunae of little importance, the inscription is now complete, and can be read from beginning to end. We can therefore now perceive and interpret its general sense.

---

houses against the walls, carelessly driving their beams into the marble, and using the solid masonry as a support for their brick and mud party-walls. All the skill of M. Perrot and his companion M. Guillaume was required to penetrate into these inhospitable houses. When they had entered they met with still greater difficulties. It was necessary to demolish the walls, take away the beams and support the roofs in order to reach the ancient wall. This was but little. The wall was hammered and cracked, blackened by dirt and smoke. How could the inscription that covered it be deciphered? It was necessary to remain for weeks in dark and foul rooms, or on the straw of a loft, working by candle-light, throwing the light in every direction on the surface of the marble, and thus gradually winning each letter by extraordinary efforts of courage and perseverance. This painful labour was rewarded by complete success. Of nineteen columns of Greek text, the English traveller Hamilton had copied five completely and fragments of another; M. Perrot brings back twelve entirely new ones. One only, the ninth, could not be read; it was behind a thick party-wall that it was found impossible to pull down. These twelve columns, although they have suffered much from the ravages of time, fill up in great part the lacunae of the Latin text. They make us acquainted with entire paragraphs of which no traces remain in the original; and even in passages where the Latin was better preserved they rectify at almost every step mistakes that had been made in the interpretation of the text. M. Egger, in his *Examen des historiens d'Auguste*, p. 412 *et seq.*, has carefully and critically studied the inscription of Ancyra. M. Mommsen, with the help of M. Perrot's copy, is preparing a learned work on this inscription, after which, no doubt, nothing will remain to be done. (M. Mommsen's work, that was announced in the first edition of this book, has since appeared under the title: *Res gestae divi Augusti ex monumentis Ancurano et Apolloniensi.*)

I.

The first characteristic that we notice when we read the Ancyran inscription, is its majestic tone. It is impossible not to be struck by it. We see at once, by a certain air of authority, that the man who is speaking has governed the whole world for more than fifty years. He knows the importance of the things he has done : he knows that he has introduced a new state of society, and presided over one of the greatest changes of human history. Accordingly, although he only recapitulates facts and quotes figures, all he says has a grand air, and he knows how to give so majestic a turn to these dry enumerations that we feel ourselves seized by a sort of involuntary respect in reading them. We must, however, be on our guard. A majestic tone may be a convenient veil to hide many weaknesses ; the example of Louis XIV., so near to our own times, ought to teach us not to trust it without examination. We must not forget, besides, that dignity was so truly a Roman characteristic, that its appearance was preserved long after the reality had disappeared. When we read the inscriptions of the latter years of the empire we scarcely perceive that it is about to perish. Those wretched princes who possessed but a few provinces speak as though they ruled over the entire universe, and their grossest falsehoods are expressed with an incredible dignity. If we wish, then, to avoid being deceived when studying the monuments of Roman history, we must be on our guard against a first impression, which may be deceptive, and look at things closely.

Although the inscription that we are studying is called "An account of the deeds of Augustus," it was not really his whole life that Augustus meant to relate. There are great and intentional lacunae ; he did not intend to tell everything. When, at the age of seventy-six, and in the midst of the admiration and respect of the whole world, the aged prince reviewed his past life to make a rapid summary of it, many memories must have disturbed him. There is no doubt, for instance, that he must have been very reluctant to recall the earlier years of his political life. It was needful, however, to say something about them, and it was more prudent to try and gloss them over than to preserve a silence that might give rise to much talk. He extricated himself in the following manner: "At nineteen years of age," he says, " I raised an army by my own exertions and at my own expense; with it I restored liberty to the republic, which had been dominated by a faction that oppressed it. In return, the senate, by its decrees, admitted me into its number, among the consulars, conferred upon me the right of commanding the troops, and charged me together with the consuls C. Pansa and A. Hirtius to watch over the safety of the state with the title of pro-praetor. Both the consuls having died the same year, the people put me in their place, and appointed me triumvir to put in order the republic." In these few lines, which form the beginning of the inscription, there are already some very singular omissions. One would infer from them that he had obtained all the dignities that he enumerates, in serving the same cause, and that nothing had happened between the first offices that he had received and the triumvirate. Thanks to the *Philippics* we know those decrees of the senate which are here alluded to with a certain shamelessness. The senate congratulates the young Caesar "for defending the liberty of the Roman people," and for having defeated Antony; now, it was after having concerted with Antony to enslave the Roman people, in that dismal interview at Bologna, that he received, or rather took the title of triumvir. The inscription preserves a prudent silence on all these things.

What followed this interview was still more difficult to relate. Here especially Augustus desired forgetfulness. " I exiled those who had killed my father, punishing their crime by the regular tribunals. Then, as they made war against the republic, I conquered them in two battles." It will be remarked that there is no mention of the proscriptions. What, indeed, could he say about them? Could any artifice of language diminish their horror? On the whole it was more becoming not to speak of them. But as, according to the fine reflection of Tacitus, it is easier to keep silence than to forget, we may be assured that Augustus, who says nothing here of the proscriptions, thought of them more than once during his life. Even if he did not feel remorse, he must often have been embarrassed by the terrible contradiction between his past and his later policy ; for, whatever he might do, the memory of the proscriptions always belied his official character as a clement and honourable man. Even here, it seems to me, he betrays his embarrassment. His silence does not entirely satisfy him, he feels that in spite of his discretion unpleasant memories cannot fail to be awakened in the minds of his readers ; and, therefore, to anticipate and disarm them, he hastens to add : "I carried my arms by land and sea over the whole world in my wars against the citizens and foreigners. After my victory, I pardoned the citizens who had survived the combat, and I chose to preserve rather than to destroy those foreign nations whom I could spare without danger."

This difficult place once passed it became easier to relate the rest. Nevertheless, he is still very brief with respect to the earlier times. Perhaps he feared lest the memory of the civil wars should interfere with that reconciliation of parties which the universal exhaustion had brought about after Actium? There is certainly not a single word in the whole inscription to revive the former rancours. He says scarcely anything of his old rivals. There is at the most but a single disdainful word about Lepidus, and an ill-natured but passing accusation against Antony of having seized the treasures of the temples. The following is all he says of his war with Sextus Pompey which gave him so much trouble, and of those valiant seamen who had vanquished him : " I cleared the sea of pirates, and in that war I captured thirty thousand fugitive slaves, who had fought against the republic, and delivered them to their masters to be chastised." As to that great victory of Actium, which had given him the empire of the world, he only recalls it to state the eagerness of Italy and the western provinces to declare themselves in his favour.

Naturally he prefers to dwell upon the events of the later years of his reign, and we feel that he is more at ease when he speaks of victories in which the vanquished were not Romans. He is justly proud to recall how he had avenged the insults the national pride had suffered before him : " I re-took, after victories gained in Spain and over the Dalmatians, the standards that some generals had lost. I forced the Parthians to restore the spoils and ensigns of three Roman armies, and humbly to come and demand our friendship. I placed these ensigns in the sanctuary of Mars the Avenger." We can understand also that he speaks with satisfaction of the campaigns against the Germans, being careful, however, to pass over in silence the disaster of Varus, and that he is anxious to preserve the memory of those distant expeditions that impressed so strongly the imagination of his contemporaries. " The Roman fleet," he says, " sailed from the mouth of the Rhine towards the quarter where the sun rises, as far as those distant countries where no Roman had yet penetrated either by land or sea. The Cimbri, the Charydes, the Semnones and other German tribes of those countries sent ambassadors to ask my friendship and that of the Roman people. Under my orders and direction two armies were sent almost at the same time to Arabia and Ethiopia. After having conquered many nations, and taken many prisoners, they reached the city of Nabata, in Ethiopia, and the boundaries of the Sabaeans and the city of Mariba, in Arabia."

But whatever interest we may find in these historical recollections, the interest of the Ancyra monument does not specially lie in them. Its real importance consists in what it tells us of the internal government of Augustus.

Here again we must read with caution. Politicians are very seldom in the habit of posting up on the walls of temples the principles that guide them, and of imparting the secrets of their conduct so generously to the public. It is evident that Augustus, who wrote here for all the world, did not intend to tell everything, and that if we wish to learn the exact truth, and to know thoroughly the character of his institutions, we must look elsewhere. The historian, Dio Cassius, gives us the most complete information on this subject. Dio is very little read, and it is not surprising, for he has none of the qualities that attract readers. His narrative is constantly interrupted by interminable harangues, which repel the most patient reader. He was a man of narrow mind, without political capacity, taken up with ridiculous superstitions, and he attributes the same characteristics to his historical personages. Truly it was worth while to have been twice consul in order to tell us seriously that, after a great defeat, Octavius took courage on seeing a fish leap out of the sea to his feet! What adds to the annoyance he gives us is, that as he has often treated of the same subjects as Tacitus, he constantly suggests comparisons that are unflattering to himself. We must, however, take care not to underrate him; tedious as he is, he renders us very useful services. If he has not the broad views of Tacitus, he devotes himself to details and does wonders. No one has ever been more exact and minute than he. I think of him as a zealous government official who has passed through all the grades and grown old in his profession. He knows thoroughly that official and administrative world in which he has lived; he speaks of it accurately, and loves to speak of it. With these inclinations, it is natural that he should be interested in the reforms introduced by Augustus into the internal government of the empire. He is anxious to let us know them in detail; and, true to his rhetorician's habits and to his unbridled love for fine speeches, he assumes that it was Maecenas who proposed to Augustus to establish them, and he takes advantage of the opportunity to make him speak at great length.[1] The discourse of Maecenas contains, in truth, what we may call the general theory of the empire. This interesting sketch, which was realized later, aids us greatly in understanding that part which we have still to examine of the inscription of Ancyra. We should always bear it in mind in order to apprehend thoroughly the spirit of the institutions of Augustus, the motive of his liberalities, the hidden meaning of the facts he mentions, and above all the character of his relations with the different classes of citizens.

Let us begin by studying the relations of Augustus with his soldiers. "About . . . thousand Romans,"[2] says he, "bore arms under me. I established in colonies, or sent

---

[1] Dio, lii. 14—40. See what M. Egger says of Dio in his *Examen des hist. d'Aug.* ch. viii.

[2] The figure cannot be read either in the Latin or Greek.

back to their municipia after their term of service, rather
more than three hundred thousand. I gave land, or money
to buy it, to all of them." On two different occasions, after
the wars against Sextus Pompey, and against Antony,
Augustus was at the head of about fifty legions; he had
only twenty-five when he died. But this number, reduced
as it was, still weighed intolerably upon the finances of the
empire. The immense increase of expenditure that the
creation of great standing armies threw upon the treasury
prevented Augustus for a long time, notwithstanding the
prosperity of his reign, from having what we should now call
a budget in equilibrium. Four times he was obliged to aid
the public treasury from his private fortune, and he reckons
the amounts that he presented to the state at one hundred
and fifty million sesterces (£1,200,000). He had much
trouble to remedy these financial difficulties, of which the
expenses of the army were the principal cause. This gave
him the idea of creating a sort of military pension fund, and
of appealing, in order to fill it, to the generosity of the allied
kings and cities, and of the richest Roman citizens; and in
order to stimulate others by his own example, he gave one
hundred and seventy million sesterces (£1,360,000) at one
time. But these voluntary gifts being insufficient it was
necessary to impose new taxes, and to fill the treasury of
the army with the proceeds of a tax of a twentieth on
inheritances and a hundredth on sales. Yet it seems that,
notwithstanding these efforts, pensions were ill paid, since
this was one of the grievances that the legions of Pannonia
alleged in their revolt against Tiberius. It is certain that
the army of Augustus was one of the greatest anxieties of
his administration. His own legions gave him as much
trouble as those of the enemy. He had to do with soldiers
who felt that they were the masters, and who for ten years

had been corrupted by flattery and promises. On the eve of battle they were very exacting because they knew how much they were required; after victory they became unmanageable from the pride with which it inspired them. In order to satisfy them, it would have been necessary to expropriate all the inhabitants of Italy in a body. Octavius had consented to this at first, after Philippi; but later, when his policy changed, when he understood that he could not found a stable government if he drew on himself the hatred of the Italians, he resolved to pay the proprietors handsomely for the lands that he gave his veterans. "I reimbursed the municipia," he says, "in money, the value of the lands that I gave to my soldiers in my fourth consulship, and later under the consulship of M. Crassus and Cn. Lentulus. I paid six hundred million sesterces (£4,800,000) for the lands situated in Italy, and two hundred and sixty million sesterces (£2,080,000) for those situated in the provinces. Of all those who have established colonies of soldiers in the provinces and in Italy, I am, up to now, the first and only one who has acted thus." He was right in boasting of it. It was not at all the habit of the generals of that time to pay for what they took, and he himself had given another example for a long time. When, a little later, he dared to resist the demands of his veterans, he had to maintain terrible struggles in which his life was more than once in danger. In every way, his demeanour towards his soldiers at that time is one of the things that do him most honour. He owed everything to them, and he had none of the qualities which were necessary to master them, neither the abilities of Caesar nor the defects of Antony; and yet he dared to make head against them, and succeeded in obtaining the mastery. It is very remarkable that, although he had gained his power solely by war, he was able to maintain the predominance of the civil element in the government that he founded. If the empire, in which there was no longer any other element of strength and life than the army, did not become from that period a military monarchy, it is assuredly owing to his firmness.

Nothing is more simple than the relations of Augustus with the people. The information that the Ancyra inscription furnishes upon this subject is quite in accord with the discourse of Maecenas: he fed them and amused them. Here, to begin with, is the exact account of the sums he expended to feed them: "I reckoned to the Roman people three hundred sesterces (£2 8s.) a head according to my father's testament, and four hundred sesterces (£3 4s.) in my own name, out of the spoils of the war during my fifth consulship. Another time, in my tenth consulship, I gave a gratuity of four hundred sesterces to each citizen, from my private fortune. During my eleventh consulship I made twelve distributions of corn at my own cost. When I was invested for the twelfth time with the tribunitian power, I again gave four hundred sesterces a head to the people. All these distributions were made to no fewer than two hundred and fifty thousand persons. Invested for the eighteenth time with the tribunitian power, and consul for the twelfth, I gave sixty denarii (£1 10s. 4d.) a head to three hundred and twenty thousand inhabitants of Rome. During my fourth consulship I had one thousand sesterces (£8) for each of my soldiers, previously deducted from the spoil, and distributed in the colonies formed by them. About one hundred and twenty thousand colonists received their share in the distribution that followed my triumph. Consul for the thirteenth time, I gave sixty denarii to each of those who then received distributions of corn; there were rather more than two hundred thousand." After these truly startling liberalities Augustus mentions the public games he gave to the people, and although the text has several lacunae here, we may suppose that it did not cost him less to amuse the people than to feed them. " I gave shows of gladiators[1] . . . . . times in my own name, and five times in the names of my children or grandchildren. In these different *fêtes* about ten thousand men fought. Twice in my own name, and three times in the names of my son and grandson, I had combats of wrestlers whom I had brought from all countries. I celebrated public games four times in my own name, and twenty-three times in place of magistrates who were absent or could not support the expense of these games . . . I showed twenty-six times in my own name, or in the names of my sons and grandsons, African wild beast hunts, in the circus, on the Forum, or in the amphitheatres, and about three thousand five hundred of these beasts were killed. I gave the people the spectacle of a naval combat, beyond the Tiber, where the wood of the Caesars now is. I had a canal dug there one thousand eight hundred feet long by one thousand two hundred feet broad. There thirty ships armed with rams, triremes, biremes, and a large number of smaller vessels fought together. These vessels contained, besides their rowers, a crew of three thousand men." Here, as it seems to me, is a curious and official commentary on the famous expression of Juvenal, *panem et circenses*. We see clearly that it was not a sally of the poet, but a veritable principle of policy happily invented by Augustus that his successors preserved as a tradition of government.

The relations of Augustus with the senate, we can well

[1] The figure cannot be read. The great number of gladiators who fought, and no doubt perished in these bloody *fêtes* will be noticed. Seneca, to show how far men can become indifferent to death, relates that, under Tiberius, a gladiator complained of the rarity of these grand massacres ; and alluding to the time of Augustus said : " That was a good time ! *Quam bella aetas periit !* "

understand, were more difficult and complicated. Even
after Pharsalia and Philippi it was still a great name that it
was necessary to treat with consideration. Depressed as it
was, the old aristocracy still caused some fear, and seemed
to deserve some regard. This is well seen by the care that
Augustus takes in his testament never to speak of the senate
but with respect. Its name comes up at every turn with a
sort of affectation. We should say indeed, if we trusted
to appearances, that the senate was then the master, and
that the prince was contented to execute its decrees. This
is what Augustus wished to be believed. He passed all his
life in dissembling his authority or lamenting about it. From
his royal dwelling on the Palatine he wrote the most
pathetic letters to the senate asking to be relieved of the
burden of public affairs, and he never appeared to have a
greater aversion for power than at the moment when he was
concentrating all powers in his own hands. It is not extraordinary that we find these methods again in his testament: they had succeeded too well with his contemporaries
for him not to be tempted to make use of them with posterity.
Accordingly he continues to play the same comedy of moderation and disinterestedness. He affects, for instance, to insist as much upon the honours that he refused as upon those
that he accepted. "During the consulship of M. Marcellus
and L. Arruntius," he says, "when the senate and people asked
me to accept an absolute authority,[1] I did not accept it. But
I did not refuse to undertake the supervision of supplies in
a great famine, and by the expenditure that I made I delivered the people from their fears and dangers. When,
in return, they offered me the consulship annually or for

[1] There is some probability, according to a passage of Suetonius (*Aug.*
52), that what the Greek text of the inscription calls absolute authority
(αὐτεξουσιὸς ἀρχὴ) was the dictatorship.

life, I refused it." This is not the only time that he dwells on his own moderation. More than once again he refers to dignities or presents that he would not accept. But here, indeed, is something that passes all bounds; "In my sixth and seventh consulship, after having suppressed the civil wars, when the common voice of all the citizens offered me the supreme power, I restored the government of the republic to the senate and people. As a recompense for this action I received the title of Augustus by a decree of the senate, my door was encircled with laurels and surmounted by a civic crown, and a golden shield was placed in the Julian curia with an inscription recording that this honour was awarded me as a mark of respect to my virtue, clemency, justice, and piety. From this moment, although I was above the rest in dignity in the offices with which I was invested, I never claimed more power than I allowed to my colleagues." This curious passage shows how inscriptions may deceive if we trust them blindly. Would it not seem that we should be right in concluding that in the year of Rome 726, the republic had been re-established by the generosity of Augustus? Now it was exactly at this period that the absolute power of the emperor was delivered from all fear of attack from without and, being quietly accepted by everybody, was finally established. Dio himself, the official Dio, who is so ready to take the word of the emperor, cannot accept this falsehood of Augustus; he ventures to show that he is not deceived, and has no difficulty in proving that this government, under whatever name it is disguised, was at bottom a monarchy; he might have added that there was never a more absolute monarchy. A single man constituted himself the heir of all the magistrates of the republic, and united all their powers in himself. He ignored the people whom he no longer consulted; he is the master of the senate, which he chooses and forms at will; at once consul and pontif, he regulates actions and beliefs; invested with the tribunitian power, he is inviolable and sacred, that is to say, that the least word let fall against him becomes a sacrilege; as censor, under the title of praefect of morals, he can control the conduct of private persons, and interfere, when he likes, in the most private affairs of life.[1] Everything is subordinated to him, private as well as public life, and his authority can penetrate everywhere from the senate to the most humble and obscure hearths. Add to this that the boundaries of his empire are those of the civilized world; barbarism begins where slavery ends, and there is not even the sad resource of exile against this despotism. Yet it is the man who possesses this appalling power, whom nothing in his immense empire escapes, and from whose empire it is impossible to escape, it is he who has just told us with a bare-faced assurance that he refused to accept absolute power!

It must be acknowledged that this absolute power, which he veiled with so much precaution, sought also by every possible means to reconcile men to itself. All the compensations which might make a people forget its liberty were given to the Romans by Augustus with a free hand. I do not speak only of that material prosperity which made the number of citizens increase by nearly a million in his reign;[2] nor even of the repose and security which, at the

---

[1] I have only summed up here a very curious chapter of Dio Cassius (*Hist. Rom.* liii. 17). We see there clearly how the Roman constitution, in which the separation of powers was a guarantee for liberty, became, by the sole fact of their concentration, a formidable engine of despotism.

[2] The Ancyra inscription gives most precise information on the subject of this increase. In 725 Augustus took the census for the first time after an interruption of forty-one years: 4,063,000 citizens were

close of the civil war, was the most imperious need of the
whole world, but also of that incomparable splendour with
which he adorned Rome. This was a sure means of pleasing
the people. Caesar knew this well, and had expended one
hundred million sesterces (£800,000) at one time, simply
in buying the ground on which his Forum was to stand.
Augustus did still more. The Ancyra inscription contains
a list of the public buildings he constructed, but it is so
long that it is impossible to quote it all. He mentions fifteen
temples, several porticoes, a theatre, a senate house, a Forum,
a basilica, aqueducts, public roads, etc. ; in truth Rome
was entirely reconstructed by him. We may say that no
public building was passed over by him, and that he restored
all those that he did not rebuild. He completed Pompey's
theatre and the Forum of Caesar, and rebuilt the Capitol ;
in a single year he repaired eighty-two temples that were
falling into ruin. He did not expend so many millions
without a purpose, and all this profusion in such a careful
ruler covered a profound political design. He wished to
dazzle the people, to intoxicate them with luxury and
magnificence in order to divert them from the intrusive
memories of the past. That Rome of marble that he

counted in this return. Twenty-one years later, in 746, the numbers
returned amounted to 4,233,000. In 767, the year of Augustus' death,
there were 4,937,000. If, to the figures that Augustus gives, we add
the number of women and children who were not comprised in the
Roman census, we shall see that in the last twenty years of his reign
the increase had reached an average of very nearly 16 per cent. This
is exactly the figure to which the increase of population in France rose,
after the Revolution, from 1800 to 1825 ; that is, like political circumstances produced like results. It might be thought, indeed, that this
increase of population under Augustus was due to the introduction of
foreigners into the city. But we know, from Suetonius, that Augustus,
contrary to the example and principles of Caesar, was very chary of
the title of Roman citizen.

built was intended to make them forget the Rome of
brick.

This was not the only compensation that Augustus offered
to the people; he made them nobler amends, and thus
sought to legitimatize his power. If he demanded the
sacrifice of their liberty he took care to gratify their national
pride in every way. No man compelled the respect of
foreign nations for Rome more than he; no man gave her
more reason for pride in the ascendency she enjoyed among
her neighbours. The latter part of the inscription is filled
with the gratifying recital of the marks of respect that the
remotest countries of the world paid to Rome under his
reign. He was eager to direct their attention towards this
external glory, lest they should fix it with some regret on
what was taking place at home. Those citizens whom the
aspect of the deserted Forum and the obedient senate
depressed, he pointed to the Roman armies penetrating
among the Pannonians and the Arabs, to the Roman fleets
navigating the Rhine and the Danube, to the kings of the
Britons, the Suevi, and the Marcomanni, refugees at Rome,
imploring the support of the legions, to the Medes and
Parthians, those terrible enemies of Rome, who asked of
her a king, to the most distant nations, the least known and
the best protected by their distance and their obscurity,
moved by this great name that reaches them for the first
time and soliciting the Roman alliance. "Ambassadors
came to me from India, from kings who had never yet sent
to any Roman general. The Bastarnae, the Scythians,
and the Sarmatians who dwell on this side the Tanaïs,
and beyond that river, the kings of the Albanians, the
Hiberi and the Medes sent ambassadors to me asking our
friendship." It was very difficult for the most discontented
to hold out against so much grandeur. But his greatest

master-stroke was that he extended this consideration for
the glory of Rome even to the past. He honoured all who
had laboured for her at all times, says Suetonius,[1] almost as
much as the gods; and to show that none was excluded
from this veneration, he raised again the statue of Pompey,
at the base of which Caesar had fallen, and set it up in a
public place. This generous conduct was also a wise policy.
By claiming a share in the glories of the past, he disarmed,
by anticipation, those men who might be tempted to use
them against him, and, at the same time, gave a species of
sanction to his authority by attaching it in some sort to
these old memories. Whatever difference might distinguish
the government that he founded from that of the republic,
both agreed on one point : they sought the greatness of
Rome. Augustus tried to reconcile the past with the
present on this common ground. He also had adorned
Rome, defended her frontiers, extended her empire, and
made her name respected. He had continued and completed that work on which they had laboured for seven
centuries. He might, then, call himself the continuator
and heir of all those who had set their hand to it; of Cato,
Paulus Emilius, and Scipio, and rank himself among them.
He did not fail to do so when he built the Forum that bore
his name; we know from Suetonius that, under those
porticoes raised by him and filled with the records of his
actions, he ranged all the great men of the republic in
triumphal costume. This was the highest point of his
political skill, for by connecting them with his glory he
received in turn a share of theirs, and thus turned to his
own advantage the greatness of the political order which he
had overturned.

These compensations that Augustus offered to the Romans

---

[1] Suet. *Aug.* 31.

in exchange for their liberty seem to have satisfied them. Every one quickly got accustomed to the new government, and it may be said that Augustus reigned without opposition. The plots which more than once threatened his life were the crimes of a few isolated malcontents, of young thoughtless fellows whom he had disgraced, or of vulgar and ambitious men who desired his position; they were not the work of political parties. Can it even be said that there were any political parties at this moment? Those of Sextus Pompey and Antony had not survived the death of their chiefs; and, since Philippi, there were scarcely any republicans. From that moment all wise men adopted the maxim "that the vast body of the empire could not stand upright and stable without some one to direct it." A few obstinate men alone, who were not yet converted, wrote violent declamations in the schools under the name of Erutus and Cicero, or allowed themselves to speak freely in those polite gatherings which were the *salons* of that time: *in conviviis rodunt, in circulis vellicant.* But those were unimportant exceptions which disappeared in the midst of the universal admiration and respect. During more than fifty years the senate, the knights, and the people used all their ingenuity to find new honours for him who had given Rome internal peace, and who maintained her grandeur so vigorously abroad. Augustus has been careful to recall all this homage in the inscription we are studying, not in a fit of puerile vanity, but to represent that agreement of all orders in the state which seemed to legitimatize his authority. This idea is shown especially in the last lines of the inscription, where he recalls that circumstance of his life which was most dear to him, because in it the agreement of all citizens had most strikingly appeared: "While I was consul for the thirteenth time, the senate, the order of knights, and all the people gave me the name of Father of our Country, and desired that this should be inscribed in the vestibule of my house, in the curia, and in my Forum, below the quadrigae which had been placed there in my honour by a decree of the senate. When I wrote these things I was in my seventy-sixth year." It was not without reason that he reserved this detail for the end. This title of Father of his Country, by which he was saluted in the name of all the citizens by Messala, the old friend of Brutus, seemed to be the legal consecration of a power acquired by illegal means and a sort of amnesty that Rome accorded to the past. We can well understand that Augustus, even when dying, dwelt with satisfaction on a recollection which seemed like an absolution, and that he was anxious to terminate in this fashion his review of his political life.

II.

I should like to give, in a few words, the impression that the analysis of this remarkable inscription makes upon me as to its author.

The whole political life of Augustus is contained in two official documents which, by singular good fortune, have both come down to us; I mean the preamble of the edict of proscription that Octavius signed, and, according to all appearance, drew up himself, which Appian has preserved; and the inscription found on the walls of the temple of Ancyra. The former shows us what Octavius was at twenty, fresh from the hands of the rhetoricians and philosophers, with all the genuine instincts of his nature; the latter, what he became after fifty-six years of uncontrolled and unlimited power; it is sufficient to compare them in order to discover the road he had traversed, and the changes that the knowledge of men and the practice of public affairs had wrought in him.

The possession of power had made him better, a thing which is not usual, and after him Roman history only gives us examples of princes depraved by power. From the battle of Philippi to that of Actium, or rather to the moment when he seems formally to ask pardon of the world by abolishing all the acts of the triumvirate, we feel that he is striving to become better, and we can almost follow the steps of his progress. I do not think that we could find another example of so strong an effort at self-conquest, and so complete a success in overcoming one's natural disposition. He was naturally a coward, and hid himself in his tent in his first battle. I know not how he did it, but he succeeded in acquiring courage ; he became inured to war in fighting against Sextus Pompey, and even courageous in the expedition against the Dalmatians, in which he was twice wounded. He was cynical and debauched, and the orgies of his youth, as related by Suetonius, do not yield to Antony's ; yet he corrected himself at the very moment that he became absolute master, that is just when his passions would have met with the fewest obstacles. He was naturally cruel, and coldly cruel, a disposition which does not often change ; and yet, after having begun by assassinating his benefactors, he ended by sparing those who attempted his assassination, and the philosopher Seneca could call the same man a clement prince [1] whom his best friend, Maecenas, had once called a common executioner. Certainly the man who signed the edict of proscription hardly seems to be the same as the man who wrote the testament, and it is indeed matter for wonder that a man who began

---

[1] *De Clem.* 9 ; *Divus Augustus mitis fuit princeps.* It is true that elsewhere he calls his clemency a wearied-out cruelty.

as he did was able to change so completely, and to assume a virtuous character, or the appearance of one, in the place of all the vices that were natural to him.

Nevertheless we should find it difficult to love him, whatever justice we are bound to do him. We may be wrong after all; for reason tells us that we ought to appreciate people more for the qualities they acquire by thus triumphing over themselves than for those they have by nature, without taking any trouble. And yet, I hardly know why, it is only the latter that please us; the former lack a certain charm that nature alone gives and which wins our hearts. The effort is too apparent in them, and behind the effort some personal interest; for we always suspect that a man has taken so much pains only because there was some advantage to be gained. This sort of acquired goodness, in which reason has a greater share than nature, attracts no one, because it appears to be the product of a calculating mind, and it is this feeling that causes all the virtues of Augustus to leave us unmoved, and to seem at the most but the results of a profound sagacity. They want a touch of nature and simplicity in order to affect us. These are qualities that this stiff and formal personage never knew, although according to Suetonius he gladly assumed an appearance of plain manners and good-nature in his familiar intercourse. But one is not a good fellow simply through wishing to be it, and his private letters, of which we have a few fragments, show that his pleasantries lacked ease, and that his simplicity was the result of effort. Do we not know, besides, from Suetonius himself, that he wrote down what he meant to say to his friends, in order to leave nothing to chance, and that he even occasionally wrote down his conversations with Livia beforehand?[1]

[1] Suet. *Aug.* 84.

But, after all, that which spoils Augustus in our opinion is that he stands so near Caesar; the contrast between them is complete. Caesar, not to speak of what was really great and brilliant in his nature, attracts us at once by his frankness. His ambition may displease us, but he had at least the merit of not hiding it. I do not know why M. Mommsen exerts himself in his *Roman History* to prove that Caesar did not care for the diadem, and that Antony, when he offered it, had not consulted him. I prefer to hold to the common opinion which, I think, does not do him wrong. He wished to be king, and to bear the title as well as to exercise the power. He never made pretence of waiting to be asked to accept honours that he passionately desired, as Augustus did. He was not the man to make us believe that he only retained the supreme authority with reluctance, and would not have dared to tell us, at the very moment that he was drawing all powers into his hands, that he had restored the government of the republic to the people and senate. We know, on the contrary, that after Pharsalia he said frankly that "the republic" was a phrase without meaning, and that Sulla was a fool to have abdicated the dictatorship. In everything, even in questions of literature and grammar, he was a bold innovator, and he did not display a hypocritical respect for the past at the very time that he was destroying what had come down from it. This frankness is more to our taste than the false appearance of veneration that Augustus lavished on the senate after reducing it to impotence; and whatever admiration Suetonius may express for him, when he shows him to us, obsequiously saluting each senator by name, before the sittings commenced, I am not sure that I do not prefer the disrespectful behaviour of Caesar to this comedy, Caesar who at last went so far as not to rise when the senate visited him. Both appeared weary of power, but it never came into any one's mind to think that Augustus was speaking the truth when he asked so earnestly to be restored to private life. The distaste of Caesar was deeper and more sincere. That sovereign power, that he had sought after for more than twenty years with an indefatigable persistence, through so many perils, and by means of dark intrigues the remembrance of which must have made him blush, did not answer to his expectations, and appeared unsatisfying to him though he had so eagerly desired it. He knew that he was detested by the men whose esteem he most desired; he was constrained to make use of men whom he despised, and whose excesses dishonoured his victory; the higher he rose, the more unpleasing did human nature appear to him, and the more clearly did he see the base greed and cowardly treachery of those who intrigued at his feet. He came at last, through disgust, to have no interest in life; it seemed to him to be no longer worth the trouble of preserving and defending. It is, therefore, the same man who said, even at the period when Cicero delivered the *pro Marcello*: "I have lived long enough for nature or for glory;" who later, when he was pressed to take precautions against his assassins, answered in a tone of despondency: "I would rather die at once than live in fear;" who might well have said with Corneille :

> " I desired the empire and I have attained to it ;
> But I knew not what it was that I desired :
> In its possession I have found, instead of delights,
> Appalling cares, continual alarms,
> A thousand secret enemies, death at every turn,
> No pleasure without alloy, and never repose."

These fine lines please me less, I admit, put into the mouth of Augustus. This cautious politician, so cold, so self-

C C

possessed, does not seem to me to have really known that noble sadness that reveals the man in the hero, that melancholy of a heart ill at ease, notwithstanding its successes, and disgusted with power through the very exercise of power. Whatever admiration I may feel for that fine scene in which Augustus proposes to abdicate the empire, I cannot avoid being a little vexed with Corneille that he took so seriously and depicted so gravely that solemn piece of acting which deceived nobody in Rome, and when I wish to render my pleasure complete in reading the tragedy of *Cinna*, I am always tempted to replace the character of Augustus by that of Caesar.

I add, in conclusion, that all these insincere affectations of Augustus were not only defects of character, but also political errors which left most unfortunate effects on the government that he had created. It was precisely the uncertainty that the interested falsehoods of Augustus had thrown upon the real nature and limits of the power of the earlier Caesars that rendered their tyranny insupportable. When a government boldly states its principles we know how to behave towards it ; but what course is to be followed, what language held when the forms of liberty are united with the reality of despotism, when absolute power hides under republican fictions? In the midst of this obscurity every course has danger and threatens ruin. Men are ruined by independence, they may also be ruined by servility; for, if he who refuses anything to the emperor is an open enemy who regrets the republic, may not he who eagerly grants everything be a secret enemy, who wishes to show that the republic no longer exists? In studying Tacitus we find the statesmen of this terrible period moving at random among these wilfully accumulated uncertainties, stumbling at every step over unseen dangers, liable to displease if they are silent or if they speak, if they flatter or if they resist, continually asking themselves with dread how they can satisfy this ambiguous and ill-defined authority whose limits escape them. This want of sincerity in the institutions of Augustus may be said to have been the torment of several generations. All the evil came because Augustus thought more of the present than of the future. He was an able man, full of resources in escaping from embarrassing and difficult situations; he was not in reality a great politician, for it seems that his view seldom extended beyond the difficulties of the moment. Placed face to face with a people who bore the kingship uneasily, and who were not fit for anything else, he invented this sort of disguised kingship, and allowed all the forms of the old government to exist by its side without endeavouring to conform them to it. But if he was not so great a politician as it has been pretended, it must be admitted that he was an excellent administrator; that part of his work deserves all the praise that has been lavished on it. By co-ordinating all the wise observances and useful regulations that the republic had created, by putting in force lost traditions, by himself creating new institutions for the administration of Rome, the service of the legions, the handling of the finances and the government of the provinces, he organized the empire and thus rendered it capable of resisting external enemies and internal causes of dissolution. If, notwithstanding a detestable political system, the general lowering of character, and the vices of the governors and the governed, the empire still had a time of prosperity and lasted three centuries, it owed it to the powerful organization it had received from Augustus. This was the really vital part of his work. It is important enough to justify the testimony that he bears to himself in that haughty phrase of the Ancyran inscription : " I made new laws. I restored to honour the examples of our forefathers which were disappearing from our manners, and I have myself left examples worthy of being imitated by our descendants."

III.

It was no doubt about the middle of the reign, when he who was the absolute master of the republic was pretending to restore the government to the people and senate, that Cicero's letters appeared. The exact date of their publication is unknown ; but everything tends to the belief that it should be placed in the years that followed the battle of Actium. The power of Augustus, become more popular since it had become more moderate, felt itself strong enough to allow some liberty of writing. It was mistrustful before that time because it was not sufficiently consolidated ; it became so again later when it perceived that public favour was passing from it. This reign, which began by proscribing men, ended by burning books. Cicero's correspondence could only have been published in the interval that separates these periods.

No one has told us what impression it produced on those who read it for the first time ; but it may be fearlessly asserted that it was a very lively impression. The civil wars had only just ended, up till that time men were only occupied with present ills ; in those misfortunes no man's mind was sufficiently free to think of the past, but in the first period of tranquillity which that troubled generation knew, it hastened to throw a glance backward. Whether it sought to account for the events that had happened or wished to enjoy that bitter pleasure which is found, according to the poet, in the recollections of former sufferings, it retraced the sad years it had just traversed, and wished to go back to the very beginning of that struggle whose end it had seen. Nothing could satisfy their curiosity better than Cicero's letters, and it cannot therefore be doubtful that everybody at that time eagerly read them.

I do not think that this reading did any harm to the government of Augustus. Perhaps the reputation of some important personages of the new government suffered a little from it. To have their republican professions of faith disinterred was unpleasant for men who boasted of being the private friends of the prince. I suppose that the malicious must have diverted themselves with those letters in which Pollio swears to be the eternal enemy of tyrants and in which Plancus harshly attributes the misfortunes of the republic to the treason of Octavius, who himself was not to be spared; and these lively recollections of a time when he held out his hand to Caesar's assassins and called Cicero his father, were not favourable to him. All this provided subjects of conversation for the malcontents during several weeks. But upon the whole, the mischief was small, and these railleries did not endanger the security of the great empire. What was most to be feared for it was that imagination, always favourable to the past, should freely attribute to the republic those qualities with which it is so easy to adorn institutions that no longer exist. Now, Cicero's letters were much more suited to destroy these illusions than to encourage them. The picture they present of the intrigues, the disorders, and the scandals of that time did not permit men to regret it. The men whom Tacitus depicts to us as worn out with struggles and eager for repose, found in it nothing that could attract them, and the bad use that men like Curio, Caelius, and Dolabella had made of liberty, rendered them less sensitive to the sorrow of having lost it.

The memory of him who wrote these letters gained most by their publication. It was very common at that time to speak ill of Cicero. Notwithstanding the manner in which the court historians narrated the meeting at Bologna and the honourable part they attempted to give Octavius in the proscriptions,[1] they were none the less unpleasant recollections for him. His victims were calumniated in order to diminish his faults. This is what Asinius Pollio wished to do, when he said, in his speech for Lamia, that Cicero died like a coward.[2] Those whose devotedness did not go so far, and who had not enough courage to insult him, took care at least to say nothing of him. It has been remarked that none of the great poets of this time speak of him, and we know from Plutarch that at the Palatine it was necessary to read his works in secret. Silence therefore fell, as far as it was indeed possible, around Cicero's great glory; but the publication of his letters recalled him to the memory of everybody. When once they had been read, this intellectual and gentle figure, so amiable, so human and so attractive even in its weaknesses, could not again be forgotten.

To the interest that the personality of Cicero gives to his letters, a still more vivid interest is added for us. We have seen, in what I have just written, how much our time resembles that of which these letters speak to us. It had no solid faith any more than our own, and its sad experiences of revolutions had disgusted it with everything while inuring it to everything. The men of that time knew, just as we do, that discontent with the present and that uncertainty of the morrow which do not allow us to enjoy tranquillity or

---

[1] See especially Velleius Pat. ii. 66.　　　[2] Sen. *Suas.* 6.

repose. In them we see ourselves; the sorrows of the men of those times are partly our own, and we have suffered the same ills of which they complained. We, like them, live in one of those transitional periods, the most mournful of history, in which the traditions of the past have disappeared and the future is not yet clearly defined, and know not on what to set our affections, and we can well understand that they might have said with the ancient Hesiod: " Would that I had died sooner or been born later ! " This is what gives Cicero's letters so lively though mournful an interest for us ; this is what first attracted me towards them ; this is what, perhaps, will give us some pleasure in spending a short time in the society of the persons they depict, who, in spite of the lapse of years, seem almost to be our contemporaries.

INDEX

393